"Uniquely polyphonic and dialogical in its structure, *Dante and the Other* is not yet another volume of essays on Dante but rather a one-of-a-kind course that employs diverse and promising disciplines, such as phenomenology and psychoanalysis, in retrieving anew all the wonder of encountering the Florentine's universe (as if) for the first time. Here are included some exemplary interpretations that will awake interest, provide context, and clarify difficulties for a new generation of Dante's readers to come."

J.P. Manoussakis, Associate Professor of Philosophy,
College of the Holy Cross; Editor-in-Chief of the
Journal for the Continental Philosophy of Religion;
author of *The Ethics of Time*

Dante and the Other

Dante and the Other brings together noted and emerging Dante scholars with theologians, philosophers, psychoanalysts, and psychotherapists, bridging the Florentine's premodern world to today's postmodern context. Exploring how alterity has become a potent symbol in religion, philosophy, politics, and culture, this book will be of interest to many related fields.

The book offers a thorough foundation in approaching Dante as proto-phenomenologist. It includes an informative review of literature, historical insight into Dante's poetics-toward-ineffability as alternative to modern scientism, a foray into science fiction, existential elaborations, phenomenological analyses of *Inferno's* Canto I, and applications to psychotherapy and qualitative research. It also contains a poem from an imagined Virgil retiring in Limbo, and a meditation on Dante's complicated relationship to homosexuality.

Dante and the Other presents the mystical passion of apophatic spirituality, the millennia-spanning Augustinianism of radical orthodoxy, Levinas, Heidegger, and many others—all driven by Dante's Labors of Love. It is essential reading for Dante scholars, as well as readers interested in his works.

Aaron B. Daniels is a Research Fellow at Psychology & the Other at Boston College, and a Senior Lecturer of Psychology at Curry College. His publications include *Jungian Crime Scene Analysis: An Imaginal Investigation* (2014), and *Imaginal Reality, Volumes 1 & 2* (2011). Before entering academia, he practiced clinical psychology for ten years in community and private practice, where he achieved LGBT specialist status.

THE PSYCHOLOGY AND THE OTHER BOOK SERIES

The *Psychology and the Other* book series highlights creative work at the intersections between psychology and the vast array of disciplines relevant to the human psyche. The interdisciplinary focus of this series brings psychology into conversation with continental philosophy, psychoanalysis, religious studies, anthropology, sociology, and social/critical theory. The cross-fertilization of theory and practice, encompassing such a range of perspectives, encourages the exploration of alternative paradigms and newly articulated vocabularies that speak to human identity, freedom, and suffering. Thus, we are encouraged to reimagine our encounters with difference, our notions of the 'other,' and what constitutes therapeutic modalities.

The study and practices of mental health practitioners, psychoanalysts, and scholars in the humanities will be sharpened, enhanced, and illuminated by these vibrant conversations, representing pluralistic methods of inquiry, including those typically identified as psychoanalytic, humanistic, qualitative, phenomenological, or existential.

For a full list of titles in the series, please visit the Routledge website at: https://www.routledge.com/Psychology-and-the-Other/book-series/PSYOTH

Dante and the Other

A Phenomenology of Love

Edited by
Aaron B. Daniels

LONDON AND NEW YORK

First published 2021
by Routledge
2 Park Square, Milton Park, Abingdon, Oxon OX14 4RN

and by Routledge
52 Vanderbilt Avenue, New York, NY 10017

Routledge is an imprint of the Taylor & Francis Group, an informa business

© 2021 selection and editorial matter, Aaron B. Daniels; individual chapters, the contributors

The right of Aaron B. Daniels to be identified as the author of the editorial material, and of the authors for their individual chapters, has been asserted by them in accordance with sections 77 and 78 of the Copyright, Designs and Patents Act 1988.

All rights reserved. No part of this book may be reprinted or reproduced or utilised in any form or by any electronic, mechanical, or other means, now known or hereafter invented, including photocopying and recording, or in any information storage or retrieval system, without permission in writing from the publishers.

Trademark notice: Product or corporate names may be trademarks or registered trademarks, and are used only for identification and explanation without intent to infringe.

British Library Cataloguing-in-Publication Data
A catalogue record for this book is available from the British Library

Library of Congress Cataloging-in-Publication Data
Names: Daniels, Aaron B., editor. | Boston College sponsoring body. | Psychology and the Other Conference (5th: 2019: Boston College)
Title: Dante and the other: a phenomenology of love/edited by Aaron B. Daniels.
Description: Abingdon, Oxon; New York, NY: Routledge, 2021. | Series: Psychology and the other | Chapters are based on papers presented at a Dante Salon during the 5th Psychology and the Other Conference, held in 2019 at Boston College. | Includes bibliographical references and index.
Identifiers: LCCN 2020037234 (print) | LCCN 2020037235 (ebook) | ISBN 9780367675868 (hbk) | ISBN 9780367675851 (pbk) | ISBN 9781003131892 (ebk)
Subjects: LCSH: Dante Alighieri, 1265-1321–Criticism and interpretation–Congresses. | Dante Alighieri, 1265-1321–Psychology–Congresses. | Other (Philosophy) in literature–Congresses. | Love in literature–Congresses. | Phenomenology and literature–Congresses.
Classification: LCC PQ4413 .D34 2021 (print) | LCC PQ4413 (ebook) | DDC 851/.1–dc23
LC record available at https://lccn.loc.gov/2020037234
LC ebook record available at https://lccn.loc.gov/2020037235

ISBN: 978-0-367-67586-8 (hbk)
ISBN: 978-0-367-67585-1 (pbk)
ISBN: 978-1-003-13189-2 (ebk)

Typeset in Times New Roman
by Deanta Global Publishing Services, Chennai, India

Contents

List of Contributors ix
Preface: The Labors of Love xiv
Acknowledgments: A Note of Gratitude for Support of this Work xix

PART I
Dante and Phenomenology 1

1 Introduction: Dante and Phenomenology:
A Review of Literature 3
AARON B. DANIELS

2 Representing the Other: Dante, Duns Scotus, and the Crisis
of Representation in the Modern Age 51
WILLIAM FRANKE

3 1321: A Space Odyssey: A Response to Franke 72
AARON B. DANIELS

4 Dante, Selfhood and Significant Journeying 80
JOHN TOOK

5 A Response to Took's "Dante, Selfhood, and Significant
Journeying" 92
DOROTHY CHANG

6 From Poetics to Phenomenology: Consciousness in Dante's
Divine Comedy 97
CHRISTIAN Y. DUPONT

7 Gateways to the Ineffable: Dante's Poetry as
  Proto-Phenomenology   113
  AARON B. DANIELS

PART II
Dante: Yesterday, Today, and Forever   **143**

8 When Bici Said Come   145
  HATTIE MYERS

9 Dante and the Medieval 'Other'   147
  PETER S. HAWKINS

10 Surprised by Grace: Hermeneutic Reflections on Dante's
   Judgments: A Response to Hawkins   155
   JAMES M. KEE

11 *Purgatorio*: A Liturgy of Forgiveness and Restoration   164
   DOMINIC AQUILA

12 Storytelling: Dante, Freud, and their Models of Eros   183
   HATTIE MYERS

13 Purgatory as a Metaphor for Therapy and Associated Ethical
   Implications   189
   K. L. MCFARLAND AND TOMMY GIVENS

14 Dante's Economy of Words after Marx   201
   MATTHEW ELMORE

   Index   223

Contributors

Dominic Aquila is a tenured professor of history and director of assessment and institutional effectiveness at the University of St. Thomas in Houston, Texas. He served as dean of Arts and Sciences and then provost of St. Thomas from 2007 to 2017. Before his appointments at the University of St. Thomas, Professor Aquila held faculty and administrative appointments at Ave Maria University, Schoolcraft College, Franciscan University of Steubenville, and the Rochester Institute of Technology.

Professor Aquila took his bachelor's degree from The Juilliard School and an MBA from the Stern School of Business at NYU. He began his doctoral work under Christopher Lasch at the University of Rochester, completing it at the University of South Africa. His research interests include interdisciplinarity, liberal education, Dante, Marshall McLuhan, Father Walter Ong, and musical semiotics. In Fall 2020, Ave Maria Press is bringing out Professor Aquila's *The Church and the Age of Enlightenment, 1648–1848*: *In Defense of Reality*. He has manuscripts in progress on Edward Elgar's *Dream of Gerontius* and the influence of Dante's *Commedia* on Puccini's *Il Trittico*.

Professor Aquila is the recipient of the *Spes Nostrae* award in support of Catholic education, and distinguished service awards from the Michigan Liberal Arts Network for Development and the Council of Independent Colleges.

Dorothy Chang is a PhD student and teaching fellow in the theology department at Fordham University in the historical theology track. She earned her MA in religion from Columbia University and her BA in religion from Rutgers University. Dorothy is interested in theological anthropology, Byzantine theology, Reformation, religious poetry, early modern theology, and critical theory. Her dissertation will examine Jonathan Edwards's understanding of light and seeks to explore the extent to which Edwards's theology of light was influenced by or a break from earlier medieval theologies of light since they were informed by different scientific frameworks than Edwards.

Aaron B. Daniels is a research fellow at Psychology & the Other at Boston College and a senior lecturer in psychology at Curry College in Milton, Massachusetts. He holds a bachelor's degree in psychology from Baldwin-Wallace College, a master's degree in psychology with an existential-phenomenological emphasis from Duquesne University, and a doctorate in clinical psychology with a depth psychology focus from Pacifica Graduate Institute. He is the author of *Imaginal Reality, Volume 1: Journey to the Voids* (2011), *Imaginal Reality, Volume 2: Voidcraft* (2011), and *Jungian Crime Scene Analysis: An Imaginal Investigation* (2014). He practiced clinical psychology in both a community mental health and private practice setting in Seattle for a decade where he achieved LGBT-specialist status. He is the recipient of the 2015 Alan L. Stanzler Award for Excellence in Teaching from Emerson College and the 2020 Curry College Award for Excellence in Partnerships & Collaborations. He is a frequent lecturer on phenomenology, mindfulness, horror, and apophatic spirituality. He resides in Boston, Massachusetts.

Christian Y. Dupont is a Burns Librarian and Associate University Librarian for Special Collections at Boston College. He previously served as director of special collections at the University of Virginia and Syracuse University, and held curatorial and reference positions at the University of Notre Dame, where he earned a doctorate in theology. He holds a master's degree in information science from Indiana University.

Christian has led the formulation of national standards for archival practices. With a commercial software development firm, he created and promoted an online request and workflow management system now used by more than nearly 100 libraries and archives.

Christian's academic and publication interests range widely. He has published a book and articles based on his doctoral research, including *Phenomenology in French Philosophy: Early Encounters* (Springer, 2014). A book he edited on the Declaration of Independence was selected for recognition by the National Endowment for the Humanities. He writes a regular feature for the *Irish Arts Review* and occasionally contributes to library professional literature.

An expert on the reception of Dante in America, Christian has published a series of essays on the formation of Dante collections at American universities. His articles have appeared in *Harvard Library Bulletin*, *Papers of the Bibliographical Society of America*, *Dante Studies*, and *Italica*, among other journals, as well as edited collections. Forthcoming publications include essays on women readers of Dante in New England and illustrations of *Inferno*. Since 2014, Christian has served as secretary and librarian for the Dante Society of America.

Matthew Elmore is a doctoral student at Duke Divinity School, where he is conceiving a project at the intersection of bioethics and political theology. His academic focus covers three areas: the relation of words and material culture; medical language and political power; and nature as articulated by the body of Christ. Before coming to Duke, Matt occupied several spaces in healthcare, most recently working as a clinical researcher in cardiology. He is a co-author of several studies published in the *Journal of American Cardiology*, *EuroIntervention*, and others. He holds an MA from the University of Nottingham, where he wrote his thesis for John Milbank on Dante's *Commedia*.

William Franke is a Dante scholar, a philosopher of the humanities, and professor of comparative literature at Vanderbilt University. He has also been professor of philosophy at University of Macao (2013–2016); Fulbright-University of Salzburg Distinguished Chair in Intercultural Theology; and Alexander von Humboldt-Stiftung research fellow.

In addition to two monographs on Dante—*Dante's Interpretive Journey* (Chicago, 1996) and *Dante and the Sense of Transgression* (Bloomsbury, 2013)—Franke's critical theory books include *Poetry and Apocalypse: Theological Disclosures of Poetic Language* (Stanford, 2009) and *A Theology of Literature: The Bible as Revelation in the Tradition of the Humanities* (Cascade, 2017). These works follow up on books tracing prophetic poetry from Homer and Virgil to Dante (*The Revelation of Imagination*, Northwestern, 2015) and then forward from Dante through Chaucer, Shakespeare, Milton, Blake, Leopardi, to more recent modern classics including Baudelaire, Dickinson, and Yeats (*Secular Scriptures: Modern Theological Poetics in the Wake of Dante*, Ohio State, 2016).

In conjunction with his work on prophetic poetry, Franke has developed what he calls *A Philosophy of the Unsayable* (Notre Dame, 2014), reconstructing the apophatic tradition in *On What Cannot Be Said* (Notre Dame, 2007, 2 vols.). His *Apophatic Paths from Europe to China* (SUNY, 2018, Chinese Philosophy series) extends this project into an intercultural philosophy. His *On The Universality of What is Not: The Apophatic Turn in Critical Thinking* (Notre Dame, 2020) explores applications of this philosophy to media studies, postmodern identity politics of race and gender, and cognitive sciences in their struggle with the humanities.

Tommy Givens holds a ThD in theological ethics and New Testament from Duke University. He is the author of *We the People: Israel and the Catholicity of Jesus* (2014) with Fortress Press and of articles in various academic journals including the *Journal of the Society of Christian Ethics*, *Journal for the Study of Christian Ethics*, and *Journal of Scriptural Reasoning*. His research focuses on biblical interpretation, political theory, and ecology, and he is currently writing a book on the Gospel of Matthew entitled, *Light in the Shadow of Death*.

Peter S. Hawkins is professor of religion and literature emeritus at Yale Divinity School. His work has long centered on Dante: *Dante's Testaments: Essays on Scriptural Imagination* (1999), *The Poets' Dante: Twentieth-Century Reflections* (2001), co-edited with Rachel Jacoff, and *Dante: A Brief History* (2006).

The poet features as well in his expansion of his 2007 Beecher Lectures on Preaching in *Undiscovered Country: Imagining the World to Come* (2009). His research in the history of biblical reception has led to three co-edited volumes to which he also contributed essays, *Scrolls of Love: Ruth and the Song of Songs* (2006), *Medieval Readings of Romans* (2007), and *From the Margin I: Women of the Hebrew Bible and their Afterlives* (2009). Together with Paula Carlson he edited the Augsburg Fortress four-volume series, *Listening for God: Contemporary Literature and the Life of Faith*. He has also written on twentieth-century fiction (*The Language of Grace*), utopia (*Getting Nowhere*), and the language of ineffability (*Naming the Unnamable from Dante to Beckett*). His most recent book, co-authored with Lesleigh Cushing Stahlberg, is *The Bible in the American Short Story* (2017).

James M. Kee was a member of the English Department at the College of the Holy Cross from 1981–2016. He earned a BA from the University of Notre Dame in 1972. After a brief sojourn as a high school teacher and a graduate student in religious studies at Yale, Kee studied English literature at the University of Virginia and earned a PhD in 1982.

Throughout his career, Kee has been a student of the relationship between the Bible and literature. He is editor of *Northrop Frye and the Afterlife of the Word* (*Semeia* 89, 2002), and has published essays on Langland, Milton, Wordsworth, and Keats. He has also published essays on the relationship between religion and the intellectual life in the so-called 'postmodern' context, including, most recently, "The Religious Obligation to Be Intelligent," in *Tradition and Pluralism: Essays in Honor of William M. Shea* (2009). He is currently working on Chaucer's relationship to Dante.

At Holy Cross Kee taught a wide variety of courses and received the College's Distinguished Teaching Award in 2007. In addition to several courses on medieval literature and Chaucer, Kee regularly taught courses on tragedy, literary theory, and literary responses to the Bible, and offered seminars on such topics as the analogical imagination and poetry and philosophy. He served as chair of the English Department, associate dean of the College, and was twice appointed interim vice president for Academic Affairs.

K. L. McFarland is a PsyD candidate at Fuller School of Psychology and Theology Doctoral student at Fuller Theological Seminary. They have a background in theater arts and are currently engaged in research examining the intersection of art, psychology, and theology. They will complete their dissertation "The Arts as an Embodied Agent of Systemic Change, in Theory and Clinical Practice" in the upcoming year. This theoretical work proposes that the arts can provide an embodied 'Other' experience that provokes a recalibration of a client's systemic way of being.

Hattie Myers is a training and supervising analyst at the Institute for Psychoanalytic Training and Research (IPTAR), where she has been on faculty and was past director of the IPTAR Clinical Center. She did her undergraduate work at Oberlin College before getting her masters at Columbia University and her PhD at NYU School of Social Work. She completed her analytic training at IPTAR. She has been on faculty at NYU School of Social work, National Institute of Psychotherapy (NIP), the Institute of Contemporary Psychotherapy (ICP), and at IPTAR in the respecialization and adult analytic program. She co-edited the books *Terrorism and the Psychoanalytic Space* (Pace University Press, 2003) and *Warmed by the Fires: The Collected Papers of Allan Frosch* (IP Press, 2019). She is the founder and editor-in-chief of *Room: A Sketchbook for Analytic Action*, winner of the 2018 *Gradiva* Award in Psychoanalysis in New Media (analytic-room.com). *Room* is an interdisciplinary magazine conceived after the 2016 US election as an agent of community building and transformation. Intersecting psychoanalysis, politics, art, and culture, *Room*'s innovative forum brings different perspectives to bear on the complex problems facing us, while inviting greater familiarity with psychoanalysis as an important lens for personal, cultural, and political discourse. The unique relationship between Dante's work and Freud's has been of special interest to her for many years.

John Took is professor emeritus of Dante Studies at University College London. He graduated from the University of Leeds with a first-class degree in Italian in 1968 and with a Doctor of Philosophy in 1971 on the basis of a thesis entitled *Dante and John of Paris*. Prominent among his publications are *L'Etterno piacer: Aesthetic Ideas in Dante* (Oxford University Press, 1984); *Dante Lyric Poet and Philosopher: An Introduction to the Minor Works of Dante* (Oxford University Press, 1990); *Dante's Phenomenology of Being*, in the series Italian Research Studies (Glasgow University Press, 2000); *Dante Alighieri, Il Fiore (The Flower); Introduction, Text, Translation and Commentary* (Lewiston-Queenston-Lampeter: The Edwin Mellen Press, 2004); and *Dante* (Princeton University Press, 2020), with a further book entitled *Why Dante Matters* to be published later in 2020 by the Bloomsbury Press in London.

Preface
The Labors of Love

Aaron B. Daniels

This volume is a labor of love. The authors included in this text are inspired to cross disciplinary boundaries because of a deep passion to give fuller voice to what they read in Dante's work—and hear within their lives and selves in response to this call. Simultaneously, this volume is about the Labors of Love—the Love that transforms. That is the Love, as Dante comes ultimately to say, that "moves the sun and the other stars" (*Paradiso* XXXIII:145). This is Love as the fundamental, driving, and gratuitous principle of life. This journey through and to Love is found across all of Dante's works. Through this journey comes the transformation of Dante the poet, the pilgrim, the philosopher, the political theorist, the theologian, the human. But the names we lob from our twenty-first-century disciplinary segregations fall short and do a disservice to one whose sojourn refused to stay confined into any one role. His discourse overflowed then and overflows now the containers.

Love unites these essays even when we do not read that word. Perhaps this silence is out of apophatic respect. That is, might the word and our habitual containment of 'love' get in the way of this fundamental orientation of being? The word 'love' takes on and has taken on so many meanings—meanings that Dante struggles with across his lifetime. Frozen, distorted, or lesser loves surely mark the cosmic landscape of the *Commedia*.

This volume grows out of a 'Dante Salon' at the 2019 Psychology and the Other Conference held at Boston College. (That salon itself was the result of several years of my research and lecturing that I briefly outline in my acknowledgments after this preface.) We gathered together over a day and a half, in the beautiful Burns Library generously prepared by its director, Christian Y. Dupont, whose phenomenological essay appears later in this volume. The scholars presented papers, commentary, responses, and posters that asked what Dante can tell us today. The 'other'—Levinas's Other—was firmly in mind for speakers as they brought contemporary perspectives to bear on the Florentine's work. The conviviality and warmth of the gathering was remarkable—a testament to this 'Love that moves.' As Took states later in this collection (p. 84),

> Dante's is an ethic turning quintessentially on the bringing home or the gathering in and harvesting of one love-impulse to another, on the kind of

love-organization whereby, entirely without prejudice to its proper legitimacy, the occasional is taken up in the ontological on the plane of properly human loving.

With his meditation placing 'harvesting' as the divine gravity of the *Commedia*, Took expands on an ancient Christian theme. In the first chapter of the Christian New Testament's *Epistle to the Ephesians*, the author presents a Christology, eschatology, and explanation of the Gospels. In verses 9 and 10, one reads that God,

> has made known to us the mystery of his will, according to his good pleasure that he set forth in Christ, as a plan for the fullness of time, to gather up all things in him, things in heaven and things on earth. (*New Revised Standard Version*)

Thus it was that the many diverse voices gathered together for the 'Dante Salon.'

A brief word regarding 'Christianity' in this volume. To ignore Dante's Christianity is a risky undertaking. Dante's faith was idiosyncratic, to be sure. For instance, a strong case can be made that Beatrice is, for Dante, Christ. Moreover, Dante advances a cosmology that stretches beyond the very limits of expression and is simultaneously scandalously personal. Nevertheless, the reader encounters a Dante that is Christian in metaphor, mission, and method. In addition to existential, phenomenological, psychoanalytic, Marxist, and numerous other discourses, many of the scholars in this volume draw on explicit Christian sources in their analyses. Other authors utilize implicitly Christian perspectives with various shades of mystical sensibilities represented. Still other contributions represent fundamentally humanistic epistemologies. And the range of interpretative frameworks stretches beyond these bounds, which is part of the power of this collection—from the premodern to the postmodern. Driven by this diversity, all of the authors believe Dante to be describing something very real; or, perhaps more accurately, something that forms the foundation of one's ability to know what is real.

With the modern sensibilities of many readers, a first time through *Inferno*—almost always the introduction to Dante—leaves them alternately baffled or smug at the Florentine's seeming sadism, archaic religiosity, and crossword puzzle of medieval references. Several authors in this volume struggle with these issues as well and go further to point out odd inconsistencies that may, however, reveal other possibilities. When taken as a whole, the *Commedia*, let alone Dante's entire literary output, speaks to such a radically different world and worldview that only an extended journey with him can begin to present profoundly new possibilities to his reader. Rather than only a divine cosmology of punishments and rewards, his is a life-long meditation on the orientation of the heart—that is, on the capacity to love. Many of the 'inconsistencies' the careful reader detects are cracks in our modern narratives waiting to let a vastly different light in. Thus, the necessary recourse to ostensibly Christian sources is actually a recourse to the depth of nearly two millennia of Western European scholarship. This volume, therefore, holds the audacious potential to enable its readers to see anew a legacy of classical and post-classical scholars who address shockingly contemporary existential, hermeneutic, psychological, ethical, and theological issues.

This collection's authors walk in many worlds simultaneously: psychoanalysis, academia, ministry, theology, language studies, and many more. Some are world-renowned Dante scholars. A few others, like me, cannot even conversationally speak Italian. Yet, as the Psychology and the Other conferences exist to show, these exterior differences can yield to deeper common discourses. These authors have a very clear vision and vocation that, for them, hearkens to a unity. Nonetheless, as one reads these authors' works, one will move between diverse dialogues. This is absolutely true to the spirit of Dante. In the *Commedia*, the reader experiences Dante move between the Pilgrim; the Poet he becomes by the end of the *Commedia*—and, thus, the author of the epic; and Dante the Poet reflecting on the process of writing; among other interstitial shifts each canto brings.

Hence, these authors also move between their scholarship, their experience of reading Dante, their personal journeys of transformation and growth, and their various philosophical and theological stances. To read these essays is to transit between ships in motion. Before encountering the minds at work in this volume, my own philosophical disposition moved me to think of these as epistemological journeys: to see the motion of these crafts as evolving ways-of-knowing that develop through encounters with their limitations. After all, the postmodern scholar tends to embrace epistemology's relativism that stubbornly refuses totalizing discourses or truths. However, as the careful reader of Franke's works realizes, he presents hermeneutics as the more all-embracing undertaking. His approach acknowledges that totalizing statements are troublesome; but, for him, this is because we are all longing for the Ineffable. That is, although the ultimate referent may exist well beyond the ken of the individual, all life is ultimately in relationship to this Ineffability. These essays are crafts driven to a point beyond the horizon of horizons, and the wind and current that carries them toward this polestar is Love.

These authors do not all agree with each other and that is wonderful. Finding those differing emphases and interpretations is part of the joy of returning to these essays again and again as I have. But the prospective reader should not be daunted by the heights of scholarship to which these authors reach. This volume provides background and references to an extent that it can serve as a primer for engaging with interdisciplinary Dante scholarship. In that pursuit, one will encounter the unspeakable, the ineffable, the conviction that life's impasses are invitations to transform, and the realization that the struggles of expression are the struggles of growth.

A brief narration of this volume: In the first part of this collection, "Dante and Phenomenology," the authors offer ways in which Dante can be seen as trying to give voice to the nature of human experience, which is the agenda of phenomenology. In the introduction, I offer the reader a detailed review of the works of authors who have attempted exactly that analysis. In chapter two, William Franke traces a key moment in the history of Western thought when Duns Scotus and Dante approached the same challenge and shared many convictions but fathered radically different traditions. In my response to Franke's thoughts, in chapter three, I situate the crisis born of this divergence in both our scientistic era and in science fiction. John Took offers the fourth chapter in which he concisely presents the existential phenomenology Dante offers in the *Commedia*. Dorothy Chang responds to Took's vision in chapter five by parsing Took's argument and raising key questions about ultimate Being in relation to Heidegger and whether the journey to selfhood is necessarily solitary. Christian Dupont offers the sixth chapter in which he executes an incisive phenomenological analysis of Dante's Canto I of the *Commedia*. Part one of our journey finishes with chapter seven in which I synthesize the contents of this half of the book and present Dante as a proto-phenomenologist.

I title the second part of this volume "Dante, Yesterday, Today, and Forever" because the contents of this second half span the seven centuries since Dante completed his *Commedia* and challenge readers to see the vital necessity of Dante's insights for formulating a more authentic path through the twenty-first century. The title is a reference from Peter Hawkins's chapter where he questions "those who embrace the poet as a bulwark against change, the paragon of values that are the same 'yesterday, today, and forever'" (p. 148). Hawkins is challenging that conservative stance by offering a gentle blasphemy in which Dante substitutes for Christ in the original quote from *The Epistle to the Hebrews* 13:8. No such parallel is intended with my choice of title for this second part, since Dante is decidedly *not* the same to each era that receives him. Dante comes to readers where they are. What might be 'the same' is his ultimate referent; but it is, as noted above, one that stretches beyond readers' capacities, wherever they may be.

Part Two begins with a poem from Hattie Myers in which she offers Virgil a chance to reflect from the relative comfort of Limbo on the nature of his time with—psychoanalysis of?— the Florentine. In chapter nine, Peter Hawkins considers Dante's conflicted relationship to the Other, especially when the other is one we would label today as 'homosexual.' James Kee responds to Hawkins in chapter ten, highlighting further tensions current readers may feel around Dante's various condemnations and offering hermeneutic phenomenological insights leading to an examination of Dante's evolving relationship to grace. In chapter eleven, Dominic Aquila presents the rhythms of *Purgatorio* in light of the liturgical references and enactments the pilgrim Dante encounters and participates in on the mountain's slopes and summit. Hattie Myers returns in chapter twelve to examine the stories of eros told by both Freud and Dante. In chapter thirteen, K. McFarland and Tommy Givens look to the imagery of Purgatory for a vision of psychotherapy that might ethically honor both the living and the dead. To complete this volume, in chapter fourteen, Matthew Elmore interrogates the idea of 'scarcity' as lived out personally, ethically, economically, and linguistically today, and offers the reader Dante's theological supersession of scarcity's tyranny, stretching toward Ineffable Love.

On behalf of myself and all the authors of this volume, we wish you a rich and challenging journey through this material. We mean this work at least to blur the boundaries between the personal, ethical, theological, and many other discourses. May it enable you once again to see the stars.

Acknowledgments
A Note of Gratitude for Support of this Work

This labor of love could not have been undertaken nor completed without the generous support of many scholars, colleagues, and friends. In the early 2000s, I began to teach Dante as part of clinical courses at St. Martin's University's Master of Arts in Counseling program in Lacey, Washington. These efforts evolved at New England College in Henniker, New Hampshire, where I used Dante to illustrate personality as a process. I presented an early sketch of my interpretations of the Three Gates at the University of West Georgia in Carrollton, Georgia, where I received encouragement and excellent insights. In Boston, Professor Peter Hawkins's unparalleled knowledge and warmth have been incredibly helpful. In my research phase, the staff of Curry College's Levin Library in Milton, Massachusetts, under the wise leadership of Katherine Garrett Eastman, provided invaluable assistance. In particular, Librarian Kimberly Doorley's support was indispensable. David Goodman of Boston College and Donald Wallenfang of Walsh University in Canton, Ohio, both provided excellent guidance at key moments. Professor Robert Smid of Curry College and his colleagues in the Boston Theological Society graciously assisted me in wrestling with key doctrinal issues. I presented early draft portions of my contributions to this volume at the Society for Qualitative Inquiry in Psychology conferences in Pittsburgh in 2018 and in Boston in 2019. Thanks to Dr. Renée Spencer of Boston University for her encouragement of tracking the shifting of reflexivity in the research process, which expanded my work on the Three Gates. I also offered provisional ideas from this work at the Psychology and the Other conferences in Boston in 2017 and its Dante Salon in 2019. A thank you to Facebook user Giovanni de Silentio in the 'Phenomenological and Existential Studies' group for bringing the Heidegger passage to my attention. Thank you also to Adam McLean for finding his alchemical comment buried deep in his site's message board. This work has also benefited immensely from the ongoing spiritual direction of Alden Flanders. David Goodman more than merits a second expression of gratitude for his creation and shepherding of the space that enabled the 'Dante Salon' to happen, the Psychology and the Other conferences. Finally, as always, my deepest and abiding gratitude to Laura Daniels for her love, support, honesty, and Light.

Part I

Dante and Phenomenology

Chapter 1

Introduction
Dante and Phenomenology: A Review of Literature

Aaron B. Daniels

This project grows out of an observation Helen Luke makes in her insightful analytic psychological text, *From Dark Woods to White Rose: Journey and Transformation in Dante's* Divine Comedy (1975/2001). She presents the famous opening three lines to Canto I of the *Inferno*. "Nel mezzo del cammin di nostra vita/ Mi ritrovai per una selva oscura/ Che la diritta via era smarrita." Luke offers Dorothy Sayers's translation: "Midway this way of life we're bound upon,/ I woke to find myself in a dark wood,/ Where the right road was wholly lost and gone" (p. 4).

Canto I serves as an introduction to the *Commedia*'s three parts: *Inferno*, *Purgatorio*, and *Paradiso*. Moreover, this opening image in the dark woods frames much of the poem's purpose. To deepen the portent, Luke (1975/2001) offers a nuance to one Italian word that opens new possibilities, not emphasized in Sayers's version:

> For Dante does not say, "*mi ritrovai **in** una selva oscura*"—he says, "***per** una selva oscura*"—and although it is perfectly correct to translate *per* as "in," the more usual and basic meaning of the word *per* is nevertheless "through" and not simply "in." (p. 4)

Luke extends this issue of translation to emphasize that this very darkness, lostness, and confusion is what brings the shock that awakens. One reflexively 'comes to' or 'recovers oneself'—"mi ritrovai"—through the process, *through* the experience itself in its often-baffling specificity.

Luke's (1975/2001) Jungian metaphor easily translates into the phenomenological. (Later in this volume, Dupont delves into phenomenological interpretations of this same passage, challenging some elements of Luke's translation, but not its phenomenological potential.) Phenomenology demands that one remain focused on experience itself and avoid the seductions of facile seemingly-objective explanations if those explanations distance oneself from the immediacy of the phenomenon. This same phenomenological fealty to experience also demands one not slip into sentimental or flowery archsubjectivity, as this reflexivity can just as easily betray the truth of an unfolding phenomenon. As Part One of this current volume hopes to show, this tension and eventual transcendence of the subject/object split mark both the phenomenological discipline and Dante's pilgrimage.

At the heart of this inquiry is a question bridging Dante's premodern era to the postmodern questions phenomenology cultivates. That is, can the 'per' by which Dante came to himself in those dark woods not also be the 'very way in which' in Heidegger's variously translated definition of phenomenology from *Being and Time* (1927). On page 34 of the German original, Heidegger asks that the phenomenologist let "that which shows itself from itself be seen *in the very way in which* it shows itself from itself."

This introductory chapter strives to provide a foundation from which scholars can advance the study of the relationship between Dante and phenomenology—both viewing Dante's work phenomenologically, but also, perhaps, more importantly, seeing Dante as a proto-phenomenologist. To those unfamiliar with either Dante or phenomenology, the summaries presented here aspire to provide a foundation that will aid in encountering the essays in the rest of this volume. Moreover, as is a central goal of this collection, the authors hope to bridge the centuries that divide today's discrete disciplines from the *philosophia* of Dante's time.

Throughout the scholarly literature from both psychological and literary perspectives, many authors seek to hear Dante's own voice rather than begin with formulaic and symbolic interpretations. In their works, three interlinked and simultaneous themes emerge.

1) Dante seeks to give voice to some sort of lived reality—even when that voice must appeal to supernatural landscapes.
2) He wrestles with his own growth and development.
3) He progressively strives to create language and forms adequate to describe the experience of his own contentious meaning-making.

On all three accounts, a phenomenological approach seems especially fecund. Yet, searching scholarly databases reveals just a few hundreds of items that explicitly link Dante and psychology in general. Narrowing the search to any specific school of psychology yields less than 100 hits. Sharpening the focus even more to phenomenology garners only a dozen sources that make an explicit link to Dante. Why is this?

Interpretations of Dante's works are quite popular with depth psychologists at cocktail parties. Moreover, psychological sensibilities also loosely color the literary scholarship addressing Dante—whether biographical to the Florentine or diagnostic of his landscapes. Examinations of Dante in the depth tradition are often components of much larger works, but only a few psychodynamic authors offer book-length examinations of the *Commedia*, let alone his other works. Luke's (1975/2001) provocative work is, by the author's own admission, a sketch—a lifetime in the making but also a call to future scholars to continue her work.

When psychoanalytic psychologists address Dante, they too often struggle to let Dante speak for himself. Instead, they apply reductionistic psychoanalyses, such as Shaw's approach in "A Pathway to Spirituality" from 2005, wherein he compares the spirituality of Wordsworth to Dante. Shaw decides that Dante has mother issues, is in denial about death, and has created Beatrice as a sort of spiritual teddy bear.

This chapter seeks to see Dante's work with new eyes and to gain some sense of the eyes by which Dante saw.

1) The examination begins by giving a sketch of Dante's two major poetic and biographic works, the *Vita Nuova* and the *Commedia*.
2) It then describes three Roman Catholic Saints—Aquinas, Francis, and Augustine—who inform not only Dante's theology but his ontology and phenomenology as well.
3) By addressing varying currents within phenomenology and parallels to Dante's project, the discussion turns to what a proto-phenomenology might look like, concluding with a comment on poetics as phenomenology.
4) The examination next turns to Dante's role as a father to the Renaissance and its humanism with necessary questions about the values of modernism.
5) To begin the fuller review of literature, this study summarizes three major works (Harrison, 1988; Took, 2000; Asay, 2014) overtly linking phenomenology to Dante and those sources responding to these works.
6) The works of Franke come next. His examinations of Dante often present hermeneutics as phenomenology in the course of examining larger philosophical, literary, and theological questions.
7) The review of the literature concludes with those few articles and chapters that make the link between the Florentine and phenomenology.

With this background, the reader can then proceed to the subsequent chapters by Professors Franke, Took, and their respondents. Part One of this volume concludes with Dupont's aforementioned phenomenological analysis of the opening of Dante's Canto I followed by my synthesis and application of themes linking Dante and phenomenology. Part Two grows out of this foundation, and its authors offer broadening perspectives of how Dante's perspectives may cast new—albeit centuries-old—light on contemporary issues and disciplines.

An Overview of Dante's Two Major Poetic Works

Dante has two major poetic works, *La Vita Nuova*—The New Life—and the *Commedia*—the so-called Divine Comedy. In its own way, each work describes Dante's progressive struggles to give voice to what is most real and true. Each work also ends at a frontier of the Ineffable.

Vita Nuova

In the *Vita Nuova*, published in 1295, a young Dante gives sketches of his remembrances of his childhood, adolescent, and young adult encounters with the incomparable Beatrice and his response to her death when she was 25. Between these moments, Dante recalls vivid visions that instruct him in his journey of faith, art, and love. The work follows a *prosimetrum* form, alternating between poetic experiments and prose explanations. Through this rhythm, Dante wrestles with how to create a poetic sensibility and form that remain true to both his experiences and his longings.

The Dante of the *Vita Nuova* feels two competing pulls. On the one hand is the desire to import and adapt the troubadour's fevered love and layered theological references into a poetic form and language. In fact, Dante and his contemporaries do just that. Dante later labels it in *Purgatorio*'s Canto XXIV, the "dolce stil novo" [sweet new style] of which the *Vita Nuova* is an important development. Written in the vernacular language of the time and region, this style looks inward for the nature of experience while also embedding layers of reference and allusion. The pull that competes with these poetic aspirations is perhaps less soul-wrenching, but equally seductive. It is the call of natural philosophy. Dante is an apt pupil and a voracious learner who could easily lose himself in the pursuit of knowledge for its own sake. Thus, poetry and science pull equally on the youthful Florentine. Nevertheless, by the end of the *Vita Nuova*, he realizes he must undertake a great pilgrimage to grow in his expressive capacity and transcend such divisions. At the end of the work, in *La Vita Nuova*, XLII, he expresses his realization that his current understanding, expressive capacity, and very way of life are not adequate to the call of his Beatrice: "After this sonnet there appeared to me a marvelous vision in which I saw things which made me decide to write no more of this blessed one until I could do so more worthily" (Alighieri, 1295/1969, Reynolds translation, p. 99).

Commedia

In many ways, the culmination of Dante's ontological and epistemological pilgrimage, begun at the end of the *Vita Nuova*, finds expression in the *Commedia*. That is, the 'New Life' called for in the earlier work begins with the realization of the necessity of a greater journey. The *Commedia*, completed in 1320, is Dante's crowning achievement. From the dark woods entered at the beginning of this chapter, Dante fails in his attempt to bootstrap his way out of his midlife morass. Thus, the great Roman poet Virgil manifests to guide Dante into the depths of a Hell most symbolized by frozen stuckness. Then, on a Mountain of Purgatory that is a proportionate global convexity to Hell's concavity, Dante undertakes voluntary sufferings to prepare himself for his ascent through the progressive sublimities of Paradise. Guided now by Beatrice instead of Virgil, each circle of Heaven becomes vaster and more all-embracing until the very end when, looking at the farthest frontier, Dante paradoxically sees the center—the Cosmic Rose. Here,

Dante audaciously suspects he sees something of the human form, but again confronts an ultimate ineffability. In the final canto, *Paradiso* XXXIII:130–145, he describes this last intuited image:

> Within itself and in its coloring
> Seemed to be painted with our human likeness
> So that my eyes were wholly focused on it.
>
> As the geometer who sets himself
> To square the circle and who cannot find,
> For all his thought, the principle he needs,
>
> Just so was I on seeing this new vision
> I wanted to see how our image fuses
> Into the circle and finds its place in it,
>
> Yet my wings were not meant for such a flight—
> Except that then my mind was struck by lightning
> Through which my longing was at last fulfilled.
>
> Here powers failed my high imagination:
> But by now my desire and will were turned,
> Like a balanced wheel rotated evenly,
>
> By the Love that moves the sun and the other stars. (Cotter translation, 2000)

Three Saints

Many readers of the Florentine find that medieval history and especially theology create profound barriers to engaging with his greatest poem. Moreover, by twenty-first-century standards, Dante's epistemology seems to blithely shift between disciplines of philosophy, poetic theory, science, rhetoric, astronomy, political science, church polity, history, soteriology, theology, and many others. Today, various academic silos divide against each other. But for Dante, these divisions are not so palpable nor insurmountable.

Dante's writing represents an invitation to a way of meaning-making that defies the categorical thinking that dominates scholarship today. His writing also invites the reader to become steeped in his inspirations. The landscapes of the *Commedia* are a realized theology. Thus, although it represents a contentious issue between scholars such as Harrison and Franke discussed below, issues of faith, religion, and theology are integral to understanding Dante.

Three of Dante's theological inspirations make a theocentric—and also a life-affirming—case that brings the reader more fully into the Presence of the Divine.

This section examines them in reverse chronological order to allow the provenance of these surprisingly radical ideas to deepen.

Thomas Aquinas

Closest in time to Dante is Thomas Aquinas (1225–1274). Although Dante did not live to see Aquinas canonized in 1323, his writings already exercised an outsized influence during Dante's life. Drawing upon his reclaiming of Aristotle, Aquinas offers a structure of human experience rooted in common but irrational emotions, such as love, sorrow, and anger. He calls these 'the passions.' These passions can be taken up in different ways and require the exercise of the intellect to direct. The influence of Thomistic theology on Dante is most visible in the repeated structure of the whole *Commedia*. The passions that are perverted in the stuckness of *Inferno* become the longing of the voluntary sufferings in *Purgatorio*, which are refined to the sublime transcendences of *Paradiso*. Dante's audacity reaches a fevered pitch at the end of *Paradiso* when he offers what Aquinas would call the 'Beatific Vision.' Aquinas places the Beatific Vision as the goal of human existence, but one that can only be achieved after death.

At their heart, all experiences contain an invitation to the Divine. In Thomistic theology, experience does not necessarily negate or obscure the Divine impulse. Rather, a fundamental virtuous structure permeates all phenomena and becomes available to those who trim the sails of their intellect to hearken to the yearning that is this call to the Divine.

Francis of Assisi

A further step back into the medieval yields Francis of Assisi (ca. 1181–1226). The lived world of Francis is brimming over with God's creations singing praise and adoration of Divine love. Only sin deafens humans to this chorus. Francis holds for Dante the promise that, seen and loved aright, our seemingly fallen world may become known as Paradise. Thus, at the top of the Mountain of Purgatory, in Canto XXVII, Dante steps through the final purgation, a wall of searing flames, and sees Paradise on Earth. The fires through which Dante passes are the flames of the angel's sword barring Adam and Eve from Eden. Dante's struggles up Purgatory's slopes, which teach him to loose his clutching dependence on vice, have finally liberated him to accept God's Grace. Only then can he see again his beloved Beatrice.

Franciscan spirituality embraces Christ's humanity. It is a profoundly incarnational epistemology in which, known and loved aright, life-as-lived can open the wonder of God's gratuitous creation. In this way, Dante's pilgrimage has been one of coming back to the place he began—his life—and seeing it as if for the first time. In a sense, a Franciscan spirituality is far less dependent on an afterlife. It offers the hope of abundant true life. That is to say, our experiences contain within them an invitation to a God-centered participation in God's creation.

Augustine of Hippo

Preceding these towering figures in Christianity is Augustine of Hippo (354–430). Of particular interest is Augustine's idea of *Presence*. Augustine contends that any effort to assert being is a reflection, moreover a hunger, for what is only true of God. For Aquinas, we cannot 'know' being; we can only lean closer to or further from it. Asay in his 2014 dissertation, discussed below, makes the specific connection that Dante is addressing Augustine and the Presence for which we long. Asay takes the further step of stating that Dante's Augustinian project is a phenomenology—an existential phenomenology, in fact. Thus, in Asay's work, Augustine's 'greater being' as we lean closer to the reality of God's Presence becomes Heidegger's engaged and fulsome authenticity; and Augustine's 'lesser being' becomes empty and nihilistic inauthenticity. This Presence is truth; living in denial of it distorts one's thinking, feeling, and aspiration.

(Proto)Phenomenology

'Phenomenology' takes on many meanings, depending on the author's discipline. The term existed before Husserl—for instance, Hegel's *Phenomenology of the Spirit* from 1807. And, although some intriguing essays discuss Hegel's phenomenology and Dante (cf. Dobbins & Fuss, 1982, "The Silhouette of Dante in Hegel's Phenomenology of Spirit"; and Shannon, 1998, "The Journey of the Mind of God to Us: Hegel's Ladder and Harris's Graduate Seminars"), that phenomenology is unique to Hegel.

Adding another grove to these dark woods, 'phenomenology' in the hands of some Dante scholars takes on any number of idiosyncratic meanings. Such is the case with Trovato in 1990 who, in an effort to show how Dante moved beyond what Trovato calls a mere 'phenomenology' to 'integral realism,' actually makes—if one ignores the terminology—a wonderful case for how Dante expresses a very sophisticated phenomenology. Trovato presents a Dante for whom theological and philosophical divisions are irrelevant and inauthentic. This is a Dante who offers an intentional reality, where sacred ideas embody. One can arguably see Trovato making the case for Dante's proto-phenomenology. But phenomenology was not to become the epistemology of modernity. The subsequent Renaissance forces of emerging modernity and its materialism muffled the call for an art and science of experience until the twentieth century.

For the purposes of this discussion, 'phenomenology' can mean several interlinked things:

1) First, it is a critical philosophy challenging both materialist approaches to the human condition as well as those forces that seek to divide a human science from other disciplines—or to turn human science into a mere expression of the neurosciences.
2) It is also a seminal qualitative research methodology growing out of these philosophical considerations.

3) It is a theoretical ground for several clinical approaches that value engaging with the client's—and practitioner's—lived worlds, as well as giving voice to the co-constituted experience in the consulting room between the therapist and client.
4) It is finally also an emerging current in theological discourse.

The following discussion of these branches of the phenomenological tree provides more than background for this current chapter. This context is essential for understanding some of the more contentious debates surrounding the interpretation of Dante and the theoretical stances advocated for by those authors discussing him.

Phenomenology as a Critical Discourse

Arguably, the original impulse of phenomenology as a distinct approach, if not discipline, is as a critical philosophy allied, eventually, to critical psychology. As summarized by Moran and Mooney in 2002 in their canon-defining work, the movement grew out of Brentano, was created by Husserl, was redirected by Heidegger, perhaps peaked with Merleau-Ponty, and faced ongoing revision through Levinas, Ricœur, Derrida, and others. From its beginning, this movement reacted against examining humans with a materialist, natural scientific epistemology and thus ignoring human experience itself. This leads to the second expression of phenomenology as a core qualitative method.

Phenomenology as a Qualitative Method

Husserl, often cited as phenomenology's founder, gave voice to the impulse to reject a materialist—and thus quantitative—approach to the human condition and moved to a qualitative methodology. He wanted to create a discrete discipline adequate to the challenges of describing the structures of consciousness. His ideas evolve across his writings, and many of the conflicts regarding the interpretation of Husserl's intentions and phenomenology arise from attempting to generalize his whole project rather than addressing discrete writings and phases of his thought.

As much as Husserl's oft-repeated axiom calls for a return to 'the things themselves!', his relationship to materialism is contentious at best. His famous *epoché*—a bracketing aside of the natural attitude of belief in these material things—seeks to cast light on the natural flow of consciousness relating to the things rather than the physical and physiological processes at work in sensation and perception. Husserl does not deny matter so much as seek to focus on the nature of experience too-easily overshadowed by matter's assumed existence. Heidegger takes up Husserl's call to 'the things themselves,' but seeks to emphasize where the attention ought to be cast in his definition of phenomenology cited above. Heidegger asserts that 'the very way in which' things show forth must be carefully interrogated in an authentic phenomenological project.

Husserl never completed his project of phenomenology, and successive generations took up his call in often-idiosyncratic ways. Nevertheless, the profusion of approaches that may loosely call themselves 'phenomenology' share this modest assertion that describing the nature of human experience itself is a worthy undertaking—one that arguably can be done in a rigorous and scientific fashion, albeit firmly and unapologetically qualitative in its method.

Phenomenology remains an important part of Continental Philosophy's discourse. And given the attention that phenomenology receives from postmodern authors such as Derrida, Deleuze, Levinas, and others, a reader could be forgiven for imagining phenomenology to be solely a branch of philosophy. Nevertheless, phenomenologists are responsible for creating rigorous qualitative research methodologies and serve as inspiration for methods widely used in anthropology, sociology, and other human sciences—with psychology, certainly in proportions, being the least of which. Whether the researchers analyze subject protocols following the structure of the Giorgi, Fisher, and von Eckartsberg method of phenomenological reduction, refine their themes pursuing a grounded theory research project, or track their shifting sense of self in participatory action research, they are applying and developing core ideas of the wider phenomenological mission. At its heart is the question: How do we best give voice to human experience in ways that reveal what is too-easily covered over by quantitative methodology?

Phenomenology in Clinical Settings

The third current of phenomenology grew out of these first two expressions. Across the twentieth century, phenomenology also powerfully influenced clinical psychological practice. Boss, Frankl, Perls, May, Yalom, and others all rely on the power of the clinical encounter as a phenomenon worthy of primary attention. Existential themes vary in their emphasis by these and other authors; nevertheless, the nature of the practice itself relies much more on phenomenological sensibilities. Though existential-phenomenological psychotherapies may bear strong resemblances to more psychodynamic approaches, the phenomenological fealty to the *how* over the *what* guides the existential-phenomenological practitioner to a greater extent than any post-Freudian practitioner. Regardless, by the end of the twentieth century, this process-focus had come also to inform many psychodynamic practitioners.

Phenomenological Theology

A fourth important current in phenomenology coalesced toward the end of the twentieth century: a religious, and typically Christian phenomenology. In many ways, this emergence is more of a coming together of currents implicit from the foundation of phenomenology. Heidegger and others are often responding to Augustine, and the contributions of the Duquesne University current of phenomenological thought is strongly inflected by the work of the school's

Spiritan Brothers. Moreover, authors such as Hans Jonas (1903–1993) and John Macquarrie (1919–2007) integrated existential phenomenology with theological themes. Nonetheless, with writers such as Michel Henry (1922–2002) and Jean-Luc Marion, theological threads have come to create a whole-cloth phenomenological theology. In this perspective, the phenomenological investigation of experience leads to a frontier of theological revelation. Complementarily, other researchers shift to an examination of currents within theology, which are best understood phenomenologically. Liberated from the dualism that materialism inevitably foists upon theology, phenomenology offers these theologians clearer access to the ground of being. Several authors addressing Dante's work phenomenologically come to theological conclusions, perhaps most explicitly William Franke. This chapter addresses his work examining this theological convergence in phenomenology below, and he contributes a chapter in this volume.

This 'theological turn,' however, is not without controversy. In 1991, Dominique Janicaud (1937–2002) published a monograph in which he simultaneously introduces this shift and expresses his ambivalence about its bona fides as a 'phenomenology.' The argument turns on rooting phenomenology's provenance in Husserl. By 2000, the essay had been translated into English and became the opening to a text, which then included works by Jean-François Courtine, Paul Ricœur, Jean-Louis Chrétien, Jean-Luc Marion, and Michel Henry. These additional authors offer a 'new' grounding to a theological phenomenology that redefines the practice, referent, and intent.

Dante's Premodern Position Relative to Phenomenology

Given these four currents in phenomenology, it merits asking what is Dante's phenomenology? Is it descriptive of experience? If so, what experience? For Robert Pogue Harrison in *The Body of Beatrice* (1988), described below, it is a phenomenology of our longing for the raw stuff of experience. In Franke's many chapters and essays on the topic, however, Dante presents a phenomenology of the hermeneutic meaning-making that is itself the substance of experience. As will become clear later, Franke eventually accuses Harrison of a naïveté regarding phenomenology and materialism. His accusations echo back to ambivalences in Husserl's fundamental project. Both Harrison and Franke agree that Dante is posed with the same struggles as phenomenologists. Through the practice of poetry, Dante gives voice to what may not be accessible to the arts and sciences of today when they stand divided against each other. Dante's premodern era may provide the phenomenologist with privileged access to a moment before these divisions became insurmountable.

If Dante does offer the reader access to an important perspective, it is in large part because he predates cultural, intellectual, psychological, and spiritual divisions that structure today's modern world. As outlined above in the first current within phenomenology, in the nineteenth century, the fear that psychology and other human sciences would become purely materialistic, natural scientific undertakings drove early phenomenologists. In the quest for 'objective' measures of mental phenomena, psychology—outside of the psychodynamic tradition—rapidly took on quantitative approaches that ignored the vagaries of human experience in favor of physiological or neurocognitive processes, or observable behavior. Phenomenologists sought to establish another theoretical and research tradition to complement if not counter these reductionist trends. If they were to avoid the reductionistic betrayal of human experience, phenomenologists would have to reconceive of some of the essential building blocks of the philosophy of science. This would necessitate an examination of history.

The Historical Origins of the Problems Phenomenology Seeks to Address

Although Victorian-era materialists may have wanted to approach humans with the same parsimony as a biologist addressing a mollusk, they clearly inherited their paradigm from an earlier source. Setting aside those phenomenologists that trace the philosophic malfeasance back to Aristotle, many phenomenological theorists came to indict the flowering of modernity in the Enlightenment and especially Descartes's dualism as the source of the problem. Descartes's famous meditations surely begin with a perfectly phenomenological grounding in questioning the nature of experience. Descartes found he could doubt everything, except that he was doubting. Many phenomenologists would concur with this conclusion. Nevertheless, Descartes eventually proffers a map that divides 'mind' from God from *res extensa*—the stuff of the material world. Whether or not Descartes is to receive credit or blame for the division of the academic disciplines and sciences, he certainly gives voice to critical epistemological schisms.

Descartes is not the first to offer these distinct categories. As Franke illustrates in his chapter in this current volume, the groundwork for divorcing theological discourse from the natural sciences within European scholarship was laid by Dante's contemporary, Duns Scotus (1266–1308). Scotus advocates distinct discourses for these emerging disciplines. Indeed, if one concedes Scotus's and Descartes's divisions, each of these domains necessarily demands fundamentally different methods for addressing them appropriately. Theology addressing God and the natural sciences addressing the things of *res extensa* will become estranged from each other in large part because they cannot agree on what constitutes 'evidence.' Hence, should not the challenges of a subject as mercurial as mind arguably necessitate the development of a distinct methodology adequate to the task? But the seductions of certainty offered by the natural sciences and their approach to this *res extensa* proved too strong and, in efforts to understand experience, came to blot it out. Franke would add that divorcing the discourse of the ineffable inherent in some forms of theology from these other fields leaves them infected with a stifling certainty. Natural science methods have, today, become the dominant paradigm for addressing any subject scientifically—whether things, humans, or God. In fact, 'empiricism,' 'rigorous,' and 'science' have become synonymous with a materialist epistemology to such an extent that phenomenologists' efforts to claim these terms are often only acknowledged within their own ranks.

A Return to Dante's Privileged Perspective

Thus, if the hegemony of materialism can find its paternity in Dante's contemporary Duns Scotus and its expansion in the budding modernity of the post-Renaissance Enlightenment with Descartes, might not Dante's historical position offer an important perspective on a premodern epistemology? Cultivating the soil from which the Renaissance grew, Dante, as presented by Trovato in his 1990 article, still exists before the Renaissance and is thus unencumbered by modernity and its fracturing of *philosophia* into discrete disciplines. God, mind, and matter are not inexorably divided for Dante nor the saints that inspired him. One can even read the greater arc of the *Commedia* as a synchronization if not rectification of God, matter, and mind.

In a 1977 article, Silverman links Dante to a moment and movement that undoes our habitual separation of philosophy from experience. Summarizing a course taught by Merleau-Ponty, Silverman emphasizes that Merleau-Ponty's phenomenology ultimately leads to the dissolution of philosophy, moving firmly into the realm of experience itself. "Living, expressing, and acting are philosophy at work, philosophy negating itself as separate philosophy" (p. 223). Silverman observes that Merleau-Ponty's goal is not a disembodied intellectual exercise so common to the Western philosophical canon:

> What appears is philosophy that has denied its theoretical stance in order to be its greatest achievement. This dialectical phenomenology is a non-philosophy,—thought become the texture of an inter-human world of experience—the world of Dante, Shakespeare, and Beethoven, but also of the common man. (p. 223)

Dante's Poetics as Phenomenology

As much as the case for Dante as a proto-phenomenologist may cast a new light on twentieth- and twenty-first-century debates regarding materialism, a question of semantics bears mentioning. In a 2017 conversation with Dante scholar Peter S. Hawkins, an essay from whom appears in Part Two of this current volume, he noted that much of what this chapter and others may present as a proto-phenomenology in the Florentine's works, would in the fourteenth century be seen as simply 'poetics.' It is, after all, painfully anachronistic to speak of a pre-Renaissance 'phenomenology.' There is no need for a phenomenology, per se, because *philosophia* has not yet been irreparably dismembered. The necessity of phenomenology's critical stance against addressing and treating humans with a natural scientific epistemology is, arguably, five centuries away.

And yet, Dante struggles in the *Vita Nuova* with the charms of (natural) philosophy versus the fervid yearning of poetry. Thus, one may, in Dante, see someone who chose a different path—a path devoted to pursuing lived experiences to the edges of expression—but chose it on the very cusp of an era in which so many others would not.

Nevertheless, if Dante is indeed an advocate of this integrated lived world, what is the reader to make of the frequent citations of him as a grandfather of modern humanism?

Dante, Humanism, and the Renaissance

Can one realistically put Dante forth as a counterpoint to modernism? Is he not a humanist—a Renaissance man before his time? He gives himself and his experiences a central place in all his works. However, so too does Augustine in his fourth-century *Confessions*. Dante's audacity may indeed be critical to the later establishment of the humanism of the Renaissance and later Enlightenment. Certainly, the Florentine's reclaiming of classical literature and philosophy informs these movements. Nevertheless, if by 'humanism' one refers to a philosophy appropriating Protagoras's 'man is the measure of all things,' then the theocentric Augustinian, Franciscan, and Thomistic currents in Dante are too strong to make him that sort of humanist.

In his *Body of Beatrice*, Harrison (1988), whose work receives attention below, places the provenance for humanism later. Harrison looks to the next generation, soaked in Dante's rhetoric and poetry, to find a true origin of fourteenth-century humanism. Harrison sees Petrarch, with(out) his absent muse Laura, facing the same longing as Dante. However, Harrison's Petrarch is in a static swoon of elegy, not a realization of the temporal unfolding of being that Harrison credits to Dante. When Petrarch focuses almost exclusively on his subjective versus phenomenological experiences, Harrison sees Petrarch is much more a father of a modernity lost in the eternal present of lament. Harrison insinuates but does not pursue the idea that Petrarch laments more than his absent Laura. His lamentation may be a prophetic call heralding a nihilism so familiar as to be invisible to the denizens of the modern world. Petrarch may be lamenting a God as well as objects that seem in perpetual retreat from his inward gaze.

In his *Dante's Phenomenology of Being* (2000), also discussed below, Took concurs with the separation of Dante's discourse from modernity. In the latter part of his work, Took addresses Dante's use of language relative to the definition of being. Took is clear that Dante is neither existential nor postmodern in his understanding of language, yet the crisis of meaning to which Dante speaks in his mid-career works, preceding the *Commedia*, bears striking parallels to today's postmodern conditions. Dante, however, can evade the vagaries of the postmodern groundlessness by fealty to his pilgrimage of faith. Took also offers an essay in this current volume where he concisely summarizes his conceptualization of Dante in existential-phenomenological terms.

As noted above, in his earlier works, Dante grapples with remaining true to experience itself. He could tip easily into the arch-subjectivism of the lyric genre he inherited. He could also find himself pursuing the pleasures of academic studies, especially in the emerging natural sciences. Dante wavers, but ultimately commits to a much harder path—becoming lost in neither the pining yet pedantic literary conventions of his contemporaries nor the sterile seductions of secular study as embodied by the 'Donna Gentile.' This Gentle or Noble Woman is, in one sense, the embodiment of *philosophia*, the sweet pleasures of study. Near the end of the *Vita Nuova*, she first appears in a window above a Dante disconsolate from the death of Beatrice. But, as Harrison (1988) notes, she is only a reflection. For Harrison, the moment Dante can see himself via the gaze of the Donna Gentile is key. Harrison describes "a visual specularity whereby the self returns to itself through the image of the other in a reflective medium, in this case a window" (p. 115). She "is pure reflection, framed in a window as a mirror, stripped of otherness" (p. 116). This is the Donna Gentile who could seduce Dante into purely rational investigations of the natural world, abandoning his yearning for a language to describe experience itself. Is not this abandonment of experience, from which Dante ultimately turns away, the mark of modernity's materialism that the phenomenologists seek to indict? Is not conversely the solipsism of Petrarch also the endless hermeneutic regression so familiar to postmodern scholars? In the end, either path quickly leads to recursive nothingness.

Further discussing these snares of rationalism, De Monticelli (2000) cites a critical impasse where this formerly-reassuring rationality—great achievement of the ego—betrays Dante. De Monticelli's article is notable for the clinical, historical, philosophical, theological, and literary elements skillfully woven together in her presentation. Dante's potentially fatal moment occurs in the *Inferno*, across Cantos VIII and IX, at the gates of Hell's inner metropolis of Dis.

To this point, Dante and Virgil have successfully navigated any impasses the demons and denizens of Hell have concocted for them. When demons block their way, the Italians declare themselves to be on a divine mission or invoke the Will of God, or other verbal shibboleths. But now, the demons will have none of it, and the Furies mount the ramparts. They call for the Gorgon, Medusa, to come out and petrify the Italian pilgrims where they stand. Neither Virgil nor Dante can talk or think their way out of this impasse and through the gates of Dis. Virgil exhorts Dante to cover his eyes, but then further adds his hands to shield them in impotent terror. The passage in Canto IX:58–66 begins with Virgil warning Dante:

> 'Turn your back and keep your eyes shut,
> for if the Gorgon head appears and should you see it,
> all chance for your return above is lost.'
>
> While my master spoke he turned me round
> and, still not trusting to my hands,
> covered my face with his hands also.

> Oh you who have sound intellects,
> consider the teaching that is hidden
> behind the veil of these strange verses. (Alighieri, 1320/2000, Hollander & Hollander translation)

Neither of the poets can explain away the inscrutable, terrifying gaze of the Medusa threatening from the battlements. And De Monticelli (2000) sagely notes that Dante's aside to the reader singles out those of "li'ntelletti sani" [sound or sane intellects] to hearken to his implicit message. This message indicts those very intellects upon which the comment's audience relies. In the face of this rationally insurmountable challenge, only an angel, God's Grace, swiftly racing to the hellgates can overcome the dire threat of Medusa's paralyzingly nihilistic wrath from Dis's walls. The angel is indignant and, after effortlessly opening the gates with a wand, chastises the demons. The pilgrimage of faith will not continue on the previously sure feet of the intellect but on a path set by a far greater will.

Thus, as De Monticelli (2000) warns her readers, Dante clearly discovers that empty rationalism will not carry the day—will not allow the true pilgrimage to continue. Matter divorced from the inherent intentionality of a lived world will freeze one into a stasis of helpless certainties. So too will endless self-reference stall, regardless of how poetic. Neither objectivity nor subjectivity offers a path forward. Therefore, Dante rejects these empty pursuits for the rich engagement of the pilgrimage. With this commitment, the Beatrice of *Commedia* can transform from the distant romantic ideal of a youthful Dante's *Vita Nuova* as well as the self-satisfied comprehensiveness of the Donna Gentile. In the *Commedia*, Dante embraces with a mature ardor the poet's journey of describing rather than labeling experience. Though he may face the same questions as the modern or postmodern seeker, Dante's faith carries him through the paralysis of self-enthrallment and describes an intentional, lived world that defies and transcends the materialist's nihilism of our current era.

Dante offers phenomenology a rich inheritance and mission. Neither the dead convictions of materialism nor the subjectivism of the arts can give voice to the nature of human experience. A path that transforms the researcher is, in fact, the message here. One cannot separate oneself from one's investigations and hope to be true to oneself and one's research. This reflexivity is not, however, mere commentary. As will unfold over the rest of this chapter, the subjectivity is an objective fact which may be encountered rigorously.

With this foundation of Dante preceding much of the entrapping positivism of the modern era as well as the subjectivist swoon of postmodernity, this essay now turns to the book-length works addressing the Florentine and phenomenology.

The Major Texts

Three major works explicitly link Dante and phenomenology: Harrison's *The Body of Beatrice* (1988); Took's *Dante's Phenomenology of Being* (2000); and

Asay's doctoral dissertation, *The Phenomenology of Frames in Chaucer, Dante and Boccaccio* (2014). Nevertheless, taken as a whole, Franke's works form the largest collection of writings on this topic. Thus, his works occupy the fourth section of this review of major texts.

Harrison's *The Body of Beatrice*

Harrison's *The Body of Beatrice* (1988)—a reworking of his doctoral dissertation from 1984—takes a loosely phenomenological approach, akin to the poetics of Bachelard, and focuses on the *Vita Nuova*, in which a young Dante searches for a language adequate to his yearning and experience. As sketched above, in Harrison's gloss of the *Vita Nuova*, Dante, through a series of visions, reaches a threshold of ineffability and must undertake a pilgrimage to discover a means of growing in his expressive ability—to essentially transform himself to be present to that which lies beyond his youthful ken. He achieves this sublime expression well after the events of the *Vita Nuova*, at the end of *Paradiso*, again facing a frontier of ineffability, but a far more rarefied and ontologically radical one.

Harrison's (1988) phenomenology seeks to "restore to the [*Vita Nuova*] its strangeness, its remoteness, its thought-provoking quality" (p. 1) in the face of Dante's own in-text interpretations as well as the centuries of critical scholarship. Nevertheless, Harrison's reluctance to deal directly with phenomenological sources can prove frustrating for scholars. In an interview with de Bruyn (2009), Harrison admits to being steeped in Heidegger and provides rich descriptions of a method that values literature as "a phenomenon *par excellence*" (p. 193). Harrison sees literature as a wise philosophy and notes its ability to inform the reader of "how much of the phenomenon remains enveloped in shadows" (p. 193). Yet, despite these later expressions, the influence of phenomenologists remains almost entirely implicit in *The Body of Beatrice* (1988). Harrison only makes his phenomenology explicit in the de Bruyn (2009) interview and an article (Harrison, 1990) he wrote to respond to critics' desire for an explanation of his avowed methodology in *The Body of Beatrice*. There, Harrison portrays the Dante of the *Vita Nuova* as a phenomenologist striving to create a method to portray lived experience most authentically—a phenomenological poetics.

In *The Body of Beatrice*, Harrison (1988) makes the archly existential assertion that the *Vita Nuova* marks Dante's discovery of time—through the presence and death of Beatrice and through Dante's shift in tone, tense, and project over the course of the work. Harrison wants to show "the projective if not the prophetic character of being in time, which attends upon the future as the ultimate source of 'meaning'" (p. 94).

Harrison's work (1988) rests on Dante's first enigmatic dream—the 'Marvelous Vision'—in which a newly smitten adolescent Dante dreams of Beatrice's nude body draped in a sanguine cloth. Harrison believes that this vision is central to everything that will happen in the rest of the *Vita Nuova* and later. Thus, he makes the phenomenological move to the hermeneutics of the vision itself, resisting the dismissive tone of a Freudian interpretation of pubescent libido. Rather than a phantasm or mere projection, the intermediary of the sanguine cloth asserts Beatrice's very real corporeality. Only the specificity of the experience, not a distancing symbolic interpretation, will yield reality. The crimson cloth is, for Harrison, the sacramental substantiation of Beatrice—her phenomenality.

> All other oneiric images and events become refractions off the cloth ... Its accessibility only through a phenomenal veil binds Dante's new life to the aesthetic order, binds it, in short, to a quest for revelation through the poetic enterprise. (p. 28)

At this point in his text, Harrison makes it clear that we all yearn for—and may ignorantly assume the reality of—the object; but we are exiled from its reality. A genuine phenomenology must start from this epistemological truth, leaving us to wrangle with only the representations and interpretations that constitute our experiences.

Harrison (1988) seems to exercise a type of imaginal epoché, seeing Dante as bracketing away "anything like a real world outside the poet's imagination" (p. 52). Yet, this lived world, known through imagination, now becomes the proper place for love and transcendence. This imagination, this transcendence—these experiences are the sum of lived reality. Dante's world is, nonetheless, one of embodiment. Beatrice's reality, "both body and image" (p. 53), exceeds mere fantasy. Harrison sees her reality, her radical alterity overflowing any containment. Thus, the "unrefinable dimension of her otherness ... keeps Dante moving" (p. 53). That is, only Beatrice's inscrutable alterity foils the seduction by the purely rational—represented by the aforementioned Donna Gentile. With this shift, Harrison challenges his readers' assumptions. Beatrice's body exists beyond Dante's experience, beyond his interpretations, and beyond the visions. Is Harrison asserting a transcendent alterity that drives our expressive—phenomenological—journey? Is this an uncited reference to Augustine's *Presence*, perhaps even Levinas's primacy of the Other? Or is Harrison attempting to address the enigma of matter's seeming reality in the face of the seeming-primacy of phenomenology? Harrison's writing remains ambivalent on these questions.

Beatrice's death, some seven years after the Marvelous Vision, devastates Dante; but before he can fully fall into the consolations of natural philosophy offered by the 'Gentle Lady,' Dante witnesses pilgrims seeking the Veil of Veronica—a 'true image,' as 'Veronica' etymologically implies, of Christ. Dante then has a 'Miraculous Vision'—not the earlier Marvelous Vision with the crimson drape. He does not recount this new miraculous vision because he *cannot* recount this vision. Harrison explains that Dante must revise what he thought was his project. In this revision, Dante not only changes his future but rewrites his past. Harrison sees this as an awakening to a "Christian existentiality" (p. 132). Thus, by the end of the work, Dante creates the New Life of the book's title. Beatrice's crimson veil has become the fabric of the book itself.

Critical Responses to Harrison

Harrison's *The Body of Beatrice* (1988) is the first full-length examination of phenomenological themes in any of Dante's work. The critical response to the work is mixed but leans toward the positive (cf. Ward, 1992; Wetherbee, 1991). Most agree how beautifully and poetically written the work is. Several reviewers note a thinness of citations (e.g., Tambling, 1991). Franke (1988), in his first review of *The Body of Beatrice*, while still completing his doctoral studies for which Harrison would be a reader, interprets Harrison's citational lacunae to be an issue of respectful silences. Given that Franke has since become known as an authority on apophatic spirituality, in which the unspoken, unspeakable, and ineffable are at stake, the critique is canny. Harrison's neglect of Christian scholarship particularly upsets the aforementioned Trovato (1990). Phillippy (1990) feels Harrison cherry-picked and stretched timelines to make his thesis fit. She also worries Harrison missed the problem of the male gaze, an issue which Wallace (1990) conversely feels Harrison ably navigates. Nevertheless, through all these reviews, the phenomenological perspective in which Harrison claims to sit receives scant notice.

Within the first few years of publication, perhaps the most substantial criticism of Harrison's work comes from Stillinger (1990). Stillinger ultimately finds the work provocative and important but is left wondering on what ground Harrison finally means to stand regarding Beatrice as Dante's inspiration. Like Phillippy (1990), Stillinger (1990) worries about Harrison's failure to address the male gaze. His greatest criticism also contains fascinating praise: Stillinger feels Harrison displays much of the same ambivalence in his work, as does Dante.

> *The Body of Beatrice* is a meditation on the relations between writers and their objects, and it is haunted, like the *Vita Nuova*, by a vision of unproblematic vision: the lover's fixed gaze, the critic's extended close reading. Yet the *claim* to unproblematic vision can obscure, as in this title, the very object of vision. Such an eclipse seems to inspire, in both books, writing that is by turns feverishly speculative and eloquently incisive. *The Body of Beatrice* is valuable for its paradoxes, for its thoughtful playfulness with academic forms, and for its perceptive close readings; if its vision of truth is less satisfying, it is at least true to the fixations of the *Vita Nuova*. (p. 404)

A far more full-throated criticism of Harrison's phenomenology comes later from Franke (2011), but will receive attention with the review of Franke's works below.

Took's *Dante's Phenomenology of Being*

The second major work is Took's *Dante's Phenomenology of Being* (2000), a masterful synthesis of existential phenomenology and Scholastic theology. Took offers a structure-of-being rooted in the nature of experience itself. He makes a powerful case for the recovery of Christian Scholasticism and the examination of Dante as far more than poet and moralist, but an important philosopher for all times.

Took's (2000) work is a complex, narrated outline exercising an existential-phenomenological distillation of Dante's perspectives in the *Commedia*. Fundamentally, the work grows out of an existential-phenomenological application—by way of Gadamer and Heidegger—of Augustine's idea of greater and lesser being, paralleled to authentic versus inauthentic being. Falling into things is to fall away from God, dangerously near to—but never fully into—nothingness. In short, ethics, theology, and ontology are indistinguishable.

Like Asay (2014), in his dissertation discussed below, Took (2000) places central importance on Dante not dissolving into the mystic numinous. Harrison (1988) implies this point as well in *The Body of Beatrice*. For Took (2000), Dante is always firmly *there* in his specificity—transformed, but always human in his existence. This includes, importantly, that alterity never dissolves. Again, the relationship to otherness transforms, matures, and becomes fuller, but alterity remains to the very furthest frontiers of Paradise. And this encounter with otherness becomes the communion and the heart of Dante's ongoing engagement with his topic, his reader, and himself.

The thereness to which Took (2000) speaks is not a naïve access to a transcendent here-and-now. Took carefully structures how being stretches ahead of itself in teleology, beside itself in self-scrutiny, and many other configurations. As Took states, the Poet is committed to "the description and dramatization of being under the aspect of its manifestness, of the forms-under-which it 'gives' itself to the mind as knowing" (p. viii). Although Harrison (DeBruyn, 2009) may proclaim a deep affinity to Heidegger, Took (2000) is far closer to the Bavarian philosopher's early existential-phenomenological works in his enterprise and presentation.

The reader of this current volume can partake of Took's penetrating formulations in an essay later in this volume in which he summarizes much of the thought contained in *Dante's Phenomenology of Being*. Took also offers the student of the Florentine a great gift in his recently published *Dante* (2020), a masterwork that covers the entirety of Dante's life and works. In it, Took collects, advances, and interweaves his decades of study and analysis.

Asay's *The Phenomenology of Frames in Chaucer, Dante and Boccaccio*

The third major work linking Dante and phenomenology is Asay's 2014 dissertation. To guide his examination of medieval authors—Dante, Boccaccio, and Chaucer—Asay chooses the idea of frame narratives. These are grounding narratives that create a space for stories within stories. In these tales, the telling itself is at issue. Asay states, "the framed word acts both to push us out of the frame into our own temporality and to draw us into fictional times and spaces" (p. iv). Without using the term, Asay courts the imaginal, noting how we become more aware of the fiction-making in our own lives when facing these narratives-within-narratives.

From Husserl and Fink to Heidegger to Bergson and to Levinas, Asay (2014) uses the genealogy of twentieth-century phenomenology to interrogate the Augustinian idea of *Presence*—that is, the present moment, the presence of the object, and the very idea of present-ness. For Asay, we all find ourselves negotiating "relationships to a presence from which [we] have always already slid away" (p. 29). Rather than placing alterity in people's encounters in the lived world, Asay places otherness in the "presence that refuses their approach even as it hurtles them into historical being" (p. 30).

Asay's (2014) real goal is to give the reader fresh eyes to read Augustine and medieval mystics who saw God as Presence. Bridging 1700 years or more of philosophy, Asay notes that the methodology to approach presence must be tangential since, although human subjects are always responding to presence, they cannot actually perceive it. Therefore, cutting through all his twentieth-century references is this same pervasive enduring inability to know time and being in their truth because of human's "normal intellectual habits" (p. 37). Appealing to Augustine and Pseudo-Dionysius's sense of Presence, Asay sees yearning permeating our lives. Those who seek this presence "progressively record the poignancy of the presence that is other to themselves" (p. 42). Asay, thus, sets up Dante's own struggles throughout his writings, especially with the language of exiles and pilgrims.

Asay's (2014) thesis is that his medieval subjects, but especially Dante, create narratives that embody the otherwise abstruse discourses of medieval mystics and theologians. By creating these framed stories, he sees these authors admitting "the inescapability of lived existence, and they work to locate transcendence within that existence rather than outside it" (p. 56). Asay sees an "incarnational poetics" (p. 56) in which Dante's audacity becomes critical. By spatializing Paradise, Asay feels Dante "reintegrated time and presence" (p. 60).

> Presence is lodged within every significant experience, just beyond the horizon ... we only approach that horizon, however, when we fall under the erotic spell presented to us by some object in the physical world—in Dante's case, his beloved, Beatrice. (pp. 61–62)

Dante's goal is to extend this 'erotic spell' to every object, making them mirrors of the divine. God is no longer opposed to matter. Rather, matter comes to tell the stories by which "we approach the infinite generativity of presence" (p. 64). When every object can be intentional, Asay says one achieves "[t]he beatific vision" (p. 64) in which the specificity, the uniqueness of every experience, every object unfurls in an endless drive to the horizons of being. Thus, in Dante, "Sin became salvation; the tendency of objects, in and for themselves, to absorb our attention became the means by which we transcended our limited perception of them to glimpse the horizon of the divine" (p. 65). In Asay, one can see themes from Augustine, explicitly, but also Francis and Aquinas. Through attending to the call within the lived world, that is God's creation, one can come into more abundant life. Again, this is not some dissolution into the divine, but a call to the lived world in its specificity, in its instantiation. And if this is true of Dante's searing transcendent visions in Paradise, it is also true of the sufferings of Hell. Asay notes how the "contrapassi"—the perversely appropriate punishments in the *Inferno*—are a powerful expression of the world the characters narrated for themselves (p. 81).

Through all of his interpretations, Asay (2014) keeps a firm grip on the central role of language—of poesis—in this project. "The same presence [Dante] encounters [in Paradise] is available in any space when we hold the aesthetics of language in constant tension with its meaning" (p. 88). And the holding of this tension then leads to the realization of any identity as secondary: who I take myself up to be is a sediment from the presence-longing solution of experience. Asay concludes that Dante "recognizes poetry as what it always was: a representation, which fundamentally assumes the absence of whatever it represents" (p. 108). For Asay, this pilgrimage of conversion—Dante's journey—is how the soul progressively attunes itself to presence.

The Contributions of Franke

Although Harrison's *Body of Beatrice* (1988) may have inaugurated the full-voiced examination of Dante from a phenomenological perspective, Harrison's scholarship has since moved on to other areas of study. With John Took, William Franke is among the world's leading Dante scholars who read Dante's works as existential and phenomenological discourses. Rooted in theology and apophatic spirituality, Franke's works go well beyond the Florentine and seamlessly integrate Continental, Scholastic, theological, and hermeneutic/phenomenological themes together. Franke, however, continues to return to Dante as a central focus or aspect of his ongoing publications. Franke's 1991 dissertation *Dante's Divinatory Hermeneutic: Towards a Poetics of Religious Revelation*, for which Robert Pogue Harrison was a reader, sets the tone for many of his subsequent works.

If one loosens the definition of phenomenology, the researcher would face the satisfying task of reading much of Franke's total output over the last twenty-five or more years to understand the nuances of his examination of Dante's phenomenology. As can be seen in one of his most recent books, *The Revelation of Imagination* (2015), in his discussion of Augustine, Franke is weaving themes of the acts of writing and reading, stretching toward the ineffable, and memory and interiority in a way that deeply indicts the convenience of separate academic disciplines and speaks to a phenomenology of revelation. Perhaps the most important point is that, for Franke, meaning-making is primary, if not originary. That is, he transcends the subject/object split as well as the matter/mind debate by refocusing his reader on hermeneutics. Outside of phenomenological and imaginal circles, this shift is likely inconceivable; but Franke consistently presents a vision of experience as the process of meaning-making. Franke's stance speaks to a powerful current within the world of phenomenological literature. Nevertheless, although he makes frequent reference to hermeneutics in a way that the reader might profitably see as a species of phenomenology, he does make discrete and specific references to phenomenology in some of his discussions of Dante. Thus, for the purposes of this chapter, the focus will remain on the explicit references to Dante and phenomenology.

Franke's Dante's Interpretive Journey *(1996)*

The idea that a reciprocal illumination can exist between Dante and twentieth-century philosophers, Heidegger and Gadamer, for instance, is core to Franke's 1996 text. Franke furthermore asserts that the specificity of Dante's historicity—often criticized as curtailing any claim to transcendence—is the very means, perhaps the only means, by which Dante can achieve any stretching toward transcendence. Franke explains that,

> Dante presents the supreme and absolute truth of Christianity, which his poem would propound, in a way that makes it indissociable from the story of his own individual search and journey. The way of understanding put in practice in Dante's work, as in all works of interpretation, consists in finding oneself in the midst of what is to be understood and so understanding oneself and it in relation to each other. (p. 4)

In a substantive appendix (pp. 113–118), Franke (1996) establishes his *bona fides* as an existential-phenomenologist. In the preceding chapter, Franke had established that the hermeneutic project pervades the entirety of Dante's *Commedia*. Like De Monticelli (2000), Franke (1996) analyzes the impasse at the Gates of Dis in *Inferno* IX and its direct address to those of 'sound intellects' as a key moment in Dante's hermeneutic project. Thus, in this appendix, Franke begins by noting that the hermeneutic stance to apply to Dante's work is not a cipher, explanation, or mere allegory; rather, it "consists in disclosing, literally unveiling, something that can be seen, some phenomena" (p. 113). Franke states that this is Dante's hermeneutics. Franke does not contrast this hermeneutic phenomenology to the primacy of perception; rather, he challenges, in concert with his reading of Merleau-Ponty, the idea that perception is ever naïve. We see, embody, and live our understandings. Thus, Dante challenges us to see aright so we may live and understand aright. In undoing 'common-sense' or unexamined assumptions that constitute our experience, Dante brings us to the heart of phenomenology all the more adamantly.

Meditating on Dante's frequent and nuanced use of the verb 'to appear,' Franke (1996) sees a shift from nineteenth-century phenomenology, which equated phenomena to mere appearance, to Heidegger's early work in which what is hidden by appearance becomes constitutive of that very appearance. More pointedly, Franke clearly explains that to discuss phenomena is to discuss being. Heidegger asserts that being itself is that which we have in question, but it is a profoundly anxiety-provoking question. Thus, inauthentic but temporarily distracting projects, which cover over that there ever was a question of being, dominate most of our lives most of the time. These distractions and misdirection are at stake in our taking-up of our experience. The phenomena, and thus the question of our being, become obscured by our seizing upon the assumed objects of our perception. Thus, Franke emphasizes that the difficult hermeneutic work of uncovering becomes essential. This is the very phenomenology in which he views Dante partaking. Being itself is the revelation; it is the showing itself from itself. Ironically, the Husserlian 'things themselves,' if unexamined in the Heideggerian 'very way in which they show themselves,' obscure being and showing. Being is lost, and the very question of being considered pointless or tautological when such seemingly obvious objects of inquiry distract our attention.

Franke's (1996) phenomenology puts meaning at stake. Being shows itself to be the meaning-making and the meaning. Therefore, Franke can smoothly bridge a phenomenology rooted in ontology—the being of beings—to the 'presencing' or Presence of Augustine. That is, one recovers the wonder and awe of authenticity when being no longer sits as a banal, Cartesian *res extensa*, but a vibrant ongoing and unfolding taking-up-the-question-of-being—which is each person's state of being. Thus, being-there or being-in-the-world, Heidegger's *dasein*, can only be encountered in its specificity. And, in our specificity, each of us provisionally, hermeneutically takes up our own being, which, in our constant provisionality, is inherent to being itself—understanding, interpreting, revising.

Thus, Franke (1996) can read Dante's audacious move of inserting himself into cosmic matters as less a matter of narcissism and more an elevation of the ontological to the primary matter of human expression. The specific human life is not only worthy of such elevated discourse, not only demands it, but life is, moreover—whether overtly acknowledged or not—these very efforts of expression and understanding. It is no surprise then that Dante, in a lightning flash at the farthest frontier of Paradise, can intuit something of the human in the divine, but finds his language fails to express it.

Literality, Franke (1996) states, distances us from the real questions behind the seeming reality of things. Franke reclaims Husserl's epoché, the bracketing of the natural attitude. This natural attitude that assumes the being of things can now be seen as an abstraction that distracts one from the abiding reality of the question of being. Instead, the epoché enables a new, more authentic perspective. "[B]y giving up our preconceived notions about what is real we can become consciously participant in the actual self-revelation and realization of Being" (p. 116).

This is not essentialism. Being is not a destination nor an object. Thus, one must speak in terms of revelation and not discovery. In this way, the flow of experience precedes any subject or object—terms that are derivative of various stances by which we take up phenomena.

> The breakthrough of phenomenology is enacted in a primordial way by Dante's project of writing a poem whose fiction is that it is not a fiction ... But this turns it immediately into a sort of reality, the reality of what shows itself. (Franke, 1996, p. 116)

This sentiment finds strong resonance in Asay's (2014) later discussion of the stories within stories of frame narratives, pointing the reader to more vital truths. Yet, if being is not to be a thing among things discovered, then it also cannot be some code or further reference to another more abiding truth.

> The phenomenon has a reality of its own independent of what it signifies, and this reality is fully manifest in it ... the phenomenon is the open manifestation of Being ... What is transformed in phenomenology and, I propose, in Dante's gnoseological method and presuppositions are the relations between immanence and transcendence of what is known as real or true with respect to the phenomena that manifest it ... Similarly, if Dante claims in the world of his poem to reveal the true world of Christian faith, not only to comment upon Christian revelation but to mediate it more directly, to make it occur historically, then the Christian truth must be capable of being manifest immanently within the phenomenon that the Divine Comedy is or can become in reading. (Franke, 1996, p. 117)

In establishing this link, Franke firmly makes the phenomenology of reading itself the event. The reader's understanding, the demand that the reader makes sense in his or her own way in the face of Dante's work, is not accidental. Franke makes a case for an existential *Lectio Divina*, the Christian tradition of contemplative reading of the scriptures with an emphasis on relating the revealed meaning to one's life and living. Franke contends that Dante cuts close enough to the existential-phenomenological project that the reader cannot avoid this hermeneutic taking-up.

> Dante's hermeneutic injunction, even with its didactic accent, by exhorting the reader to *look* at some phenomenon even while a superficial looking is exactly the danger hermeneusis must avoid, illustrates what amounts to a "phenomenological" type of hermeneusis ... What Heidegger and Dante both urge us to see is not any new object or field of objects, but rather the meaning and truth of what we already see objectively, and ultimately the meaning of Being. This truth reveals itself within the horizon of a specific temporality that for Dante is constitutive of Christian conversion. (p. 118)

This topic of Christian conversion occupies the next chapter, which contains an application (1996, pp. 138–139) of Franke's existential phenomenology to Dante's first struggle in the *Inferno*. Lost in the dark woods, Dante wants to gain some perspective and hopes to see the sun to get his bearings. He sets to climbing a hill but is quickly thwarted by three fearsome beasts—a leopard, a lion, and a she-wolf. Interpreters often gloss these creatures as historical references of Dante's time or representations of his own vices of lust, pride, and wrath or greed. Franke, however, sets to the expression and the experience Dante offers his readers. In particular, he notes the interwoven themes of appearances and temporarily. Franke sees in Dante's failure to achieve the hilltop an expression of an inauthentic entrapment in objects and the inevitable anxiety of this stance. One's temporality becomes a futile and anxiety-soaked exercise in miserliness trying to grasp fleeting time and deceptive objects, constantly leaning further away from being.

Franke's "Dante's 'New Life' and the New Testament: An Essay on the Hermeneutics of Revelation" (2011)

To begin his essay, Franke (2011) places Harrison's *Body of Beatrice* (1988) as a founding text that

> raises speculation on the meaning of Dante's prosimetric masterpiece to a level of reflection where it can become philosophically and religiously relevant for us today. I find *The Body of Beatrice*'s argumentation profound and compelling, as well as exquisite, yet I am not persuaded by its conclusions. (Franke, 2011, p. 338)

Franke then spends the rest of his essay carefully establishing links in his chain of logic whereby poetry becomes primary. The radical nature of his thesis only becomes fully apparent by the end.

Franke (2011) introduces an emerging stream of biblical exegesis in which core poems—for example, "The *Magnificat,* the *Benedictus, Nunc dimitas,* and the *Pater Noster*" (p. 340) but also Hebrew Bible sources such as Moses's or Deborah's song, the Psalms, as well as the prophets—can be viewed as urtexts from which the Bible's prose narratives spun. That is, the early Christian Church first organized around these often-ecstatic poems and their revelatory nature and celebrated them liturgically. The stories, the theology, and the dogma came later and are, thus, secondary. Franke shifts to the nature of the Gospels and prepares his reader for the argument regarding Dante's New Life. "The gospels are really about a miracle of faith within the lives of individuals in the Christian community, and only as such is the outward 'history' they tell susceptible to being comprehended" (p. 343). For those interested in the nuances of this radical revision of the Bible's provenance, Franke offers compelling evidence and hints at arguments to be found expanded in his later works. For the purposes of this current examination, the key point is that the concept of the primacy of poetry supplants some idea of unmediated experience, objective facts, or even perception. Poetry expresses, induces, and is a flow of experience too-easily masked behind explanations rife with unexamined assumptions.

In his reading of Harrison (1988), Franke (2011) sees the explanatory and narrative elements of Dante's prosimetrum form elevated above the lyric poems. In this move, Harrison (1988) would introduce the teleological and temporal elements so critical to his existential argument. Franke (2011), however, questions if the interspersed 'explanatory' prose of the *Vita Nuova* truly achieve this end. For Franke, Dante is narrating a conversion story rooted in the experience of revelation. Thus, explanations are a secondary sediment—a by-product only relevant in their capacity to point back to the revelation—the poetry itself. Although Dante would not have been aware of the radical stream of biblical exegesis Franke outlines, Franke is clear that the approach to faith, liturgy, and the Bible indigenous to Dante's world was one of revelation, not static explanation.

Thus, Beatrice is a revelation of Christ. Undoubtedly, Christological implications permeate Dante's work; but Franke (2011) goes further. 'The Event'—the revelation—is the irruption from which our meaning-making tumbles away. Beatrice cannot become a Christ if Jesus as Christ is not first known through the searing poetry that Franke posits as the core of Christian scripture. Who Jesus *is* comes before who Jesus *was*. Conveying the shift from the historical to the phenomenological, Franke explains:

> A chronicle of facts alone about this person could not reveal the person's extraordinary significance. The 'biographical' narratives subsequently elaborated are keyed to texts which do not state facts but convey, figuratively and lyrically, the meaning of a new life … This existentially verified, lived miracle, which is the presupposition for beginning the story, is first cast into a symbolic form 'lyrically' felt to embody and communicate this new and heightened life. Transposing this figural/lyrical core into a dimension of narrative, the book begins, then, with a miracle story, such as the annunciation of the angel to Mary or the apparition of Beatrice to Dante. (p. 344)

Franke goes so far as to speculate that Dante's prose explanations may even be fanciful and, regardless, they are secondary to the lyric or revelation.

Franke's (2011) argument profoundly parallels both his phenomenological sympathies as well as his devotion to apophatic spirituality. Poetry records the sounds we make in the face of the inexpressible—the revelation. The Ineffable surrounds, undergirds, indicts, and stretches our experience. Thus, the Gospels and the *Vita Nuova* stand on the same ground:

> The *Vita Nuova* and the gospel are both predicated on a common assumption that there is a subjective dimension of experience in which alone the deep reality and meaning of history or of a life-history, or even of just an event, can be perceived. Such meaning, in both cases, declared itself to memory and could be adequately represented only by a form of witness which projected an inner experience of miracle into the idiosyncratic diction of poetic language. Dante's acute awareness of this irreducibly subjective and personal

aspect of the advent of divinity and salvation shows clearly in his constant recourse to categories of dream, vision, and imagination in relating every one of Beatrice's epiphanies. (p. 347)

Franke asserts that Dante clearly demonstrates this commitment in his ongoing use of the verb 'to appear' throughout his works. For Franke, the objective reality that one has subjective experience forms an existential ground. This assertion is also synonymous with phenomenological reality. The reader could be forgiven for thinking of Jung's repeated use of the phrase 'objective psyche.'

With this ground laid, Franke (2011) can assert his objections to specific conclusions in Harrison's work (1988). In particular, Franke (2011) notes, "All this talk of appearance might induce us to make a distinction, as Robert Harrison does, between the phenomenal and the noumenal. But against this, I submit that Dante's language has not an epistemological but rather a hermeneutic import" (p. 349). Meaning-making exists in the matrix of each person's existential condition, whether in, for instance, its indeterminacy, mortality, or confrontations with its edges of knowability. Thus, the 'thing in itself' that is supposed to exist beyond or before perception—as implied by the term 'noumenal'—is actually part of the wrestling with meaning-making. For Franke, as discussed at the outset of this section, hermeneutics is phenomenology. Our meaning-making is our experience. Therefore, Franke expresses concern that Harrison posits being beyond meaning-making—an argument that cuts to the heart of Heidegger's existential phenomenology.

What then does Franke (2011) do with the objects of discussion? What of Husserl's 'things themselves'? Franke's answer appeals to Augustine's Presence, stating, "we are in a universe governed by a central transcendent Signified which turns everything else into signifiers of itself" (p. 352). Because Franke sees Harrison bracketing off the religious elements of Dante's New Life, Franke's—apophatic—theocentric ontology will, necessarily, be problematic for Harrison. The 'thing itself' for Harrison (1988) is in the title of his work—it is Beatrice's body perpetually veiled in the phenomenal. Franke (2011) repositions the encounter and asks the reader to consider the very 'presence-ing' of that body, even to the extent that the reader may wonder if Franke would consider the real referent to be the Body of Christ. Franke admits that reintegrating a discourse of faith into Dante scholarship does not accord with well-established currents in Dantology, noting,

> I think Harrison's biases are likely to be shared more generally among American Dante scholars and literary critics than my own. Nevertheless, the hermeneutics of faith should not be lost sight of in the interpretation of an author for whom a religious faith was paramount, as it ostensibly was for Dante—and even if this were only ostensibly so. (p. 354)

If Dante is to be relevant in the twenty-first century, it will not be in a discourse interpretatively sterilized of its religious elements.

In accord with Harrison (1988), Franke (2011) states that the experience of reading must be approached ontologically—how one reads and is changed in the reading will rest on existential grounds. Therefore, the meaning-making of the reader is an existential act addressing a work whose ground is fundamentally existential.

> I agree with Harrison that we must understand Dante's representations ontologically, but this is not because of what they *represent*, purportedly a real woman, but rather because of what they are: artifacts of an existential-poetic act. Dante's experience of a real woman, if that is what it was, comes to light in literature. (p. 354)

Franke's point is provocative. In his view, Harrison (1988) seeks to express the experience to which the writing refers. Franke (2011) seeks to remind us that all of Dante's works—and Franke's essay—are literature and expression itself. The expressing is the primary function—one of meaning-making.

Franke (2011) becomes more pointed in his critique. He questions if one can honestly speak of the 'primacy of perception'—hearkening to Merleau-Ponty's work of the same name—without ignoring the entanglement of subjectivities and objectivities in which meaning evolves. Thus, Franke summarizes,

> the meaning of human existence can never simply be perceived; it must rather be decided and enacted. Understanding revelation in existential terms need not stop with the primacy of perception, as Harrison would have it, but leads on to the risk and decision of interpretation, such as it has been lived and relived by believers in all ages. (pp. 355–356)

The theological is not an addition for Franke. In its yearning, questioning, indeterminacy, and lived convictions, the—poetic—theological stance is the fullest expression of the flow of experience.

Franke (2011) repeatedly challenges his reader to consider what one actually beholds in reading—entirely appropriate for reading an author like Dante who wrestles with seeing. What the reader beholds is writing that is a making of meaning. This text challenges readers to assess their own meaning-making. Regardless of what the text may refer to, the text itself is a making and remaking of meaning—the same process in which the reader engages. As Dante begins the *Vita Nuova*, he refers the reader to the 'book of his memory,' not a discerning review of documentary evidence and differing accounts of his life. Franke states, "in some sense the 'original' event must equally be considered to be writing itself—a sort of incarnation of the Word in Dante's individual existence" (p. 356). Thus, a more fundamental moment—an event, the Event—is at stake in Franke's reading of Dante. This event fractally pervades Dante's, Franke's, and the readers' experience—"it consists in the verbalization of experience or being" (p. 357).

Franke (2011) sees that Dante dodges the endless hall of self-referential mirrors—text about text about text …—by remaining firmly oriented toward transcendence. For Dante, these are the expanding frontiers of ineffability. Franke sees Dante preceding the inveigling morass of Cartesian subjectivity and thus able to attest to the inescapable encounter with alterity. Though Franke reads Harrison (1988) to raise these issues, Franke (2011) remains dissatisfied with the answers offered. Instead, Franke returns to Dante's religious context.

> Not knowing the other as an object of perception but relating through the word to an otherness that cannot be directly perceived is the way of transcendence proper to Dante's Christian medieval culture based especially on the technique of *lectio divinis*—the meditative and interpretive reading of sacred texts. (p. 358)

Repeatedly, Franke offers the privileged premodern grounding for Dante as a foil to not only his successors but also Harrison's (1988) interpretations. Franke (2011) places the revelation firmly within the pages of the *Vita Nuova* rather than deferring it to the future, as he characterizes Harrison (1988) doing. The ecstasy of the lyric is the means of this revelation.

Agreeing with Harrison (1988), Franke (2011) sees profound teleological elements, and for him, in his reclaiming of the Christian content, they are equally eschatological and existential. Beatrice's absence presents the same dilemma as does Christ's seeming absence after the Resurrection and Ascension. But it is only in Christ's absence that the longing for his Presence becomes the foundation of faith. Thus, Franke remains adamant that one ought not to reach too far beyond the bounds of the *Vita Nuova* to understand the revelation.

Finally, Franke (2011) challenges his reader to break down overly-convenient disciplinary and scholarly objectivity. He demands his reader come to terms with how life is lived when he states,

> We can decide to believe what the text witnesses to and thereby risk losing our scholarly objectivity—or we can decide to bracket such religious conviction and decision. But in either case our decision will radically determine the text as we encounter it and the possibilities of understanding and self-understanding that the text holds out to us. (p. 359)

And in doing so, Franke places Dante as a prophet and visionary of what Franke seats at the core of Christianity.

> That transcendent divinity should condescend to reveal itself in incarnate form was the germ and genius of the religion for which Dante became an ideologue and propagandist—not to say a prophet, which would be to espouse his biases and my own. (p. 359)

Thus, the fullest phenomenology is revelation—always and already. Religious discourse, setting aside political and cultural appropriations, contains an invitation to take up the meaning-making that is the stuff of experience in such a way as to free one to see the light shining at the limits of common understanding—the scintillating frontiers that are the ground of being.

For Franke (2011), whether in the Hebrew or Christian Bibles or the texts of the Florentine, the poetic is primary. Thus, the event, the revelation implicit in all phenomena, is a poetic one. Franke states it bluntly that "poetic figuration derives from existential reality" (p. 361). The fullest meaning will not be found in explanation. Meaning is meaning-making, and Franke reads the lyric poetry of the *Vita Nuova* as so profoundly rooted in life as to effect a transformation of the genre and the reader.

Franke's "Dante Studies After the Theological Turn" (2018)

In a 2018 essay for the *Oxford Critical Theory Review*, Franke addresses the return of a theological lens by which to examine Dante. Of course, the theology of the twenty-first century is not the theology of Dante's era. The theological shift to which Franke speaks leads him to review several important works defining new shared territory between theology and literary theory relative to the Florentine. Of note for this current chapter is Franke's citation of the work of French philosopher Janicaud (1937–2002) in which phenomenology and theology find shared discourse. Franke also uses this essay to praise the work of Webb, who examines the implications of Dante's challenging stance regarding personhood in *Paradiso*. Franke notes that,

> Webb unobtrusively works some of the weightiest traditions of thinking about persons, as well as some of the newer knowledge from the cognitive psychology and neurosciences, into her probes of Dante's incomparable phenomenological exploration of the experience of being a person. (p. 3)

That is, in the face of the seductive anti-gravity of theological abstractions, Dante's humanity endures and transforms through his fealty to phenomenological description.

Ultraphenomenology: Levinas, the Other, and Franke

Phenomenology, regardless of which species, relies on the idea of an object in its *assumed* reality. Phenomenology is always the phenomenology *of* … . A phenomenology will necessarily track the shifting definition of, relationship to, or sense of a perceiving self in the face of this object. To free phenomenologists from the tyranny of the object's 'reality,' Husserl's epoché was a contentious but liberating caesura in the history of philosophy and human science. It enables phenomenologists to set aside the physiological, physical, and so-called objective aspects of sensation and perception, to focus on the flow of experience. Phenomenologists place the object's objective reality—asserted by the 'natural attitude' nearly everyone holds toward a material world—aside. A phenomenology will describe the comportment of consciousness toward these bracketed objects. Many phenomenologists conveniently demur on questions of the object's ultimate reality, preferring to focus on the fecund epistemological shift the epoché effects.

The postmodern condition presents what one might think is a boon to phenomenology. In postmodernity, the object is held in a state of deep suspicion. Heidegger enshrines what was already a contentious philosophical issue when he defines *dasein*—being-in-the-world—as that sort of being which has its being in question. If my being is in question, then the being of that which I behold may be even more so. In an update to Descartes's fundamental question as described earlier in this chapter, phenomenology steps in to respond that, although my being, the being of other people, and the being of things may indeed be dubious, we cannot ignore that we have these pervasive experiences regarding all these modes of being. Yet the postmodern philosopher remains vexed by the insurmountable distance between signifier and signified.

The problem is not new. As Asay (2014) explains, Augustine placed true Presence beyond our ken. Any appeal to the being of an object or being, in general, is a leveraged transaction, borrowing from an unreachable referent. Augustine removes the transitory being, upon which every thought or action relies, from the playing field of life—placing being beyond the bounds. Therefore, what is phenomenology when the brackets of the epoché contain either an arrow-pointing-'beyond' or a promissory note? Is this a phenomenology of nihilism, a phenomenology of mystical longing?

Franke (2007) turns the reader's attention to Dante's *Paradiso* and the philosophy of Levinas to describe this territory in what he considers its native tongue: ethics. He explains that ethics is

> fundamental to any disclosure of the world and to the very consciousness of self ... Ethics in this sense is more than one branch of knowledge among others; it enfolds in embryo a comprehensive vision of the world and its conditions of possibility. (p. 209)

Ontology, epistemology, and phenomenology will all spin-off from this ethical core in Franke's examination. Franke sees this stance as native to Dante, who "follows the Latin humanist tradition in elevating ethics to a preeminent position as the sum and goal of all knowledge" (p. 210). This is a lived world that is fundamentally and unavoidably intentional. Franke bridges Dante and Levinas explaining,

> for both authors the essence of ethics is a radical transcendence of oneself in relation to an Other who is other than all one can say. This relation is constituted in language, but specifically as its limit-condition and as manifest in the

> failure of language adequately to represent or express this unapproachable, inappropriable otherness. (p. 210)

Ineffability is at the core—at the ever-present frontiers?—of Franke's (2007) undertaking. He seeks to interweave the premodern and the postmodern. A metaphysics rooted in apophatic theology "that recognizes God as ineffable and as manifest precisely in the experience of language's failure brings the Paradiso close to various postmodern modes of thinking" (p. 211). Franke singles out Dante's opening passages of *Paradiso* to remind the reader that the poem is shot through with this ineffability. "[N]either has he been able to comprehend and so remember what he 'saw,' nor would he be able to express it in words even if he had" (p. 214). Dante, after all, has set his task as a phenomenology of the Ineffability of Ultimate Alterity. This is not a lyric swoon where Dante falls into solipsistic archsubjectivity. Franke emphasizes that Dante often frames his revelations as objective realities of experience.

Franke (2007) refocuses his reader on the experience of an objectivity that has no object. This shift seeks to represent

> an ineffable one-knows-not-what. Whatever it is that they endeavor in vain to convey remains in itself irreducibly beyond expression and objectification. It cannot be properly signified by words but requires rather a first-person experience of "transhumanization" on the part of whoever is going to succeed in understanding the experience of paradise that Dante, from the very first canto, categorically renounces describing in any objective manner:
>
> > Trasumanar significar per verba
> > non si poria; pero l'essemplo basti
> > a cui esperienza grazia serba,
> > (I:70–72)
>
> [As Franke translates the passage from *Paradiso*:]
>
> > (Transhumanizing cannot be signified by words;
> > so let the example suffice for the one
> > to whom grace reserves the experience) (p. 215)

In his efforts to give voice to this experience, Dante must objectively note the limitations of his own subjectivity but acknowledge the call from the deepest of passions to stretch beyond these limits.

To categorize this undertaking, Franke (2007) finally engages the phenomenology that has been hiding just below the surface of his essay.

> Levinas is an invaluable guide into the inaccessible reaches of an ethical "experience" that is, properly speaking, beyond experience and expression. His

> ultraphenomenological explorations illuminate philosophically what may after all be the only possible path through the territory of the ineffable and unrepresentable, a territory that is also charted, however differently, by the Paradiso, in which the metaphysical imagery functions as a metaphor for what in the end demands to be understood as an ethical relation to the unrepresentable Other—whether this be God or a significant Other like Beatrice. (p. 216)

This 'ultraphenomenology' is the phenomenology of a fundamental orientation beyond oneself, beyond one's expressive capacity. Is all phenomenology an ultraphenomenology? Explicitly, obviously not. But, if any and all experiences are simply veils cast between an unknowable Other and a secondary fathomless subject? Then, ecstatically, yes. And in this encounter, the ethical is not an addition, an extrapolation, or a commentary. The ethical is the voice and substance of these ultraphenomena.

> There is no phenomenon that can make manifest, nor any words that can directly represent, this sort of contact ... Only its bearing upon me and the infinite obligations with which it binds me can genuinely be "experienced"—that is, irresistibly produce an ethical conviction in me ... [R]epresentations, not of the Other but of its effects on me, can and indeed do proliferate. This is what, according to Levinas, engenders the ethical subject, the core of the me ("le moi"), in its uniqueness. (p. 216)

The Other precedes the one who is ethically indebted to the Other. Thus, at the core of every being is this debt—*my* debt—to the Other.

As Franke (2007) describes it, Dante's flights through Heaven undo him and leave him in holy and ecstatic "vulnerability to the invasion of otherness" (p. 217). These wounds constitute what Franke characterizes as the 'Passion of the Subject'—the only authentic orientation of the subject to alterity, according to Levinas. This subject inhabits a world where every signification and all significance comes from an inarticulable—and perhaps unconscious—obsession with the Other. Franke elaborates that all meaning and significance is from "transcending the self towards the Other to whom one is ethically responsible before one is even conscious of being oneself—for this ethical responsibility vis-a-vis an Other is the bond that first makes a human being individual and 'one'" (p. 219). Ethics are the structure of reality, of reality-making, that is, of signification. The simple acts of interaction with things and the meaning-making of even the most banal of actions refer to and exist from the Other. One cannot escape this ethical ground of being that is, in truth, a vector pointing beyond one's limits.

Having set this Levinasian structure, Franke (2007) presents Dante in this light of alterity.

> Dante's whole poem ... is an attempt to describe the passion whereby one becomes possessed by the Other as "God"; in the failure of its descriptions

> it illustrates the passivity in which one is affected by the Other at the very core of and indeed before the origin of one's being. Dante's most profound reality is that of the Infinite, and it is thus wholly incommensurable with any humanly definable identity. Just as Augustine had found God to be more interior than his own self ("interior meo," *Confesiones* III,vi,ll), so Dante transcends himself as he moves towards an infinite and unknowable God at every stage of his journey through Paradise. (p. 219)

This orientation to the Other that demands an ongoing self-transcendence is synonymous with an orientation to the Ineffable that defies derivative and deceptive reifications of language and being. Franke clarifies that the *Commedia* "is the witness to what it is not, to the Transcendent that has passed through the subject's experience, leaving the subject in effect traumatized, at the same time as it constitutes the ethical subject in the first place" (p. 220). What may be implicit in Levinas's writings for some religious readers becomes explicit in Franke's reading of Dante: how one relates to God and neighbor align (p. 220). This Dantean and Levinasian subject is, at its most fundamental level, a longing and desire for what lies beyond its reach and ken, but is nevertheless its most intimate reality.

To illustrate, Franke (2007) looks to the many impasses of expression Dante narrates. Even Dante's memory buckles and fails in the face of the task of recalling what has no words. For Franke, this Levinasian 'obsession' and 'desire' drive the subject, even to the point of annihilation. Franke cites the mortal Semele in Canto XXI of *Paradiso* demanding to see the god Jove, which leads to her destruction, as well as Dante's ongoing struggle to even fully behold Beatrice in the light of Heaven. These are not mere external forces. Because one's being is founded on this debt and call to alterity, "the Other in me" (p. 222) indicts the vanity of identity from within as well. Franke elaborates that this interiority is an incarnational one of vulnerability. Rather than some spiritual abstraction, the transactions of alterity are visceral.

> Before anything definable in terms of consciousness, I am my vulnerability to being hurt, and the immediacy of my bodily existence exposed externally is the sign of this. Humanly and ethically, I am constituted by the exposure to and responsibility for the Other. This is what Levinas calls "incarnation." (p. 222)

Franke admits that Dante hedges the literality and physicality of his visions of Paradise, but not their reality. In this sense, Franke sees a powerful parallel to Paul's vision discussed in *2 Corinthians* and Paul's inability to determine whether these were 'in the body' or not.

This specific indeterminacy of the experiences is not accidental. Franke (2007) emphasizes that this journey toward what has always been the truth—that 'I' cannot even claim my own being—will undo all certainties, except perhaps one's fundamental yearning for the Other. Throughout the *Commedia*, Dante has been an audacious and presumptuous narrator and character. Yet, by the end, "*Paradiso*, undoes this whole construction, unsays the said, opens Dante's carefully constructed and strongly asserted self to an Infinity and otherness in its midst" (p. 223). God is, for Dante, the 'great sea of being' upon which his little ship has been repeatedly shattered. The reader could, thus, be forgiven for imagining that Franke is contradicting other aforementioned writers who assert that Dante maintains his uniqueness through even the final mystical vision. However, Franke reminds his reader that Dante continues to struggle with giving voice to the experience, even as he fails to find the words. Therefore, the sojourn of Dante-the-Pilgrim is

> a return home, but it is a return to an unknown, never before experienced "home" in the otherness of God, and to this extent it is a being at home in exile … "God" is the truth of a self that can never truly know itself except in the God who transcends knowledge. (p. 224)

With his elaborate cosmic landscapes, many readers count Dante's work as fundamentally metaphysical. Franke (2007) disagrees. This is a landscape of an experience, an ultraphenomenology of experience itself—and an experience that is thoroughly ethical in its discourse. Metaphysics, Franke reminds his reader, is a totalizing narrative. As audacious as Dante may be, he is wise enough not to attempt such a thing. The Other is far vaster than any cosmology can contain. In this refutation of metaphysics' agenda, Franke casts Dante in accord with postmodern thought. *Paradiso* is a narration of this essential journey of being itself. To stretch beyond our ontological boundaries, one cannot merely ignore or "suppress Being, Being is what one needs in order to go beyond. This is what Dante's poem, as a celebration of being in a self-transcending song of the self, in effect demonstrates" (p. 225). The descriptions of struggling to say what is fundamentally beyond saying, the narrative that folds in on itself as the author and character become synonymous, and a lived world driven by an intentionality toward transcendence—these mark, for Franke, Dante's final work as kin to postmodern thought. Franke uses Levinas's ethical ultraphenomenology to cast the blinding light of the Other on Dante's work and discovers ineffably radiant resonance.

Franke is the only author to date to link Dante and Levinas at any length. This absence is noteworthy since the unfolding relationship to the Other is so deeply woven into all of Dante's works, but especially the *Commedia*—from isolation to the loving mentorship from Virgil to the blazing guidance of Beatrice to the ultimate frontier of expression and being. However, because it necessitates engaging with *Paradiso*, perhaps the lack of extensive investigations is understandable. His final text is Dante's complete summation and his apotheosis. Its imagery forces the reader out of the literality of Hell and the rich symbolism of Purgatory to narratives of ineffable transcendence. Nevertheless, Levinasian examinations of Dante's work seem a rich territory for future scholars to explore.

Conclusion to Franke's Contributions

Later in this current volume, Franke challenges his reader to imagine what a modernity growing out of Dante would have looked like instead of his contemporary Duns Scotus (1266–1308). As Franke describes it, Scotus offers a 'univocal' being that enables access to all subjects through what would become the scientific world view. Franke notes that the 'crisis of representation' plagued both men, but Dante's 'emphasis on ineffability' offers edges to rationality and being that modernity's materialism cannot acknowledge. Thus, Franke extends this current chapter's thesis of Dante as a proto-phenomenologist to a complete provenance of an alternative epistemology and ontology.

Franke courts the imaginal frequently in his writings, but his is not a Jungian nor Hillmanian legacy. The primacy of theology cuts through all his works, and a particular type of theophany is the ground of being he offers his reader. In particular, Franke's interweaving of Levinas and Dante's *Paradiso* brings together several themes from Franke's other phenomenologically-oriented examinations of Dante.

With the major works that narrate the encounter between Dante and phenomenology summarized, this essay now turns to individual chapters and articles.

Articles Linking Dante and Phenomenology

This section chronologically presents articles, essays, and book chapters that circumscribe phenomenological elements in the creation, intention, and reading of Dante's works.

Nolan's "The Vita Nuova and Richard of St. Victor's Phenomenology of Vision" (1974)

Perhaps the earliest work to link the two topics is a 1974 article by Nolan. The examination centers on a moment in the *Vita Nuova* when the Lord of Love appears to Dante and asks Dante to put aside all *simulacra*—a word most associated with false idols in biblical and theological literature. Dante is to go deeper into experience rather than merely recount or symbolically interpret. The Lord mournfully follows with a description of how Dante must necessarily dwell at the circumference of the circle while the Lord is the center. Nolan interprets this as a foreshadowing of Dante's ascension into Paradise; and a reader might also read this as instructions for Dante to dwell more fully with his current experience and leave metaphysical abstractions for those who dwell in heavenly realms.

Nolan (1974) draws upon the mystical phenomenology of Richard of St. Victor, who died in 1173, to create a strongly theological gloss of Dante's early work, placing the *Vita Nuova* much more with medieval religious works than love poetry. Nolan tracks the development of Dante's 'seeing'—both externally and internally—in the work. Contemporary to Hillman's earliest publications, Nolan's essay bears a strongly imaginal/archetypal perspective, perhaps best placing it with Corbin's examinations of Sufism. Nevertheless, Nolan is in the Singletonian school of Dante interpretation—that is Christian symbolist—and tends to deal in carnal versus higher love dichotomies rather than a transformation of love that would be truer to Augustinian and Thomistic theology.

Nolan (1974) challenges her modern readers to decide what to do with mystic visionaries: Are they psychotic, hyperbolic, or, as Nolan suggests, must the sincere interpreter move to a phenomenology that renders the accounts 'true'? Nolan sees a clear phenomenology thriving in medieval mystics. Thus, Nolan tracks the transformation of Dante's visions from Beatrice's crimson drape to the ineffable frontier at the end of the work. She portrays the visions as 'sacramental'—a word that, for her, is synonymous with 'phenomenological'—that is, true to a lived world.

Shoaf's "Medieval Studies After Derrida After Heidegger" (1989)

The next work to contain phenomenological insights into Dante is a chapter by Shoaf from 1989 that arguably presents the case for the reading of Dante as a phenomenological experience of meaning-making. Significantly, Shoaf begins his essay with a vector of Heidegger's thought that others do not emphasize in their discussions of Dante, but with which Franke would clearly concur in his multiple writings, especially in emphasizing the primacy of poetry (2011). Drawing from Heidegger's *An Introduction to Metaphysics*, Shoaf (1989) quotes, "It is in words and language that things first come into being and are" (p. 9). The primacy of language, of signification, a move so instinctual to postmodern thinkers, takes on fresh significance when considering Dante's quest to create expression in the face of the Ineffable. Nevertheless, as Shoaf notes, although Dante's literary world overflows with interrelationships much as the postmodern condition leaves the subject today; unlike today, Providence guides Dante's world. Regardless, in both eras, Shoaf finds Heidegger, "and, in particular, his instruments, especially useful just because they seek the 'relation of all relations' or language" (p. 10).

In order to begin his quest to liberate Dante from doctrinaire interpretations, Shoaf (1989) extensively quotes from the "Epistle to Can Grande." Regardless of debates of authorship, the work is popularly attributed to Dante, and it serves as an introduction and interpretive guide to the *Commedia*, and the *Paradiso* in particular. Shoaf quotes this Dante: "It should be understood that there is not just a single sense in this work: it might rather be called polysemous, that is, having several senses" (p. 13). Even Dante's various levels of analysis create frictions and contrasts with one another in what Shoaf poses as a parallel to Derrida's *différance*.

Shoaf's (1989) most abiding point is a refocus on the experience of reading as a primary act. To read is to be made and to make. Reading is not an exercise in uncovering a unified intention, but a play of possibility—veiling and unveiling.

Thus, the very experience of reading becomes a phenomenon—becomes *the* phenomena. Shoaf states:

> And yet, if we attend carefully to what Dante has written, we can see, I think, how this fullness of Scripture "is" emptiness (Derrida would write this "is" *sous rature* ["under erasure"]); the extra-literal meanings clearly are to be occupied, filled, by each reader, with himself; and to be so occupied, they must, just as clearly, in some sense, be empty—to be so applicable to a given individual's discrete, historical situation, these meanings must be full only in such a way as to be empty. So also with the extra-literal meaning of Dante's poem itself: it is empty as full insofar as each of us can insert himself into the articulations of rewards and punishments—find himself or herself in a type that is also an individual. In both cases, in short, and to make the crucial point, to read the text is to write it, is to write oneself into it and ultimately after it. Every reading of these texts, every medieval reading, is a supplementary writing of the texts. And what fullness there is does not obtain without its answering emptiness. (p. 14)

In reading, one is also, thus, being written by the text as one also writes it. One becomes a story, a poem—in accord with Asay's (2014) observations regarding frame narratives. Finally, Shoaf (1989) even goes so far as to link—in Caputo-like fashion (see *The Prayers and Tears of Jacques Derrida*, 1997)—mystical emptying to postmodern deconstruction.

Just as frontiers of ineffability structure Harrison's and Franke's readings, Shoaf (1989) calls his readers to encounter emptying and emptiness in order that the play of meaning may remain fresh and vital. Shoaf states, "It is to disseminate anew possibilities of perceived relations in texts or words whose usage has hardened their fictionality or metaphoricity into a pseudo-proper, a meaningless, meaningfulness" (p. 15). In this way, Shoaf advocates, without using the word, an epoché around previous interpretations.

Traditional readings, for Shoaf (1989), block any real meaning, since meaning is always personal and must involve a simultaneous emptying and filling. Like De Monticelli (2000), seeing the Medusa as a figure of rigid rationalism, Shoaf (1989) cites that becoming locked into interpretive paradigms becomes the curse of that Gorgon appearing on the ramparts of Dis. Shoaf observes that,

> In Dante, Medusa is a figure of literalism, of the letter that kills (2 Cor 3:6), and correspondingly, of a kind of reading which insists on the letter and resists figuration, that reading which refuses to lift the veil of, indeed, if need be, to rend the veil, to see underneath. (p. 16)

Shoaf beautifully illustrates through an extended metaphor from Canto XXIV:1–15 of the *Inferno* how allowing the text to unfold without the reader rigidly clutching interpretive biases is critical.

> In that part of the young year when the sun
> begins to warm its locks beneath Aquarius
> and nights grow shorter, equaling the days,
>
> when hoarfrost mimes the image of his white
> sister upon the ground—but not for long,
> because the pen he uses is not sharp—
>
> the farmer who is short of fodder rises
> and looks and sees the fields all white, at which
> he slaps his thigh, turns back into the house,
>
> and here and there complains like some poor wretch
> who doesn't know what can be done, and then
> goes out again and gathers up new hope
>
> on seeing that the world has changed its face
> in so few hours, and he takes his staff
> and hurries out his flock of sheep to pasture. (Alighieri, 1320/1982,
> Mandelbaum translation)

Dante's pen, frost's pen, the farmer, the farmer's misinterpretation of frost as snow in Dante's simile, and the reader all participate in a complex and transformative dance of shifting interpretations. Shoaf opines that Dante himself advocates for this very polysemous practice. This awareness of shifts in meaning-making is, of course, entirely authentic to phenomenology, although Shoaf does not use that word. Shoaf further bolsters this emptying of text and reader by citing Augustine's realization that readers of the Bible may find very real truths not intended by the scripture. Shoaf quotes Augustine stating, "I should prefer to write it in such a way that a reader could find re-echoed in my words whatever truths he was able to apprehend" (p. 23). Shoaf summarizes his point with the axiom that "we humans come to truth only by wandering. For Derrida, such wandering consists of detours. For Augustine, it is pilgrimaging, to the Truth who is no one's private property" (p. 23).

This essay (Shoaf, 1989), overarchingly, establishes that approaching Dante with postmodern sensibilities is not an imposition, but an—ironically, given Shoaf's resistance to historical perspectives—historically authentic approach. Contained within Shoaf's postmodern approach is a sense that an existential-phenomenological perspective on Dante is not only viable but vital. Shoaf advocates not the certainties of modern inquiry, but the uncertainties of a postmodern reading and establishes the paternity of this freedom in Dante's own works. Moreover, Shoaf asserts that the origins of this approach might well be seen more broadly as native to the medieval approach to literature.

Scarry's "On Vivacity: The Difference Between Daydreaming and Imagining-Under-Authorial-Instruction" (1995)

In 1995, Scarry published an article that seeks to discuss authors' approaches to creating absorbing descriptions of spaces. Scarry roots her discussion in the observation that one's own imaginations are too often quite fleeting and undeveloped, yet an author can create remarkably vivid settings for a reader. This vivacity is, however, far from universal in writing. Thus, Scarry enters into an archly phenomenological discussion of how layers, both literal and figurative, can enhance the experience of vivacity. The sunlight cast through a scrim onto an opposite wall can fix a space in a way in which a description of that wall unto itself could never do. The reader of Scarry's essay might easily move to the crimson veil around the dreamed-of-Beatrice in *Vita Nuova*. And, although the text of the article itself has nothing directly to do with Dante, in an endnote, Scarry discusses a personal correspondence with the poet Robert Pinsky, known in this context for his 1995 translation of the *Inferno*:

> Robert Pinsky observes that Dante's Inferno may be "a supreme example of one kind of surface passing over another, one made more solid or opaque by the sliding." ... Pinsky calls attention to the many passages in which the ability of a physical body to displace material stones or ground is contrasted with the inability of a shade to do so. "Hell itself (and its inhabitants) is one great scrim passing over a more solid reality. Or the reverse, apparent material reality is really a scrim of transparent illusion passing over the more solid moral reality underneath." (Scarry, 1995, p. 24)

Thus, Scarry's phenomenology of imagined spaces gives way to a metaphoric interpretation of the imaginal as a foundation for 'reality.' This layering of possibilities speaks to both the challenges many readers face when first encountering the *Commedia* and also the richness of the many returns to this 'polysemous' text. Dante's premodern perspective may actually turn the habitual materialism of modernity into a primacy-of-the-imaginal that renders the various derivative materialities we take for reality.

Ardissimo and Scarini's "Fenomenologia Do Maravilhoso Na Literatura Italiana" (2011)

In a broad-reaching essay from 2011 with profuse references, Ardissimo and Scarini strike a distinctly imaginal tone without ever referencing authors from that tradition. The authors' work rests on the paradox that the fantastical in literature often seeks to speak more clearly to "dimensions of daily life and the ordinary" (p. 4) than do non-fiction or 'realistic fiction.' The authors emphasize that Dante's work stands on a fealty to everyday experience. Thus, they state, "Beatrice is, therefore, the prodigy, or the supernatural event that enters the daily life of Dante to reveal to him an unexpected dimension of existence" (p. 4). Therefore, the power of the story overcomes and transcends the stagnation of labels and pedantry of metaphysics. Ardissimo and Scarini state, "With Beatrice, Dante solves the contradiction between carnal love and spiritual love, love for Beatrice is never contrary to love for God" (p. 5). In this, the authors clearly declare that Dante identifies "Beatrice with Christ" (p. 5)—a transcendent, incarnate figure whose reality irrupts into human lives. The parallels to Asay's 2014 dissertation and several pieces of Franke's works are strong as Ardissimo and Scarini (2011) present an intentional lived world best known through fantastical fictions. An argument some might take up against a phenomenological approach to Dante is to ask how stories rife with dreams, visions, and fantastical landscapes could be considered 'phenomenological.' Ardissimo and Scarini's essay offers a powerful reply.

Shores's "Body and World in Merleau-Ponty and Deleuze" (2012)

Shores's article from 2012 rests in the most formal philosophical definition of 'phenomenology' placing it in the minority of the literature. In it, Shores pits Merleau-Ponty's canonical insistence on the unity and wholeness of experience against Deleuze's predictable emphasis on discontinuity and disruption. Shores dedicates most of the article to summarizing the integrative nature of Merleau-Ponty's project. This includes an emphasis on foreshadowing and expectation. In contrast, experience, for Deleuze as read by Shores, ought to be understood best as those elements that precisely do not fit and thus create decomposition. Shores notes, challenging a tenant of Merleau-Ponty, that neither the body nor embodied experience are adequate to hold together phenomena. Shores cites Deleuze's use of an episode from the *Inferno* to explain. In this episode, from *Inferno* VI:7–21, Dante is surrounded by the writhing bodies of the gluttonous.

> I am in the third circle, filled with cold,
> unending, heavy, and accursed rain;
> its measure and its kind are never changed.
>
> Gross hailstones, water gray with filth, and snow
> come streaking down across the shadowed air;
> the earth, as it receives that shower, stinks.
>
> Over the souls of those submerged beneath
> that mess, is an outlandish, vicious beast,
> his three throats barking, doglike: Cerberus.
>
> His eyes are bloodred; greasy, black, his beard;
> his belly bulges, and his hands are claws;
> his talons tear and flay and rend the shades.

> That downpour makes the sinners howl like dogs;
> they use one of their sides to screen the other—
> those miserable wretches turn and turn. (Alighieri, 1320/1982, Mandelbaum translation)

Shores (2012) explains Deleuze's reading:

> Rain droplets are pelting a damned soul, disrupting the composition of his skin at that location and thereby sending shock waves of decompositional forces throughout the rest of his body. Yet, to maintain his constitution, the soul turns up a new side of his body that is more able to sustain the affections. He is aware of how the rain affects him, and he thus knows how to self-affectively alter himself so to maintain his differential contact with it. Our active self-affection and adaptive interaction with the world around us is what Deleuze here calls "rhythm." (p. 203)

Shores offers further examples from Deleuze of this rhythm, for instance, in the swimmer's disruption upon encountering a powerful wave. Where and what is a body that is shot through with such vectors of power? A further example comes in the mutual disruptions and alterations of two musicians improvising with each other. One can perhaps hear the echoes of that mysticism Caputo believes rests apophatically within many postmodern theorists' works as not even human bodies or souls can maintain a continuity. Thus, what can be the shredding tortures of Hell, in Deleuze's example, could become the ineffable mystical blaze of Paradise.

To state it more succinctly, challenging the synesthetic holism of Merleau-Ponty, Shores (2012) characterizes Deleuze's idea of sensation as a decompositional rhythm in which disruption is what truly constitutes experience. Disruption, difference, discontinuity—these are what construct the wave of phenomena that humans blithely distort into consistent identity in Shores's gloss of Deleuze. At the same time, this Deleuze is not advocating for a physiological explanation—this is a 'body without organs.' Shores summarizes a vision in which Merleau-Ponty's synesthesia does not reign because there is no synthesis—solely 'waves of disruption' ripple through a space that will only temporarily distinguish its organ of experience but soon dissolve.

Nevertheless, the stance Shores (2012) presents from Deleuze may be more of an internecine innovation than a wholesale impugnment of Merleau-Ponty's legacy. Shores concludes:

> Merleau-Ponty's theory better accounts for the ongoing constitution of phenomenal objects, the familiar things in the world around us, while Deleuze's theory better explains the intensity of any given moment of phenomenal experience. Thus, although Deleuze's model in many fundamental ways contraposes Merleau-Ponty's model, we need not regard it as a critique of

phenomenology itself, but rather as a useful contribution to phenomenology's pool of theoretical ideas. (p. 207)

With these opposing visions, might the reader not be encountering contrasting modes of lived experience? The *Inferno* undoubtedly offers ample evidence of disintegrating forces staved off only temporarily by defiance, pride, contentious story-telling to cement one's legacy in the living world, and all the other vice-ridden strategies that bolster the brittle self in Hell. What then can one make of the voluntary and intentional suffering of *Purgatorio*? Is the disruption a welcome purgation of Hell's inauthentic fixations? And, moreover, in *Paradiso*, the reader witnesses epic syntheses of mounting cosmic forces. Yet, here Dante still maintains some I-Thou even unto the face of the divine, though his expressive capacities finally fail in earnest.

Although Shores (2012) remains firmly within the discourses of twentieth-century Continental Philosophy, Asay's (2014) radical interpolation of Augustine's ideas of Presence comes to mind as well in this discussion. This Presence defies one's ability to capture, yet creates and drives the ability to fervently desire to reach it through one's own ontology and expression. Does Merleau-Ponty's perspective rely on a more unified self than Augustine could endorse? Alternately, do Deleuze's discontinuities bespeak a presence that is other to the assumed subjects and objects of everyday experience?

Shores's (2012) essay offers, arguably, more potential for a traditionally phenomenological analysis of the *Commedia*, even though the Dante connection is secondary and brief. The shift is more than hermeneutic, in that the phenomenologies themselves shift rather than merely the interpretive lenses. Shores's essay offers a provocative invitation for future scholars.

Monticelli's "Fear in Dante's Inferno: Phenomenology, Semiotics, Aesthetics" (2015)

Monticelli (2015) begins his chapter with the tension between Dante the architect, author, and poet of the *Commedia*, versus Dante the epic poem's protagonist and pilgrim. Monticelli characterizes this as a "cognitive dissonance" (p. 107), but one from which Dante does not ultimately retreat, though the character often cowers, faints, demurs, and otherwise attempts to avoid what faces him. Moreover, Monticelli sees further tensions woven into the process of the creation of the epic, "in the transitions from experience to memory, from memory to intellectual conceptualisation and from there to linguistic expression" (p. 107). Though other commentators leap ahead to the resolution of this conflict with ideas of a Hegelian dialectic or Jung's transcendent function achieving a mystical synthesis in Paradise, Monticelli finds dwelling with the nature of the tension will prove essential if one is not to impose doctrine and dogma onto the poem. That is, Monticelli prefers a phenomenological fealty to the experience of Dante over any interpretive tradition. Like other commentators, he even repurposes Husserl's epoché, in this case, to bracket off previous moral, political, theological, or philosophical discourses.

Monticelli (2015) repeatedly uses the term 'pathemic' in his essay. He seems to intend the psychiatric symptom of 'pathemic aphasia' wherein a patient experiences loss of speech when overwhelmed with emotion. In this usage, Monticelli thinks of all the times Dante cannot give words to his experience and may even faint—or fear that he will—in the face of overwhelming experiences, especially in *Inferno*. Thus, Monticelli chooses 'fear' to be the exemplar of this phenomenon. Dante must discipline these pathemic spasms in the face of the unspeakable in Hell to become present to the Ineffable of Paradise. Even from the opening passage of *Inferno*'s Canto I, Dante the author experiences fear in recalling the dark woods. The fear overflows the page. Therefore, in order to understand the transformation, Monticelli (2015) proposes three disciplines, "phenomenology, semiotics and aesthetics" (p. 109).

Monticelli (2015) begins his phenomenology of fear with Aristotle, but quickly finds the Greek philosopher's conceptualization ill-suited for Dante's initial fear in the dark woods. Aristotle demands an identifiable threatening object of the fear, but Dante can scarcely be said to be afraid of trees or mere darkness. Thus, Monticelli turns to Heidegger and his concept of *angst*. Monticelli notes that Heidegger intends angst to be a sort of fear, but contrasts it to the mere fear—*furcht*—of an object. If there is something that angst is about, it is being-in-the-world itself. If hearkened to, and not sublimated into inauthentic fear of some object, angst can pull one into a world that has become insignificant. "*Angst* destroys, in other words, our familiarity with the world" (p. 113), a state that leaves one in the experience of 'not-being-at-home.' "Not-being-at-home uproots us from the everyday network of meanings that silently ensures the effectiveness of our innerworldly activities. This is why *Unheimlichkeit* [not-being-at-home] basically coincides with *Unbedeutsamkeit* [insignificance]" (p. 113). Thus, with his 'right road lost,' Dante is, in Monticelli's formulation, in the grips of angst when he speaks of 'fear.' Finding himself in these dark woods, Dante cannot recall how he got there, and Monticelli sees this as a further Heideggerian parallel with 'thrownness'—one does not come to the world, one always already finds oneself in the world. The Florentine is lost in meaninglessness, uncertainty, and alienation—a decidedly existential Dante.

Although Monticelli (2015) thinks Heidegger's angst works well to explain the opening phenomenological context of Dante's epic journey, Monticelli does not believe Heidegger's development of angst as a call toward authentic being-toward-death describes how Dante's journey unfolds. Monticelli sees Dante's movement from angst to actual fear as a sign that a Heideggerian solution is not apt. Monticelli believes that Dante needs tools and objects to work through his impasse, and that will not happen in a narrative of the 'nothing and nowhere' of Heidegger's angst. Monticelli turns back to Aristotle and his interpretation of the tragedy. The audience must viscerally experience pity and fear in order to undergo that necessary transformative fire of catharsis. Hence, Monticelli pulls Dante out of his angst and into a theatrical fear that will grant him the objects by which he can undertake his journey. The next stage of the journey will, in Monticelli's formulation, unfold in a 'Semiotics of Fear.'

Monticelli's (2015) semiotics develop over four stages. First comes the angst, which offers Dante no distance in which to make meaning. Second, Monticelli draws his reader's attention to the sun, which Dante would climb the hill to see. The possibility of a re-orienting 'seeing' arises. Third, the beasts thwart Dante's assent, and real fear returns. And, fourth, knowledge must prevail; therefore, Virgil and Beatrice enter the narrative to guide the pilgrim. The semiotic movement is from the indeterminacy of angst, to the palpability of fear, to the liberation offered by knowledge.

From this semiotic transformation, Monticelli (2015) shifts Dante to the aesthetic in the liminal spaces of Hell and reintroduces Heidegger. In Hell, Heideggerian 'innerworldly beings'—those beings which we encounter within the world—are no longer things which facilitate us falling into everydayness. These strange objects are fraught with betweenness.

> The new fear which seizes Dante uncontrollably in the infernal space lies in between *Angst* and *Furcht*: its objects are the infernal shadows [*ombre*], which can in a way be considered Heideggerian "innerworldly beings" of the strangest kind—their Being is essentially contaminated by nothingness, and their innerworldly presence is already marked by a fundamental absence. (p. 119)

The darkness of the woods transforms into the fundamental condition of Hell. Though the infernal realms are vast, the pilgrims are frequently caught in a claustrophobic foreshortening, which leaves Dante unable to see and discern anything beyond what is immediately apparent. The condemned souls who could not foresee the consequences of their life choices face a hellish contrapasso that enshrines their shortsightedness.

Monticelli (2015) offers three aesthetic strategies to work through Hell's sensory entrapment. For Monticelli, much like a Jungian analyst, conflicts must move into "full sensory perception" (p. 118) for one to adequately encounter and then transcend them. Nevertheless, the perception is overwhelming. Thus, the experience must first be given sight. Second, the intensity must be attenuated by avoiding becoming enthralled. For Dante and Virgil, this means they must keep moving to escape becoming mired in curiosity, pity, disgust, or intoxication (p. 125). Third, "[p]erception must be focused in order to avoid that indeterminacy which sets the imagination free and amplifies fear" (p. 125). The metacommentary in this third aesthetic strategy threatens to make the reader's head spin. In a work that is entirely of Dante-the-Poet's imagination, Dante-the-Pilgrim must focus his perception so as not to swoon into tremulous imagined fears. All three of these strategies have powerful therapeutic resonances that fall beyond the pale of Monticelli's work. Jung's work on active imagination springs easily to mind as analysands' images threaten to overwhelm them while they must simultaneously attempt to remain true to the images.

In conclusion, Monticelli (2015) notes that the intensity of Hell breaks Dante's no-longer-functioning epistemologies—the very ways of knowing, which brought him to the dark woods. He must endure through this pulverizing experience to be able to achieve the epistemological transcendence that Paradise will eventually unveil. Dante must discipline

> the sensitive body, which must be taught to perceive and feel in the right way in order for the textual construction to be adequately accomplished according to the general plan of the author-architect, without, at the same time, depriving the reader of the literary pleasure which is derived from pathemic interferences and the relative narrative tensions. (p. 127)

Monticelli finishes with a last plea, like many of the preceding scholars in this chapter have, that the text be left to speak for itself and not turn it into some sort of cipher for derivative interpretations.

Conclusion

This concludes this introduction's review of those texts, chapters, and articles that bring Dante and phenomenology into conversation. With these materials in mind, the reader may venture into the remainder of Part One of this volume with some foundation in the cast of characters, ideas, and conflicts that constitute the territory of a phenomenological encounter with Dante. At the end of this first part, I offer syntheses of the ideas presented in this introduction and in the subsequent chapters. This chapter also provided an overview of Dante's texts and important inspirations, which will serve the reader well in Part Two of this volume in which the examinations of Dante spread beyond the phenomenological but maintain a strong link to the question of the encounter with the Other.

References

Alighieri, D. (1969). *La Vita Nuova* (B. Reynolds, Trans.). Penguin Classics. (Original work published 1295).

Alighieri, D. (1982). *Inferno* (A. Mandelbaum, Trans.). Bantam Classic. (Original work published 1320).

Alighieri, D. (2000). *Inferno* (R. Hollander & J. Hollander, Trans.). Anchor Books. (Original work published 1320).

Ardissimo, E., & Scarinci, S. (2011). Fenomenologia do maravilhoso na literatura italiana. *Per Musi, 24*, 21–29. [Google Translation, 11 pages].

Asay, T. M. (2014). *The phenomenology of frames in Chaucer, Dante and Boccaccio*. PhD diss., University of Oregon.

Caputo, J. (1997). *The prayers and tears of Jacques Derrida*. Indiana University Press.

De Bruyn, B. (2009). Echoes of the phenomenon—A conversation with Robert Pogue Harrison. *Image [&] Narrative, 10*(1), 1–12. [e-journal].

De Monticelli, R. (2000). Dante's *Inferno*: Phenomenology of a strange passion. *Psychopathology, 33*(4), 182–191.

Dobbins, J., & Fuss, P. (1982). The silhouette of Dante in Hegel's phenomenology of spirit. *CLIO, 11*(4), 387–413.

Franke, W. (1988). Review of *The body of Beatrice* by Robert Pogue Harrison. *Rivista di studi italiani, 4*, 78–82.

Franke, W. (1991). *Dante's divinatory hermeneutic: Towards a poetics of religious revelation.* PhD diss., Stanford University.

Franke, W. (1996). *Dante's interpretive journey.* University of Chicago Press.

Franke, W. (2007). The ethical vision of Dante's *Paradiso* in light of Levinas. *Comparative Literature, 59*(3), 209–227.

Franke, W. (2011). Dante's "New Life" and the new testament: An essay on the hermeneutics of revelation. *The Italianist, 31*, 335–366.

Franke, W. (2015). *The revelation of imagination: From Homer and the Bible through Virgil and Augustine to Dante.* Northwestern University Press.

Franke, W. (2018). *Dante studies after the theological turn.* Oxford Critical Theory Review.

Harrison, R. P. (1984). *A phenomenology of the Vita nuova.* PhD diss., Cornell University.

Harrison, R. P. (1988). *The body of Beatrice.* Johns Hopkins University Press.

Harrison, R. P. (1990). Phenomenology of the "Vita Nuova". *Annali D'Italinistica* 8, Dante and Modern American Criticism, 180–184.

Heidegger, M. (1927). *Sein und Zeit.* M. Neimeyer.

Janicaud, D. (1991). *Le tournant théologique de la phénoménologie française.* L'Eclat.

Janicaud, D. et al. (2000). *Phenomenology and the "Theological Turn": The French debate.* Fordham University Press.

Luke, H. M. (2001). *Dark wood to white rose: Journey and transformation in Dante's divine comedy.* Parabola Books. (Original work published 1975)

Monticelli, D. (2015). Fear in Dante's Inferno: Phenomenology, semiotics, aesthetics. In Z. G. Barański, A. Kablitz, & Ü. Ploom (Eds.), *I luoghi nostri: Dante's natural and cultural spaces* (pp. 106–128). Tallin University Press.

Moran, D., & Mooney, T. (2002). *The phenomenology reader.* Routledge.

Nolan, B. (1974). The Vita nuova and Richard of St. Victor's phenomenology of vision. *Dante Studies with the Annual Report of the Dante Society, 92*, 35–52.

Phillippy, P. A. (1990). Review of *The body of Beatrice* by Robert Pogue Harrison. *South Central Review, 7*(1), 108–110.

Scarry, E. (1995). On vivacity: The difference between daydreaming and imagining-under-authorial-instruction. *Representations, 52*, 1–26.

Shannon, D. (1998). The journey of the mind of God to us: Hegel's ladder and Harris's graduate seminars. *CLIO, 27*(4), 573–592.

Shaw, J. A. (2005). A pathway to spirituality. *Psychiatry, 68*(4), 350–363.

Shoaf, R. A. (1989). Medieval studies after Derrida after Heidegger. In J. N. Wasserman & L. Roney (Eds.), *Sign, sentence, discourse: Language in medieval thought and literature.* (pp. 9–30). Syracuse University Press.

Shores, C. (2012). Body and world in Merleau-Ponty and deleuze. *Studia Phaenomenologica, 12*, 181–210.

Silverman, H. J. (1977). Heidegger and Merleau-Ponty: Interpreting Hegel. *Research in Phenomenology, 7*, 209–224.

Stillinger, T. C. (1990). Review of the book *The body of Beatrice* by Robert Pogue Harrison. *Italica*, *67*(3), 403–406.

Tambling, J. (1991). Review of *The body of Beatrice* by Robert Pogue Harrison. *Modern Language Review*, *86*(1), 220–221.

Took, J. F. (2000). *Dante's phenomenology of being*. University of Glasgow Press.

Took, J. F. (2020). *Dante*. Princeton University Press.

Trovato, M. (1990). Dante's poetics of good: From phenomenology to integral realism. *Annali d'Italianistica* 8, Dante and Modern American Criticism, 232–256.

Wallace, D. (1990). Review of *The body of Beatrice* by Robert Pogue Harrison. *Speculum*, *65*(3), 683–686.

Ward, D. (1992). Review of *The body of Beatrice* by Robert Pogue Harrison. *Comparative Literature*, *44*(1), 88–90.

Wetherbee, W. (1991). Review of *The body of Beatrice* by Robert Pogue Harrison. *Modern Philology*, *88*(3), 299–301.

Chapter 2

Representing the Other[1]
Dante, Duns Scotus, and the Crisis of Representation in the Modern Age

William Franke

Dante's *Commedia*, with its emphasis on ineffability, bears witness to a crisis of representation concerning God, but more generally concerning reality as a whole. Our human means of knowing are exposed as mere representation and as inadequate to God's reality. Dante's exact contemporary, John Duns Scotus (1265/66–1308), the Scholastic philosopher and theologian, feels the same crisis and works out a response of world-historical significance. He makes the concept of *esse* [being] 'univocal.' *Esse* has no special analogical senses as applied to God. It is the exact same concept for finite or for infinite being. Consequently, we are made capable of signifying God by a concept, although this does not mean that we understand God's essential being or anything else about infinite being. Still, for Scotus, the concept is the same concept, whether applied to the finite beings that we can know and understand or to infinite being, of which we have no concrete understanding.

This redefinition giving us a merely formal way of signifying God nevertheless brings incalculably far-reaching and practical consequences in its train. Scotus's metaphysical doctrine of the 'univocity of being' leads to the scientific worldview of a seamless realm of natural law and predictability, in which everything that is anything is representable. In effect, Scotus's concept of the univocity of being enables all of reality to be grasped as nature, since the Creator does not belong to another category or concept of being. This is what later becomes fully explicit in Baruch Spinoza's (1632–1677) concept of 'Deus sive Natura' [literally 'God or Nature']—the idea that the Creator cannot be distinguished from the creation. The proviso that God's own being or nature is not understood through this concept—which holds true for Scotus, though not for Spinoza—does not matter for those who are not interested in knowing anything absolutely but simply in measuring and mastering the immanent world of finite phenomena. And this latter focus of interest will prevail in producing the outlook on the universe that characterizes modern science.

Stirred by the same problem and predicament as Scotus, Dante invents a different solution to dealing with a divinity that transcends human understanding. In an age demanding rational accountability in the manner of Scholastic philosophy, with its almost unimpeachable intellectual authority, Dante's new gnoseology follows a path of poetry. He realizes that true and ultimate reality is no longer representable in any direct way as literal-historical truth. But rather than inventing a purely formal concept of being and thenceforth focusing on its finite manifestations, he produces metaphorical and analogical conceptions to convey poetically the human experience of being face to face with the incomprehensible reality of the divine at all levels of existence. Poetry thus affords subjectively conditioned and expressive access to a higher truth than that of empirical fact. Dante stretches thought beyond its strictly conceptual capacities and extends reason's reach poetically. He thereby keeps representation open to an other world of mystical-religious experience and providential history.

On this showing, the same crisis of representation that produces our contemporary secular world founded on empirical science is capable of an alternative solution that yields a poetic vision not only of this world but also of the other world. The other world is not objectively even a world so much as an unknowable dimension of mystery. Yet it is imperiously determining for human reality in ways that cannot be accounted for except mythically and poetically—like the very fact of our being here at all. In these terms, Dante's thought and work furnish clear indications for an alternative modernity along the path not taken. Some of these alternative possibilities come to fruition in Nicholas of Cusa's (1401–1464) conjectural science of analogical speculation, which makes human constructions or conjectures key to discerning the inconceivable. Similar possibilities flourish in Giambattista Vico's (1668–1744) new science, which can serve for reversing the priority of rational fact over imagination: The true, or what is real for human thought and experience, beyond the mere certitude of facts, is revealed as produced rather by metaphorical invention.

What I offer here is, in effect, a counter-Nietzschean genealogy—contra-*Twilight of the Idols*—of how the true world became a fable not through Plato and Christianity with their idealism, but rather through modern science and technology, with their reductionism—reduction of the real to empirical sense-data and the material objects that can be constructed on their basis. This latter approach ignores the affective, imaginative, and voluntary dimensions of human experience that are based on various kinds of existential commitment and belief and that determine the reality lived by human beings beyond the merely cognitive dimension. Empirical science is based on a reduction of reality to what is perceptible by the human subject's sense impressions. This intellectual revolution is a result of the same crisis that Dante resolves by propounding poetry as a higher form of knowledge.

The unknowability of the ultimately real or divine, as it becomes acutely inescapable for Dante and for Duns, forces a subjective turn in knowing. But Duns's approach leads to a transcendental reduction of the empirically real to a world of appearances—this becomes systematic in Kant; whereas Dante takes appearances not just for themselves as making up a world constituted by phenomenological objects, but rather as hermeneutic means of conjecturing and contemplating a reality that transcends all human knowing of objects. The empirical universe is thereby made to open upon the only imaginable world(s) of a nonobjective reality—the ultimate reality envisaged by religions.

Phenomenological Reduction and the Univocity of Being

The issue of how to fit God into metaphysics troubled Scholasticism and posed a major challenge to integrating the Greek metaphysical worldview with the biblical worldview based on revelation. Scotus finds a solution that, in effect, opens the way to modernity and its science in which both traditions continue their histories of effect—*Wirkungsgeschichte* as Gadamer uses it. Scotus is enabled to do so chiefly by virtue of his 'formal method' of considering his subject. He takes the manifest form that things or concepts are *for us* as the only object of knowledge that we can truly consider. He abstracts from what they may be in themselves beyond our ken. This anticipates the move that Kant later makes fully explicit with his distinction between *Erscheinungen* [appearances] and *Dinge-an-sich* [things-in-themselves]. Our human, conceptual structure of receptivity is thereby erected into a condition of the possibility of knowing—it becomes 'transcendental.' We can know nothing except in the terms dictated by our noetic apparatus. Knowing this apparatus, therefore, gives us a certain a priori, universal knowledge concerning everything knowable—to us.

Scotus's teaching of the univocity of being entails that the concept of 'being' applies to or is predicable of all beings, finite and infinite alike. Of course, this is true *for us*, or for the being and beings that we can think and conceive. And what may be beyond our conceptions, we cannot say; we can, at most, allow for such a mystery. This positions us at the source of knowing and of what is known rather than leaving us on the outside, trying to get a handle on what is already given prior to and independent of us. Being and reality are redefined in terms that make us part of them and make them inconceivable without us. In this sense, Meillassoux (2006) qualifies modern philosophy en bloc as 'correlationalism.'

We can understand this as, in crucial respects, an anticipation of the phenomenological method as it would be developed later by Edmund Husserl (1859–1938). After all, Scotus's revolution in metaphysics—like Husserl's in epistemology—consists of having introduced a formal method that outlines the limits of the discipline. A glaring difference, nevertheless, is that Husserl employs his phenomenological method as a way of returning to *den Sachen selbst* [the things themselves]. He is trying to reverse the abstraction that scientific epistemology has introduced, with the result that we know things always only relative to our conceptual framings and systems. The reality of things for the modern age that Husserl inhabits has become purely phenomenal. Manifest appearings of things *are* things themselves for such an empirical worldview. This is not the case for the metaphysical worldview of the Middle Ages, with its infrastructure informed by Neoplatonism and monotheism. Yet in Scotus's and Husserl's cases alike, there is an epistemological reduction to the manifestation of things in the event of knowing, in effect, a phenomenological reduction. Without denying the transcendent being of things, there is, in either case, a methodological decision to concentrate on just what is manifest to the knowing subject in experience or in thinking. Knowing is thereby enabled to separate strictly between the known and the unknown.

Scotus's orientation of knowing to a 'formal' object is basically what makes the scientific revolution possible. Ironically, once again, Husserl applies this formalizing move rigorously in order *to resist* the tendency of science to separate us from the *Lebenswelt* [life-world] that is the background necessary for lending our thought and lived experience their sense and meaning. Husserl's is a self-critical move that coerces scientific knowing to take account of its own entrapment in mere formality. His turn back to the 'things themselves' is an attempt to exit from the merely formal reality that was ushered in by Duns Scotus's determination to relate knowing to being in a univocal sense that is indistinctly worldly and divine, finite and infinite, accident and substance. Husserl can do this because modern thought takes for granted that there is no other being than phenomenal being and that in focusing purely on manifest phenomena, it is returning to things themselves.

The reality of 'being' with which Scotus as a thinker—and not as a believer—is concerned is the being that can be thought and conceived: a formal being, a being that is already formed by and for being known by a subject. It is essentially what Husserl treats as phenomenal being, being that is also always *for a subject*, since a 'phenomenon' is inherently an appearing to a subject. From a radically modern epistemological viewpoint, there is no other being, no being that is not phenomenal, nothing that is metaphysically real. One will have to follow phenomenology forward to its so-called 'theological turn' in *post*modern thinkers, with Levinas, Michel Henry, Jean-Luc Marion, Jean-Ives Lacoste, and Jean-Louis Chrétien, et al., in order to see it reopen in the direction of a reality that cannot be humanly conceived at all, but can only be divinely given (see Janicaud, 1991; Janicaud et al., 2000; for contextualization and commentary, see Simmons & Benson, 2013). However, with univocity, there is no longer any need to refer to any higher being or order of reality. Not that the phenomenal being that *is* referred to is fully known or even knowable. The unknowable depth of being is still there—at least for Scotus—within the sphere of immanence, although it can be ignored and has no proper language. It lurks as a penumbra of what all languages about objects cannot grasp or even discern.

The Epistemological Turn in the Formal Understanding of Being

Historians of medieval philosophy outline a 'second beginning'—after Plato and Aristotle—of metaphysics in the thirteenth century and particularly with Scotus. This second beginning is 'ontological'—and even epistemological, I wish to stress—rather than theological (Honnefelder, 2008, pp. 114–132; Boulnois, 1999, pp. 471–479). This shift makes metaphysics a science rather than a type of wisdom. It proceeds from what is first known *by us* rather than from what is first in itself or in the order of being. Knowledge now proceeds from what is first in predication rather than in ontological rank. Metaphysics becomes a transcendental science, focused finally on terms as instruments of knowing rather than on things themselves. This becomes especially clear and programmatic after Duns in the logic of William of Ockham (1287–1347), as noted by Honnefelder (2008, p. 111).

What Scotus proffers is already a form of *critical* philosophy based on self-certainty secured through self-limitation. Already in Scotus—and fully and explicitly in Ockham—our knowledge of being is fundamentally disjunctive rather than positive. Being is understood formally as simply what does not contradict being— "cui non repugnat esse in rerum natura." Being is understood modally as neither actual nor not-actual, but simply as entailing no contradiction of reality—"ens (est hoc), cui non repugnant esse" (Duns Scotus, 1300–1304, *Ordinatio* IV d. 1, q. 2, n. 8; cf. IV d. 8, q. 1, n. 2 & I d. 3, q. 3, n. 124). Duns's is a formal way of seeing things, but what he sees is not the less real for all that. In fact, it enables a whole new dimension of reality to be focused and expressed. The 'content of the form,' so to speak, opens up to view in a way that was also to be explored and exploited poetically by Dante.

Scotus's famous 'formal' manner of consideration is, after all, inclusive of the perspective of a subject—just as the phenomenological 'phenomenon' is an object as it is perceived by a subject. In effect, Scotus introduces subjectivity as constitutive of what things are when they are considered 'formally.' The various forms by which they are perceived and defined come to light through their being known from various angles of encounter in the experience of knowing subjects, yet these forms belong nevertheless essentially to the being of the things in question. Henceforth ontology, in its revealment and articulation, is conditioned by epistemology.

Duns Scotus, in this manner, anticipates the epistemological turn that essentially characterizes modern philosophy from Descartes to Kant and Husserl. Knowing becomes recognized as constitutive of things—if not absolutely in themselves, then at least as they appear to us in the world. In bringing out the subjective angulation of disclosure of what things are in the world, Duns is also in step with Dante's metaphorical method of revealing the cosmos and the truth of all things in universal history. Dante, too, writes subjective perception or 'formal' consideration into his poetic epiphany. The subjectivity of what he presents as nonetheless divine revelation flows from the same source of insight as that from which Duns Scotus draws his recognition of the 'formal' character of things as they are accessed through human knowing and experience.

Merely formal differences perceived from different viewpoints are not independently existing individuals in a purely subjectless world of objective entities. Nevertheless, these formal differences make a world of difference for Scotus, as for Dante. The tragic irony of modern intellectual history is that, subsequent to the application of Ockham's razor, this formal world of possibilities is going to be demoted to the status of an empty metaphysics or a mere fiction by the 'progress' of the modern world toward a pure positivism of strictly objective entities. This operation begins with nominalism in the Middle Ages, and it will eventually wind up in the completely digitalized universe of our own age of globalization. What is retained from Scotus's world of possibilities with real ontological roots is only a purely positive grid of objectively defined abstractions. This misprision cuts away the theological grounding of the real.

The most original path-breakers of this modern world, notably Franciscan theologians such as Scotus and Ockham, had something entirely different and even opposite to this in mind. They were contemplating the unconditioned freedom of the divine Will and the consequent contingency of the natural world. This conception entails the analogous freedom of the human mind and will self-reflectively generating a reality of their own creation. This unconditioned freedom of the individual mind and will that the Franciscan philosopher-theologians discovered and opened up in its visionary potential was for them still exercised in the image of a divine Creator. But it could also be captured and made the slave of mechanisms for controlling human thought and action by conglomerate powers that would result eventually in an asphyxiatingly managerial, technocratic culture.

Such is the formal dimension of reality that Scotus opens to view in metaphysical terms. Dante, through his work with the imagination, opens a realm of pure form that is similarly invented or discovered by human intellect. Yet, it is none the less real for all that. It is a realm of free spiritual expression. These domains of formal reality are realms of representation, whether of abstract entities or of poetic imaginings. But, in both cases, with Duns and with Dante, they call to be understood on the basis of a kind of quasi-rational faith in which reason transcends, or at least suspends, a purely or restrictively objective self-understanding—and does so on rational grounds. As such, these purely formal realms are reality-bearing traces of a higher order of metaphysical being and even of divine spirit.

However, for Duns, that higher realm is the object of only a purely abstract metaphysics and of a practical—not theoretical or speculative—theology. Human reason is sufficient unto itself and autonomous in the secular sphere. Dante, too, is a proponent of the autonomy of the secular order, but he never forgets that this very autonomy is a reference to and a vestige or repetition of divine autonomy. Dante strives in every way to reconnect the finite with the infinite. Duns's concept of the univocity of being makes both the finite and the infinite thinkable in a single concept that gives humans an apparent conceptual control over the other—the metaphysical—realm that Dante obsessively recognizes as ineffable. Univocity fosters a forgetting of the unassimilable otherness of being. It forges the conceptual tools for ignoring the ungraspable mystery of being at the ground of all beings, and thus for treating finite being, which is but a re-presentation, as absolute or sufficient unto itself.

Signification of the Real and an Autonomous Sphere for Representation

For Duns Scotus, God remains inconceivable in concrete terms by finite human beings. He can, nevertheless, be signified by language in a proper concept. This can be brought about through a concept that God himself has instituted and given to humans to be known through the biblical revelation, but it can also be achieved through an abstract metaphysical concept such as that of 'infinite being.' God's nature is not truly *conceivable* for humans, but it can nevertheless be truly *signified* by such a concept. Scotus eliminates analogy—we have no approximate knowledge of what God is like—and allows for only direct, univocal signification of God. He admits the inadequacy of our concepts to really and concretely conceive the nature of the Infinite. There is no commonly conceivable reality or *ratio* that applies to both God and creatures—"in nulla realitate conveniunt," (Duns Scotus, 1300–1304, *Ordinatio* I, d. 8, q. 3, n. 82). However, proper conceptual knowledge is not necessary for our being able to *signify* God beyond what we can actually understand.

In *De Interpretatione* (1.4–1.6), Aristotle (384–322 BCE) laid down the principle that words are the signs of thoughts, which are the signs of things. But the new semantic paradigm introduced by Scotus's Franciscan predecessor Roger Bacon (1214–1292) revised this traditional Aristotelian-Boethian model. For Bacon, signs such as words signify directly things, not their concepts or mental images. Even without our necessarily being able to conceive things accurately and completely, the signs we employ *intend* to signify things that we cannot adequately conceive—like infinite Being. The direct relation of the sign to the *res* in the new semantic paradigm enables God to be signified as infinite Being, even though there is no adequate way for finite humans to understand or conceive God—and no common *ratio* between God and creatures. In fact, Scotus freely admits this lack of any common measure. The univocal concept of Being that is common to God and creatures in intention corresponds to no common property in reality—"nihil unius rationis in re," (*Ordinatio* I d. 8, n. 138–140; cf. I, d. 31, n. 29–31). Precisely in this regard, it is a purely 'formal' object.

Scotus initiates a strong dissociation of signification from intellection as two distinct operations of thought. By separating what is the object merely of a semantic code from what is actually thought through a metaphysical concept, he creates a sphere of pure representation. This separation has many powerful applications that will not cease to disclose themselves in astonishing and fantastic ways—eventually producing quarks and quanta, supernovae and white dwarfs, antimatter and superstrings—throughout the coming age of scientific invention.

We can easily see what motivates such a secular recasting of knowledge. The human mind gains complete autonomy in a secular sphere of its own self-defined formal objects or concepts. The mind can forget its concern for the otherness of reality as such and can focus simply on the sphere that it defines for itself and manages through its own inventions in its own proper domain. This procedure evinces the power of self-reflection for creating a coherent system of concepts—which is the basis of any modern science.

Scotus dismantles the analogical thinking that Thomas Aquinas designed in order to approach, in an at least a quasi-scientific manner, a wholly other reality, of which we could never have proper, unmetaphorical, unanalogical intelligence (Pannenberg, 2007, pp. 164–165, sifts the far-reaching significance of this upheaval). Scotus replaces the doctrine of analogy and Dionysius's three ways—affirmative, negative, mystical—by three types of transcendentals corresponding to three degrees of knowing God (cf. Boulnois, 1999, pp. 320–325). This radically alters the meaning of the divine Names. The first degree comprises Names such as Good, Infinite, and Wise, which are pronounceable and knowable, but not revealed. The second degree is the Tetragrammaton, which is revealed, but not conceivable or pronounceable by humans. It is imposed by God and is a proper, revealed divine Name, but remains a foreign language for God's human creatures. We do not understand it. There is also a third degree, a common Name for God: 'Being,' as revealed in *Exodus* 3:14, is abstractly conceivable by humans *and* properly applicable in its infinite mode to God. It is per se an adequate concept of God, but it can only be imperfectly conceived by humans.

By means of these distinctions, Scotus avoids the paradoxes typical of negative theology in the tradition reaching from Dionysius the Areopagite (fifth to sixth centuries CE) through Maimonides (c. 1135–1204) to Aquinas (1225–1274) and Eckhart (1260–1328). He avoids the radical anonymity of God by distinguishing between the origin through the imposition of the Names and their intended sense. We do not need to be able to understand its meaning in order to employ a divine Name. Thus we can accurately name God, although we do not know God's own being or essence. Scotus also avoids hereby the typical Scholastic homonymy of all the divine Names. In the Divine Names tradition, Good, One, Being, True, etc. all mean the same with regard to God irrespective of the formal distinctions between them as objects of the intellect. For Scotus, even though all Names refer to the one, indivisible Being of God, they are understood under various *ratios* by the finite intellect and so have different meanings. Finally, the primacy accorded to 'Being' as *the* divine Name par excellence makes the object—but not the intellectual content—of theology coincide with the object of metaphysics and of our conceptualization. A new unity and order are brought to human knowing even of God by defining human knowing's range such that it no longer has to confront the absolute difference of the divine but can handle everything with adequate univocal concepts, even without always having a concrete intuitive knowledge of what they mean.

Of course, any treatment of God as an object is pure artifice. In this regard, Scotus is actually still a strong proponent of God's ineffability, as long as we refer to the act of trying to comprehend him and not simply to the sign representing him (*Reportatio Parisiensis*, Scotus, 1302–1307, I, d. 22, q. 1, n. 12). So Scotus does not eliminate negative theology at the level of the conception of God, which remains impossible, but only at the level of the signification of God, which *is* possible, even without our understanding what is signified by 'God' or by perfections such as 'being' or 'oneness' or 'goodness' as attributed to God. According to Scotus, created intellect comes to rest only in contemplating God as Being in the mode of infinity, which is the most perfect concept of God that we can conceive (*Ordinatio* I, d. 2, q. 2, n. 147). Even though this concept in its infinite mode is not really understandable or concretely thinkable by finite human intellect, God can nevertheless be named and signified by it.

What Scotus has done, in effect, is to erase the mysticism of the Divine Names that was cultivated in Neoplatonic and Patristic tradition. The Divine Names are no longer a privileged or even a possible path to the intellectual experience of God. Naming and language are no longer accorded ontological or gnoseological significance. They are merely instrumental to technically correct procedures of designating and denoting. Genuine knowledge in the modern age is empirical and experimental and entirely dissociated from any linguistic auras. Names are no longer considered to be infused with symbolic meaning and miraculous potency. The apophatic, negative way of theurgically uniting with God by divination through contemplation of the divine Names—and by an exercise of intuitive intellect beyond the scope, or at least the control, of concepts—is abandoned. It is left to be taken up and reinvented as a new type of verbal magic in poetry from Dante to Mallarmé, an 'alchimie du verbe' as Rimbaud calls it, for French symbolists.

As Boulnois (1999) remarks, the "primacy of the concept" has at this point "totally absorbed the naming of God" and the three ways—affirmative, negative, mystical—of Dionysius (p. 302). God can be emptily represented as 'Being,' but without any substantive knowing of the divine nature, because the constitutive negativity for finite human intellect of knowing the divine has been rejected in order to impose a positive, humanly controlled system of knowing. This production of a positive system based on human concepts is the path pursued with single-minded determination by modern science, and with the kind of 'success' that modern technology makes manifest.

Objective Representation: Beyond Naming and Desiring the Divine

This revolution of paradigms entails also abandoning the priority of the Good in Dionysius the Areopagite in order to make Being the proper Name of God and give it priority. God is thenceforth known not primarily through beneficent divine operation and the corresponding transformation of the human knower by the desire for the Good. Instead, God is *objectively represented* according to his proper Being—as humanly conceived. This is the major liability bequeathed by Scotus to modernity—the shift into dealing with representations rather than directly with reality. Formerly, dealing with the real involved inextricably also the affective reality of a subject. But science demands abstracting from such subjective affect. What Scotus started would become fully evident only much later in the seventeenth century. The rise of experimental science would consolidate this sea change from the medieval gnoseological framework based on analogy—a relational knowing by means of participation—to the new episteme based on objective representation. Incisive angles of approach to this epochal epistemological shift are outlined by Hoff (2013) building on Foucault (1966).

A direct mirror relation of identity between entities is the basis of this epistemology geared to the efficacious manipulation of things rather than to transforming *oneself* in conformity with the ideals of Truth and Being. The practice of self-expropriation in the image of the Infinite—as in the spiritual quests of antiquity and the Middle Ages—is forgotten. This is certainly a catastrophic loss and is sometimes recognized and portrayed as such. But there are also gains.

Scotus prepares the way for Spinoza's affirmative metaphysics as non-discursive and as wholly distinct from theo*logy* and from any other form of representation by a Logos. Gilles Deleuze (1992, pp. 63–67) focuses specifically on Spinoza's derivation from Scotus. This is what proves so unacceptable to Milbank and company, for whom revelation, as in the Bible, comes essentially in and through the Word. The erasure of linguistic mediation leads also to scientific positivism, which claims to investigate things directly, without any recourse to discursive traditions, but simply on the evidence of things themselves. Of course, 'things' here means empirical things appearing to the senses, and even this definition of the elements of an ontology is not free of linguistic presuppositions.

Nevertheless, Scotus opens a space for experiential and experimental—yet non-linguistic—mysticism that also inspires profoundly apophatic innovations and development in the modern age. His concept of 'haecceitas' [thisness] intends a singularity that is not accessible to linguistic-conceptual articulation. Movements of affective piety beginning in the fourteenth century will fill in this space with diverse expressions of ineffably singular experience. Bernard McGinn (1998) and Andrew LaZella (2019) demonstrate some of the far-reaching logical consequences.

The definitively anti-theological consequences of Scotus's erasure of analogy are drawn only by his successors, who eliminate contemplation of the divine. The tendency of the Radical Orthodoxy, as spearheaded by Milbank and Pickstock, to blame Scotus for the modern eclipse of God and theology can, in this respect, be corrected—or at least counterbalanced—by following the detailed and precise historical analysis offered by Boulnois (1999). Boulnois appreciates the genuinely theological passion driving Scotus, even though Scotus renders metaphysical and physical science completely autonomous from theology.

It remains, nonetheless, true that in the wake of Scotus, there are no longer any means of constructing a dynamic kind of interactive knowing of the divine through analogy. There is no longer any symbolic order connecting metaphysics and revelation. Analogical and metaphorical theology have been undermined. The supposedly scientific, univocal knowledge of God for early moderns like Francisco Suárez (1548–1617) is purely metaphysical in a merely objective sense that Kant would definitively show to be untenable.

Concrete knowing through figure and open-ended, proliferating image and metaphor is no longer viewed as a gift from God, but rather as a purely human production. This reconfiguration is determining for the whole cast of modern thinking, and it grounds the great reproach of Milbank against Scotus. (On gift as fundamental to the nature of theological knowing, see Milbank, 1995.) The dissociation between the divine gift of God's revealed—but not understood—Name and the human concepts that can be rationally elaborated and metaphysically contemplated, yet without theurgical efficacy or communication with divinity itself, is the fateful legacy of Duns Scotus. This effectively inaugurates the modern and scientific age of thought in which theology is disconnected from human concept-formation and the inventive making of metaphors. Before Scotus, making concepts and metaphors could be understood as inherently theological, as participating in divine creativity. Human words were naturally understood as reflections or as sparks animated by the divine Word or Logos.

Dante still understands language emphatically as a divine gift. However, Dante will also prove in key ways to share and integrate the new secular outlook developed philosophically by Scotus. And even Scotus himself still frames his masterwork, *De Primo Principio* (c. 1308/2001), with prayers to the Lord God, *Dominus Deus noster*, to grant him to believe and know and expound—"mihi ea credere, sapere ac proferre concedat" (para. 1.1). In fact, each of its four chapters begins with an address to God, and the treatise concludes with effusions of praise for divinity, inscribing the investigation into a God-directed discourse. Scotus, too, recognizes science as God's gift, even in giving it a rational foundation independent of theological grounding. Nevertheless, the thrust of his work as a whole relegates prayer to another register, one of willing, separate from knowing.

Whereas Aquinas and Albert (1200–1280) had attempted to integrate the new Aristotelian rational science with theology, Duns no longer deems this to be possible. He respects the internal coherence of philosophy and denies that natural reason has any need of a supernatural supplement. Reason is fully sufficient within its own domain and perceives nature likewise as self-sufficient. Theology, for Scotus, is simply another discourse that has its own positive justification in Scriptural revelation, but it is not reached through a negative—apophatic—dialectic in which natural reason would become aware of its own limits and insufficiency. Particularly the *Commentary on the Sentences*, where Scotus stages a dialogue between a philosopher and a theologian, demonstrates this. See also the prologue to his *Ordinatio* (1300–1304), First Part: "On the Necessity of Revealed Doctrine."

This latter, negative approach to knowing has made a come-back in postmodern times, for example, with Theodor Adorno's negative dialectics (1966) and with Emmanuel Levinas's abjection in facing the Other (1961). Negation stands at the origin also of French poststructuralist thinking of excess—such as with Bataille, Nancy, and others. Hent de Vries (1989) brings together these versions of contemporary quasi-negative theology in *Theologie im Pianissimo: Zur Aktualität der Denkfiguren Adornos und Levinas* translated by Geoffrey Hale as *Minimal*

Theologies: Critiques of Secular Reason in Adorno and Levinas (2005). And in this respect, Dante is much closer to the postmodern experience in registering the inadequacy and insufficiency—"questa disaggualianza" (*Paradiso* XV:83)—of his own natural being in Paradise. Scotus's emphasis on the sufficiency of human reason in its own domain, in contrast, enables its decoupling from revelation and theology and therewith the dawn of the modern scientific age.

The Good as Sought Through Will Without Intellect—Subjectivity

In modern culture, the complement of objective, scientific representation is a *will* operating without intellectual insight or any guiding vision of truth. Only its own self-posited ends and purposes can orient it and serve as values for it. The will is no longer oriented by desire for the Good as such. It no longer willfully seeks concordance with a higher reality or Will. Duns does not give up on the desire for the Good and for God as fundamental to the orientation of human existence, but he removes them from the quest of the intellect for knowledge of truth and of the Cause of the universe. Instead, he assigns impulses to seek the good to the realm of ethics and to the practice of charity. Desire for the Good belongs exclusively to the jurisdiction of the will and communicates with the divine only through commands supposedly known by revelation. Their connection with reason is thenceforth severed. Nature, too, like reason, is thereby released into its autonomy.

Human 'good will' still reasons and finds grounds for its actions, but its goodness is generated self-reflexively from itself and from its own willing of the good. It is no longer essentially determined by reason, as in the Thomistic tradition. Will does not need to be informed and motivated externally by rational discernment of what is good-in-itself. The will itself now finds reasons and uses them, *making* them good rather than simply obeying their intrinsic nature as radiating the light of the real and true. The will's goodness is no longer rooted in the cosmos. Will is itself the origin of the good rather than merely a faculty of choosing what is already in and of itself good on purely rational and natural grounds. This shift ushers in the new age of the will that is good-in-itself and leads eventually to the Kantian morality of the autonomous good will. With it is born the fact/value split that cleaves modernity into the dualism of free subjects, on the one hand, and an alienated world of mere matter, on the other.

In an attempt to forge an alternative, Henri de Lubac (1896–1991) developed a theology based on the natural desire for the supernatural, for instance, in his *Surnaturel. Études Historiques* (1946). This notion is the antithesis, as noted by Milbank (2005), of Duns's thinking that so marked the modern era. Duns makes reason sufficient and incontestable in its own nature and immanent sphere and thereby grants a charter to human—apparently self-grounding—reflection to dominate the world by its own natural and rational powers.

Even though Dante, too, allows for an autonomous secular sphere, he nevertheless turns in constant tension toward a supernatural sphere that secular reason strives to emulate. Reason has no objective, scientific means of access to this other reality, but Dante nevertheless activates and intensifies his subjective and poetic efforts to approach and conform to it as an ideal. Dante understands, at least implicitly, through his imagination, that theology has to go beyond its fixed, dogmatic representations of the other world in order to preserve an ability to connect with the real spiritual order in a dynamic, existential relationship. This is the dimension that Kierkegaard calls 'subjectivity' and brings to full expression in his radical contestation of the Enlightenment paradigm of autonomous, self-grounding science with its secular rationality. That secular paradigm for Kierkegaard was most fully achieved in the Hegelian system.

Kierkegaard's subjectivity existentially witnesses a passion for the infinite and transcendent. Dante first discovers this radical subjectivity through his realization of the inaccessibility of any properly divine reality and truth. Up against this impasse, Dante forces open a secular realm for individual expression in relation to the inexpressible. Scotus, facing the same impasse, designs the system of autonomy for free conceptual invention within the sphere of our empirical and objective reality, cordoning off the higher metaphysical reality as a matter for ethics and charitable action. This becomes the founding charter for modern science and its mechanistic worldview, on one side, and for subject-centered, eventually liberal ethics, on the other, complemented by an—optional—fideistic theology. The other route foreshadowed, instead, by Dante, opens the way to poetic understanding of the cosmos by subjective means of expression such as symbol and metaphor and to humanities disciplines as modes of interpreting every aspect of reality as engaging personal existence.

Conceptual Production of 'Objective' Being—The Way of Representation

The new paradigm prepared for and introduced by Duns Scotus is one of representation. The theory of representation turns away from the imponderables of Being itself and its incomprehensibility in the Dionysian tradition toward 'objective' being: This means intensional being or being as an object for the intellect. Objective being is being that is conceived by the intellect under some determinate aspect or *ratio* and is not simply indicated vaguely and indeterminately.

Paradoxically, 'objective' originally means being an object for a subject, the opposite of existing independently of the mind, which is the meaning that 'objective' takes on in common currency in modern times once this origin is forgotten. The formal, objective point of view forged by Scotus is thenceforth treated simply as the way things *are*. Science, consisting in formal, conceptual schemas fabricated by the mind, is taken to describe the true reality of things. The metaphysical dimension of the Other that cannot be conceived is erased, and the world as such is simply identified with this conceptual production that can be called 'objective being.' This reductive common sense, based on objective, empirical reality, is, in essence, what the phenomenological movement rebels against. Phenomenology aims to restore the reality of lived experience of phenomena as they appear to subjective consciousness in all their apparent transcendence and mystery.

Nonetheless, the reconceiving by objective science of all reality through its own categories of representation is immensely empowering for the whole human apparatus of knowing, which becomes a comprehensive system of self-reflection. Although the intellect produces its own objects, they are still intended by Scotus to correspond to real things—*res*—outside the intellect. Scotus is still a metaphysical realist. But the immediate objects of intellection are produced by the active intellect rather than being received directly from the things themselves. Aristotle has been preempted here by Avicenna (c. 980–1037). The corporeal ground of knowing has been upstaged by a more direct spiritual ground and cause, one in which the object of knowing now inheres as a formal, intensional object in a knowing subject. The incipient severance of formal knowing of intensional conceptual contents from knowing and unknowing of reality in its absoluteness and otherness becomes much sharper after Scotus, and it ushers in the fully modern paradigm of representation. ('Intension' designates the meaning, the properties or intellectual content included in—or 'intended' by—a concept, whereas 'extension' delimits the set of entities that fall under it.)

In this paradigm, the mind is trapped in a world of representations that are always only representations of other representations and can never break out of this prison house of reflecting mirrors into direct contact with another reality. The fateful consequences of this epistemological predicament of self-enclosure within representation are played out pathetically, for example, following Descartes, in the tragic theater of Racine (*Bérénice*, *Andromaque*, *Phèdre*, etc.)—an interpretation I develop elsewhere (Franke, 1993). Scotus's own theory of concepts, however, is not yet a pure representationalism because his concepts are still grounded in real things (Honnefelder, 2011). The relation of subject and object in Scotus is still correlational rather than ontologically oppositional. 'Correlational' is used here in an ontologically deeper sense than that employed by Meillassoux (2006) in *Après la Finitude*. Scotus comes before the typically modern alienation of the subject from the world and the famous fact/value split.

The Paradigm of Representation and Dante's Alternative Version

Dante enthusiastically receives the new empowerment by representation in all its self-reflexive potential. Yet he does not effectively cut off or occult its connection with real being. He does not take representation as sufficient unto itself, but rather only as analogically revealing of true and ultimate being. He incorporates the self-reflexive powers of representation into a larger paradigm governed by analogical imagination. Objective, scientific knowing is not 'absolute knowing' for him, as it would come to be more clearly in the modern age. This objectively representational knowing reaches its most reductive stage in twentieth-century logical positivism, for which even the absolute knowing proffered by Hegel's (1770–1831) science of wisdom became unintelligible nonsense.

Such conceptual shifts are not necessarily once and for all. Essentially the same shift as we are studying in medieval Scholasticism can be traced centuries later in the turn of Renaissance art and architecture to subject-centered 'linear perspective' making space a mathematizable realm dominated by the eye of a self-reflective 'I' (Hoff, 2013; and deeper in the background here stands Belting, 2008, and that text's translation by Schneider as *Florence and Baghdad: Renaissance Art and Arab Science*, 2011). The transition from a Renaissance gnoseology based on affinities between things to the 'classical' epistemology of identity inaugurated by Descartes, with his postulate of the self-reflective identity of the subject as *cogito*, reenacts it yet again (Foucault, 1966).

Knowing becomes representation in the age of Scotus; and Dante, too, works with this momentous paradigm shift. However, for Dante, all knowing is still beholden to a theological gift, and this gift can be known and made one's own only in prayer and supplication—or in prophetically-inspired creative poetic activity. Human knowing of the divine, and even of the truly real, can be approached only approximatively and conjecturally through the representations of the imagination. For Dante the poet, representation, even when recognized as a human production, is still marked as ultimately an endowment of a divine Giver. Representation is only a special manifestation of a paradigm of knowledge as revelation that is much wider in scope, and that stands on a higher ground of truth. This is patently the case, especially for Dante as prophetic poet. Revelation certainly remained a superior form of knowing for Scotus, too, but he nevertheless pried it loose from objective scientific knowing by the finite, rational faculties of the human mind, which were placed thenceforth under a regime of representation.

For Scotus, the immediate object of human knowing as 'esse objective' [objective being] is a *represented* being, and this being is actively produced by the active intellect. Paradoxically, for modern ears, 'objective' being is actually generated by an epistemological subject rather than standing as the unmediated presence of an external object. As 'objective,' it designates literally and etymologically something 'iactus' [thrown] 'ob' [in front of] a conscious subject. Scotus develops this line of thought, continuing from Roger Bacon and Henry of Ghent (c. 1217–1293), tearing the domain of the objects of thought away from natural causality and translating it into an intelligible realm of formal entities. The 'objective' realm is separated from the natural, worldly realm of efficient causality. A purely formal realm of intensional objects is conceived according to certain *ratios* that are considered to be really in things, but their mode of being in the *res* and in its representation in the intellect is no longer the same. Scotus annuls the—Aristotelian—communication of the sensible form or 'species' from the material object to the mind and substitutes—following Avicenna—an imitation or copying or reproduction of it by the intellect.

Scotus "lays here the theoretical foundation for the new paradigm of the formal object in modern thought starting from Suárez" (Boulnois, 1999, p. 94).

Knowledge is now produced not directly by the object, to which the mind is receptive, but by the mind itself through its faculty of representation. Such 'knowledge' is an interior word or concept, a representation produced by and for the knower of the object known. For Scotus himself, the mental representation is still intrinsically connected with the real thing: It is a trace that expresses the thing through a relation of partial resemblance. Yet the representation, as formal object, has a very different mode of being from the material thing or *res*: It is intelligible and spiritual, a product of the self-reflective mind. The formality of the object is mentally fashioned and therefore is not received, not 'phantasmatic' being—a sensible *species* received by perception. Gathered from elsewhere, such phantasmatic being does, in effect, in our present state, for Scotus, still guide our fashioning of formal objects (Boulnois, 1999, p. 94), but they are ontologically independent, being transparently products of our own mental reflection.

Certainly, some form of mental image as representation is already found in Thomas Aquinas and in Henry of Ghent, but Scotus makes representation a process of reproduction rather than of reception. It is a real production by the intellect distinct from reception of sensible phantasms—*species*. This opens the way to modernity—the metaphysical modernity of Suárez, but also the poetic modernity inaugurated by Dante and leading to Vico, in which imagination is not abandoned as a way of knowing. In either case, the modern relation to reality passes by way of self-reflexive, humanly defined constructs.

Thus, a new approach to knowing as reproductive representation originates here also with Dante. Dante adumbrates it in his treatises, and he develops it in his poetic works, especially through their implicit theory of art. However, according to Dante's alternative version, representational knowing is not reduced to univocal concepts but proceeds rather by metaphor, even metaphor for the Infinite and Incommensurable. Poetic expression of a higher reality than the empirical becomes the vocation, particularly of theological imagination. This other route for representation, with its self-reflexive productions as pursued by Dante, leads not to seeming mastery of the material universe through the grid of scientific concepts, but rather towards the imagination of other worlds, including higher, divine, and spiritual worlds.

Dante's self-reflexive imagination raises questions concerning the relation of all humanly attainable knowledge to theology and revelation. His answers share much in common with Scotus's because they are both creatively reacting to the same intellectual and cultural predicament. But there are also momentous divergences owing largely to the very different aims of scientific analysis versus poetic vision. My own view, which I propose as deeply aligned with Dante's outlook, is that we cannot adequately interpret this new realm generated by the self-reflective work of the imagination without using the resources of theology. However, theology here must be understood as not just a *product* of representation through an exercise of human imagination, but also as its creative source in the mind or self-understanding of God. (God's own knowledge of himself is the primary sense of 'theology' for Aquinas in *Summa Theologica* Ia, q. 1.

Cf. Ia, q. 14.) Of course, this source—God—surpasses human comprehension, but it is revealed in the imaginative *process* itself as an experience and enactment of infinity. Confrontation with the Incommensurable, as nothing that can be humanly grasped, is embraced as an essentially constitutive and eminently creative moment necessary in order to interpret the whole of our self-reflexively generated reality. Theology, so conceived, is such a self-reflectively generated discourse, but one that imaginatively strives to think beyond its own limits and calls them into question. Such theology becomes self-critical and rejects every finite concept of the Infinite as idolatrous. A self-subverting discourse, such theology is negative or 'apophatic.'

From Logical (Dis)Analogy to Imaginative Conjecture Versus the Forgetting of Being

This apophatic or negative theology takes on a new sort of pertinence in Dante's historical context of crisis concerning the metaphysical realm of revealed truth. Relation to a purportedly higher world involves analogy, but also dis-analogy. This holds for Dante, just as it holds for Dionysius, the Pseudo-Areopagite, and for the whole Dionysian tradition of apophatic mystical discourse. God's own proper being is inaccessible to natural reason. There is in this predicament already an epistemic break. It gives Dante poetic license and prophetic freedom to reinvent, in his own very personal terms, the entire other worlds of Christian damnation, purgation, and salvation. Yet, at the same time, Dante solemnly maintains that his poem is true prophetic revelation. I pursue this train of thought in the first chapter of *Secular Scriptures: Modern Theological Poetics in the Wake of Dante* (2016): "Dante and the Secularization of Religion through Literature," (pp. 9–42). Dante recognizes the mediation of imaginative representation as necessary in order to reveal the other world of the divine. Our human predicament as apophatic—our existing in relation to an unsayable Other—issues in free, creative, imaginative expression of this existential condition.

Dante retains the truth that genuine knowing is possible only on the basis of our existential involvement and is not purely objective knowing. Duns, too, realizes that our knowing of God is possible only through charitable relations and actions, but he also defends a knowledge of finite things as rationally grounded without necessary reference to the infinite. This furnishes the basis for scientific knowing—yet only at the price of forgetting the totality of the Infinite, the Cause in which all exists, and thus also of forgetting Being. Duns's univocal concept of Being renders eminently possible, if not inevitable, a forgetting of infinite Being, and this forgetting itself is then forgotten rather than retained as the final and definitive revelation delivered by finite being and its history. Dante, in contrast, remembers this condition of inadequacy, which he calls "disaggualianza" (*Paradiso* XV:83). He acknowledges programmatically this incorrigible, necessary forgetting of his paradisiacal experience as enframing the entire poem in *Paradiso* I:7–9 and XXXIII:94–96. Just such a forgetting enframes the concealment of unconcealing that Heidegger's thought strives so titanically to reverse as dominating the subsequent modern history of being.

Dante, like Scotus, is on the path of the dissolution of the medieval doctrine of allegory in the face of the newly discovered radical subjectivity of human knowing. Meister Eckhart (1265–1329), another exact contemporary, likewise uses analogy as a way that makes expression of the divine really only a subjectively mediated metaphor for what cannot be objectively known and expressed without becoming idolatrous. All beings are immediately related to God, the Infinite. The ownmost being of anything is an objectively unknowable mystery like God. Alain de Libera (1980) parses this predicament in detail. Symbolic thinking flourishes in the age subsequent to Duns Scotus, but it is not objectively grounded so much as a human and subjective way of construing things. It is, in Nicholas of Cusa's vocabulary, *conjecture*. Cusanus's *De Coniecturis* (1441–1442) directly follows-up and completes his groundbreaking *De Docta Ignorantia* (1440). Cusanus will be among the first to fully recognize and assimilate the new episteme. Pannenberg (2007) presents this transition from objective analogy to subjective symbol penetratingly in chapter VI: "Das Verblassen des Analogiegedankens auf dem Weg vom spätmittelalterlichen Platonismus zur neuzeitlichen Philosophie," pp. 181–211. A conjecture is not just an arbitrary construction: It aims at, and is called forth by, an unknown, an enigma.

Dante is able to invent—or conjecture—the world of his poem with utter freedom of imagination because the world it relates to is strictly speaking, unrepresentable. The other world does impinge on and informs his representations at every point, but there is no calculus for how or with what results. As noted by Rubenstein (2014), contemporary scientific cosmology again pullulates in imaginings of other worlds, even ones beyond time and space. This science requires us "to believe in the existence of many other universes" that "we cannot prove" and that "are accidental and incalculable" (p. 214). Subjective mediation by the personal passion of the poet—or the poetic cosmologist—becomes the condition of possibility of revelation. Dante discovers the freedom of poetic imagination, such as it can be exercised in a secular universe. The doctrine of artistic or creative *genius* will develop later in the Enlightenment, notably with Kant, to account for this productive faculty and its freedom unconfined by the apparent reality of the empirical world. Even so, already for Dante, such imagination is all geared toward and aimed at the absolute reality beyond all finite beings.

In effect, Dante exploits analogy for the very same reason that Scotus rejects it. Both understand that, in their post-Aquinian era, analogy cannot provide scientific knowledge of God and of the 'separate entities' of the other and invisible world. All this surpasses our sense-bound means of knowing, for we have no sensory intuition of purely intellectual beings. This is the predicament that Kant takes to heart as the starting point for his *critical* philosophy. Accordingly, at this juncture, representation of the other world can only be a free invention. This causes objective discourse and practices in finite realms such as jurisprudence to enter into crisis and contradiction. The upheaval in the juridical domain is examined by Steinberg (2013) in *Dante and the Limits of the Law*. Yet, on this basis, Dante pursues his poetic creation as the expression of his personal, existential relation to ultimate reality.

In *Paradiso* IV:40–42, Dante explains—through Beatrice—that even Scripture employs poetic metaphor to speak to human beings of God and angels, since human understanding takes from sense alone—"solo da sensato apprende"—that which it then makes worthy of intellection. Thus Scripture "condescends" to human faculties, attributing "hand and foot" to God and human form to angels Gabriel, Michael, and Raphael, while "e altro intende" [meaning something else] (IV:43–48). Dante's own methods of representing metaphysical reality likewise resort to sensible images as existential witness to a metaphysical experience that is otherwise ineffable.

Scotus, like Kant, and well before him, turns to the will and love as the only way of relating to this higher, supernatural reality that cannot be known theoretically, not concretely anyway, not by us, at least not in this life. And this delimitation of the realm of spirit and freedom from that of nature and necessity frees the sublunary world—in fact, the whole physical universe—to be investigated in terms of its own logic and intrinsic order. This universe becomes the domain of the natural sciences.

Duns opens a sphere of conceptual creation—just as Dante opens a sphere of imaginative creation—that is autonomous, a realm of freedom and contingency, a secular realm. Yet it still stands radically in relation to another realm, one that is inaccessible by merely human means, but that can be sounded by theology. In contrast to theological revelation, human means discover their own self-reflexive powers of establishing relations internal to reflection as a mediated way of relating to the radically exterior. These self-reflexive ways of science and imagination become radically separated from theology after Scotus; and even Dante becomes adamant against confusing the secular and sacred orders, notably with regard to their claims for authority in government. In *Monarchia*, Book III, he argues rigorously for this binary, "two-truths" type of political doctrine, which reverberates throughout his *oeuvre* from *Convivio* IV.iv to *Paradiso* XXX:133–148, with its projected celestial coronation of Emperor Henry VII. Both secular and spiritual authority, nevertheless, in Dante's teaching, are based on a direct relation to the one God, as *Monarchia* III.xv and all of *Paradiso* unequivocally attest.

Dante's imaginings of the other world become fully real as 'repetitions' in a human sphere in some way answering to what contact with the higher reality has inspired in him. He recognizes God as being inaccessible per se—as Godself—to human means and theoretical reason, as symbolized finally at his poem's end by the geometer's vain attempt to square the circle (XXXIII:133–135). Still, divinity can be mediated by repetition as enacted in poetic experience and also in the actualizations of liturgy and other religious rituals. A similar sort of status as real, even though removed to a realm of humanly created formal objects, applies to Scotus's metaphysics. Yet Scotus begins to erect a system of transcendental concepts that cordons off the humanly accessible sphere from divine intervention, and this solution remains intact through Kant. In Dante, the discovery of the autonomous sphere of representation bequeaths to modernity what we know as the world of poetic fiction and aesthetic imagination. It will be understood in the Romantic age, with its demiurgic notion of poetic creativity, as a realm of human self-determination and autonomous will. But, as I have argued extensively elsewhere (1996; and 2015, chapter 5), Dante pursued poetry rather as a subjective, interpretative re-enactment of a divine act of self-revelation.

Note

1 This chapter is adapted from William Franke's forthcoming book, *Dante's Paradiso and the Theological Origins of Modern Thought: Toward a Speculative Philosophy of Self-Reflection* (Routledge, 2021).

References

Adorno, T. (1966). *Negative Dialektik*. Suhrkamp Verlag.
Belting, H. (2008). *Florenz und Bagdad: Eine westöstliche Geschichte des Blicks*. Beck.
Belting, H. (2011). *Florence and Baghdad: Renaissance art and Arab science*. (D. L. Schneider, Trans.). Harvard University Press.
Boulnois, O. (1999). *Être et représentation. Une généalogie de la métaphysique moderne à l'époque de Duns Scotus*. Presses Universitaires de France.
Deleuze, G. (1992). *Expressionism in philosophy* (M. Joughin, Trans.). Zone Books.
de Libera, A. (1980). *Le problème de l'être chez maître Eckhart: Logique et métaphysique de l'analogie*. Cahiers de al Revue de théologie et de philosophie.
De Lubac, H. (1946). *Surnaturel. Études historiques*. Aubier-Montaigne.
de Vries, H. (1989). *Theologie im Pianissimo: Zur Aktualität der Denkfiguren Adornos und Levinas*. J. H. Kok.
de Vries, H. (2005). *Minimal theologies: Critiques of secular reason in Adorno and Levinas*. (G. Hale, Trans.). Johns Hopkins University Press.
Duns Scotus (1300–1304). *Ordinatio*. Retrieved from http://www.logicmuseum.com/wiki/Authors/Duns_Scotus/Ordinatio
Duns Scotus, J. (1302–1307). Reportatio parisiensis. In A. B. Wolter & O. V. Bychkov (Eds. & Trans.), *John Duns Scotus. The examined report of the Paris lecture: Reportatio I-A*, vol. 2 (2008). Franciscan Institute.
Duns Scotus, J. (2001). *Tractatus de primo principio: Traité du premier principe*. Librarie Philosophique J. Vrin. (Original work published c. 1308).
Foucault, M. (1966). *Les mots et les choses*. Gallimard.
Franke, W. (1993). Hermeneutic catastrophe in Racine: The epistemological predicament of 17th century tragedy. *Romanische Forschungen, 105*, 315–331.
Franke, W. (1996). *Dante's interpretive journey*. University of Chicago Press.
Franke, W. (2015). *The revelation of imagination: From Homer and the Bible through Virgil and Augustine to Dante*. Northwestern University Press.
Franke, W. (2016). *Secular scriptures: Modern theological poetics in the wake of Dante*. Ohio State University Press.
Hoff, J. (2013). *The analogical turn: Rethinking modernity with Nicholas of Cusa*. Eerdmans.

Honnefelder, L. (2008). *Woher kommen wir? Ursprünge der Moderne im Denken des Mittelalters*. Berlin University Press.

Honnefelder, L. (2011). *Johannes Duns Scotus: Denker auf der Schwelle vom mittelalterlichen zum neuzeitlichen Denken*. Ferdinand Schöningh.

Janicaud, D. (1991). *Le tournant théologique de la phénoménologie française*. L'Eclat.

Janicaud, D. et al. (2000). *Phenomenology and the "Theological Turn": The French debate*. Fordham University Press.

LaZella, A. (2019). *The singular voice of being: Duns Scotus and ultimate difference*. Fordham University Press.

Levinas, E. (1961). *Totalité et infini*. Martinus Nuihoff.

McGinn, B. (1998). *The varieties of vernacular mysticism (1350–1550)*. Crossroad.

Meillassoux, Q. (2006). *Après la finitude: Essai sur la nécessité de la contingence*. Seuil.

Milbank, J. (1995). Can a gift be given? Prolegomena to a future trinitarian metaphysic. *Modern Theology, 11*(1), 119–161.

Milbank, J. (2005). *The suspended middle: Henri de Lubac and the debate concerning the supernatural*. Eerdmans.

Pannenberg, W. (2007). *Analogie und Offenbarung: Eine kritische Untersuchung zur Geschichte des Analogiebegriffs in der Lehre von der Gotteserkenntnis*. Vandenhoek & Ruprecht.

Rubenstein, M.-J. (2014). *Worlds without end: The many lives of the multiverse*. Columbia University Press.

Simmons, J. A., & Benson, B. E. (2013). *The new phenomenology: A philosophical introduction*. Bloomsbury.

Steinberg, J. (2013). *Dante and the limits of the law*. University of Chicago Press.

Chapter 3

1321: A Space Odyssey
A Response to Franke

Aaron B. Daniels

As C. S. Lewis strives to close the loop of his framing narrative to the first novel of his Space Trilogy, *Out of the Silent Planet* (1938/2013), he has his protagonist respond to the narrator, reflecting on the purpose of sharing the story. Through these layers, Lewis is, himself, speaking to his readers regarding his objective when he writes, "If we could even effect in one per cent of our readers a change-over from the conception of Space to the conception of Heaven, we should have made a beginning" (p. 140). This sentiment can serve as a fitting epigraph to this chapter.

In October of 2019, I took on the daunting task of responding to the lecture by William Franke, of which the preceding chapter in this volume is his expansion. The Dante Salon at the 2019 Psychology and the Other conference brought together Dante scholars from around the world who bridge the seven centuries since Dante's death by bringing contemporary philosophical, theological, and psychological perspectives to bear on the Florentine's work. In the midst of a rich array of presentations, testified to by this current volume, Franke's paper was a particular joy for me, sharing as we do a deep conviction in the power of a phenomenological perspective. I resonate with Franke's message, but knew, from the start, that I could not hope to respond in Franke's terms. He is a Dante scholar of the highest caliber, and his knowledge of apophatic theology—among other fields—is equally prodigious. I am a psychologist with a weakness for philosophy and theology and a love of Dante; but, growing from our phenomenological commitments, where Franke and I meet as scholars is the essential question of this moment in history, 'where are we and how did we get here?' Historians are perhaps always addressing this question for preceding eras; yet today, like the question of being itself, this question is deeply obscured, to the point of seeming irrelevancy and even non-existence.

Thus, having read his paper in advance, I sat and listened to Franke's brilliant analysis and waited for an image to emerge. This is a tried-and-true Jungian technique favored by Jung's archetypal psychology descendants, especially Hillman, who asks practitioners to inquire 'who's here?' What gods, creatures, and stories inform this current situation?

For me, Franke's attention to Duns Scotus's intention to retain God's centrality is essential to the argument. Scotus is no atheist. Nevertheless, he discovers that a distinct discourse devoid of theological considerations enables a type of analysis of the natural world heretofore unimagined. The 'univocity of being,' which Franke sees Duns Scotus asserting, obscures the question of being. This is a simple step and, from today's perspective, seemingly common sense. Indeed, this is the common sense of today. But a partition with horizon-defining implications is the result. Dante, on the other hand, offers a vision of a phenomenologically inflected poetry. Franke reminds his readers that Duns Scotus is loath to venture too far into any description of divinity; and, although Dante will also eschew making positive and final statements about God, the driving question and the fundamental orientation of human existence toward God is the core of Dante's work. Duns Scotus adequately establishes distinct discourses such that theological imagination need play no role in other forms of inquiry.

This brought me to think about Dante's heavens as presented in *Paradiso*—so overflowing with Grace, effulgent, and driven with searing passion toward the Ineffable, and to contrast that with the vacuum of our literal heavens today: space. Thinking of what Dante would have to do to ascend the Divine Spheres today brought me to the image of the astronaut, especially as interrogated by Romanyshyn.

Romanyshyn—on equal footing in Jungian and phenomenological discourse—introduces his analysis of the astronaut in *Technology as Symptom and Dream* (1989) and develops it further in lecture. Within his book, Romanyshyn deals with questions of where we are all headed. He examines the possibility of the spacesuit becoming the 'exoskeleton' of the technological human of the not-too-distant future—if not, figuratively, our present. He imagines a "*homo sapiens astronauticus*" whose body is "turned inside out, re-dressed in terms of technical functions *on the way to being discarded*" (p. 19). In lecture, Romanyshyn sat less with the spacesuit and more with the image of the free-floating astronaut—contextless and disconnected.

When I offered this floating cosmonaut at the Dante Salon in response to Franke's paper, Professor Arielle Saiber responded, "that doesn't sound so bad to me!" That is, might we find some peace in our age of super-saturated 'information,' 'communication,' and 24/7 'access'—just breathing and floating? Indeed, one does not imagine this astronaut checking email or receiving texts. (Perhaps we would respond differently if we spent much of 2020 in personal protective equipment and in quarantine.) However, Romanyshyn does not present a generic image of an astronaut in a sort of astral sensory-deprivation apparatus. His image and the one upon which I wish to expand comes from a very specific moment in history: Stanley Kubrick's 1968 masterpiece, *2001: A Space Odyssey*.

Kubrick (1968) gives his free-floating astronaut an epic historical context. He presents the fearful impasse of the early hominids in the opening section of the film, "The Dawn of Man." Our hirsute ancestors exist among the other beasts with little distinction from them and no power over them. Living in fear of predators and driven away from resources by a rival tribe, they huddle together in a shallow cave. The tribe awakes one morning to Kubrick's iconic black monolith within their midst. The leader furtively touches it in a moment evoking the fingers of Adam and God—nearly—touching on the Sistine Chapel's ceiling's "The Creation of Adam" (c. 1512) by Michelangelo. Following his lead, the rest of the tribe touches this new presence. Soon thereafter, the hominid leader stares at a large bone and, with a bit of experimentation and a lot of Strauss's *Also Spracht Zarathustra* for soundtrack, can visualize its use as a tool—a weapon that allows his tribe to regain access to the watering hole. In his ecstasy of discovery and his tribe's victory over their rivals, he throws the bone into the air, and Kubrick edits the image into a spacecraft in orbit over Earth.

I ask my reader to leave aside the extra-textual explanation or interpretation of this monolith and focus instead on its inscrutability. A presented by Kubrick (1968), our ancestors lived in a world of fearful immediacy. Incapable of symbolism, this was a world where things were exactly what they were—if one can even make use of any form of the verb 'to be' in that context. But in his encounter with the monolith, the leader—and soon thereafter, the whole tribe—faces something that raises the question of meaning. This is the question they previously could not ask: 'What does any of this mean?' But in encountering the monolith—in spite of making use of all of their resources of smell, touch, foot-stamping, vocalizations, and every other sensate epistemology—this newly formed question of meaning resolutely received no answer. Nevertheless, without question, this monolith *was* before them. Given that the next scene shows the leader contemplating bones, one could make the existential move—the recognition of death and finitude being critical for the human kind of consciousness. Regardless, the encounter with the inexplicable, inscrutable presence of the monolith facilitates a very special kind of consciousness: imagination. The leader sees possibility and potential utilization. Meaning emerges because existence is no longer immediacy and irrefutability. Perhaps, existence has become a question. Meaning becomes possibility in unfolding engagement. That is to say, before—or without—imagination, there is no meaning. Though we as the audience may imagine what the monolith may mean or what Kubrick and author Arthur C. Clarke intended, the monolith itself defies being explained away and thus evokes, creates, *demands* imagination. Our speculations as the audience are only further testament to being those early hominids' descendants.

For my purposes in this response to Professor Franke's chapter, I want to parallel the plight of our hominid ancestors to our science fiction analogs in the remainder of Kubrick's *2001* (1968). The early hominids and the *homo sapiens astronauticus* both face impasses that can only be overcome by a radical shift in consciousness. The denizens of this future-now-passed, as exemplified by the disconnected floating astronaut, are detached, emotionless, flat. Kubrick's cinematic setup is this: Scientists discover a new monolith on the Moon—unaware of the previous prehistoric presence—and it sends a signal directed toward Jupiter. Thus, in the second section of the film "Jupiter Mission," astronauts on board the *Discovery One* on their interplanetary mission become the focus for the remainder of the film. Astronaut Frank Poole expresses nearly the same flattened affect in a video conversation with his parents as his colleague David Bowman does when the homicidal computer HAL refuses to open the pod bay doors for him. Emotionally, our characters are as disconnected as they physically are when space-suited and floating in the abyss.

As one tries to look around the corner of Kubrick and Clarke's (1968) vision, questions emerge. For instance, is this a world without religion? We are given no indication one way or the other. But this is surely the world that Franke in Chapter 2 of this current volume informs us that Scotus helped to create. The question of God, the ineffability of God, plays no role in the conversations, imagination, or ethical comportment of the characters. These are Franke's "free subjects" in an "alienated world of mere matter" (p. 62). Moreover, these denizens of a technocratic future-now-passed are not enthusiastic astrophysicists full of wonder like our Neil DeGrasse Tyson or Michio Kaku. Instead, the astronauts in *2001* (1968) fulfill functions interchangeably. Where is the meaning for these humans? Viewers are left to conjecture for themselves since Kubrick portrays what Franke will characterize as a 'world of willing,' but a groundless willing where meaning is to be self-apparent. They are things among things—a clear demonstration of Heidegger's inauthenticity of *das Mann* [the Them or they-self]. Additionally, Kubrick's division of the film into three sections places the technological advances and Moon colonization still within the "Dawn of Man" section, as emphatically noted by Camerena (2014). That is, Kubrick's (1968) audience is to take even our most advanced post-industrial technological advances to be merely part of the Dawn of Man.

I ask my reader to forgive my further artistic liberty as I attempt to parallel Dante and Kubrick. All is in the service of trying to ask the questions from the beginning of this essay, 'where are we and how did we get here?' And to add one more, 'how may we come to once again recognize the Ineffable at the heart and furthest edges of our existence?' Dante's *Vita Nuova* ends with the Florentine admitting that he does not have the words to express his greater vision but his commitment to become the Poet who can. The title of *A New Life* is, in part, a reference to this new orientation toward giving voice to what is beyond his capacity. In large part, that commitment will come to fruition with the *Commedia*. Dante awakens from his ruminations on youthful ardor and poetic technique to a realization—however distant—that he is fundamentally oriented toward something beyond his ken. At the risk of comparing Dante to a furry troglodyte, cannot one parallel this awakening to that of the hominids opening *2001* (1968)?

To further this parallel, like Dante in *Paradiso*, the technological humans of *2001* (1968) have begun to ascend the heavens. In the spacecraft *Discovery One*, the astronauts, most of them not-even-slumbering in suspended animation, venture to the orbit of Jupiter. For Dante, in *Paradiso* XVIII–XX, Jupiter is the sixth sphere, the realm of just rulers. But our astronauts do not find some sort of justice. Instead, the technology in which they have not only trusted but truly *become* betrays them. HAL, the supercomputer onboard the spacecraft, succeeds in murdering all of them except Bowman. Clarke's writing frequently wrestles with questions of technology and the idea of God. In this succinct image, Kubrick and Clarke offer the viewer a clear indictment of a complete surrender to technology. However, death is not the last word.

A snapshot becomes necessary before *2001* (1968) can reach its transformative and transhumanist climax. What the viewer has witnessed is a technological world free of any relevant theological discourse with humans nearly dissociative in their affectlessness; technology which reaches its logical apotheosis in murderous efficiency; and heavens that destroy in their abyssal vacuum, yet at its anthropological foundation, this is a humanity whose existence emerged—emerges—in the face of an inscrutable presence. Thus, are these new technocratic creatures actually human if they do not confront—cannot even acknowledge—a frontier of unknowing? In the conclusion of "The Dawn of Man," the monolith appears once again—on the Moon—and sets in motion events which will lead to a very different apotheosis. That is, the impasse of our hominid ancestors becomes the technological impasse of *2001*—and arguably today.

Before we can describe Kubrick's (1968) efforts to express this final vision, a comparison between *2001* and 2001 could prove informative. Humans, of course, had not ascended the heavens in our actual 2001. Humans had not set foot on the Moon in nearly thirty years, let alone established colonies. Spacecraft with humans aboard orbited Earth but did not venture further. Pan Am Airlines, which Kubrick portrays as launching commercial spaceflights, had been ten years in the grave by our 2001. The tenacious Hubble space telescope was eight years into its new lease on life, and uncrewed spacecraft were gradually making their way into the farther reaches of the solar system. That is, machines, not humans, were—and continue to—ascend the celestial spheres dreamed of by Dante. On Earth, 2001, of course, also became the year of the unthinkable tragedies of the terrorist attacks on America on September 11th. Although the civic and technological landscape looked starkly different from Kubrick's breathtaking visions, the impasse was all the more palpable for our humanity still bound to Earth. In a sense, the 'unthinkable' became all the more a baffle to our acknowledgment of the Ineffable. This configuration is as opposed to the pilgrim Dante who chooses to venture through the landscape of the unspeakable in *Inferno* in order to, eventually, reach the Ineffable in *Paradiso*.

These images provide some literal and some imaginal answers to the question of 'where are we and how did we get here?' But the additional question of where the Ineffable can reach us today—or, more appropriately, where we might acknowledge the abiding frontiers with the Ineffable in our lives—remains. After all, if God is God—and perhaps this should be written G-d in this case, since we are audaciously speaking of the Ineffable—then marginalizing, forgetting, or defining-out-of-rhetoric will not eliminate the Call. But our post-Scotus efforts may certainly turn that Call into a pathology—so alienated from it as we have become. Moreover, if we are looking at global consciousness, then with such layered denial creating an edifice of material certainties, the working-through of this pathology promises the sort of cataclysmic enantiodromia that finds representation in the past forty years of global disaster films—since we all are far too sophisticated to take literally any Apocalypse. Individually, rather than globally, Dante surely presents us with elaborate visions of what the journey from horrifying certainties, to deliberate transformative labors, to ascending sublimities looks like. But the intervening seven centuries have undeniably changed our imagination. Thus, a return to Kubrick (1968) and the fate of astronaut Bowman may give us some guidance, if not hope.

The third section of Kubrick's (1968) film is "Jupiter and Beyond the Infinite." Bowman has disabled HAL: regressed the machine to a child-like state—with HAL famously singing 'Daisy Bell' more and more slowly—and then deactivation. Only with HAL shut down does Bowman learn the truth of the mission—the pursuit of the signal from the Moon monolith to Jupiter. Bowman has had to strip away—*purge*—layers of technology to discover the actual telos through which he was living. *Discovery One* reaches Jupiter, and, in a small space pod, Bowman approaches a massive monolith in orbit around the gas giant. (Devotees of the film will tell you that this is when the home viewer should place the needle onto the B-side of Pink Floyd's 1971 album *Meddle*, "Echoes.") The sequence rapidly becomes psychedelic. Bowman enters the seemingly impenetrably solid monolith. He is transported through a kaleidoscope of time and space with the screen-wide shots of his face expressing a range of extreme emotions—all the more shocking after their preceding marked absence. Bowman witnesses himself aging and switches perspectives to witness himself in spacesuit beholding his aged self. All of this culminates with a Bowman of advanced years struggling to reach a monolith at the foot of the bed in which he lays. Echoing the early hominid's first encounter, he touches the monolith and the audience beholds a fetus wreathed in light floating in space above Earth accompanied, once again, by the opening to Strauss's *Also Spracht Zarathustra*.

Clarke continued to write within the mythos of *2001*. The film *2010: The Year We Make Contact* (Hyams, 1984) adapts Clarke's *2010: Odyssey Two* (1982). The later film is a decidedly less ambitious and less enigmatic creation than Kubrick's masterpiece. Nevertheless, it contains a few pieces of Clarke's ongoing symbolic journey germane to this essay. By the end of *2010* (Hyams, 1984), the viewer witnesses a flood of monoliths turn Jupiter into a new sun. The symbolism is stark, if not quite accurate in placement to Dante's cosmology. Sol, our sun, has become a ball of gas, not a source of hope, rebirth, and enlightenment. This demythologization is so profound that Sol cannot be reclaimed. Notwithstanding Bowman's transformation, only a new sun placed once again in a heavenly orbit can renew the relationship and claim a new covenant with humanity.

Jungian amplification might lead one to ask if HAL is a sort of shadow figure. With technocratic scientism occluding the possibility of a Virgil appearing in the midst of our lives, are we offered this virtual assistant as the shadow alternative? Would 'Siri' or 'Alexa' be better names today for our Virtual Virgils? Of course, these are Broken Beatrices who cannot inspire us to journey through Hell or up Purgatory and even less guide us to the very edges of Heaven. Although we may get the answers to all of our questions from disembodied voices, that may simply indicate that we aren't asking the right kind of questions. Like Bowman, we don't even know that we don't know. Nevertheless, in spite of the technological hegemony of Bowman's world, the astronaut faces the sort of lightning flash, transhumanist moments that Dante does in *Paradiso* XXXIII; but how much less prepared Bowman is! How much less prepared than Dante are we? That the astronaut's mystical transdimensional and transhumanist vision becomes Bowman-viewing-Bowman himself speaks to the necessary individuality of the experience, if only tangentially. We will not find a generic mystical path, no matter how many mystical or New Age texts we read. The Ineffable indicts the specificity of each of our denials of its inescapability. Bowman's visions align with what Franke notes in this volume when he says,

> this source—God—surpasses human comprehension, but it is revealed in the imaginative *process* itself. Confrontation with the Incommensurable, as nothing that can be humanly grasped, is embraced as an essentially constitutive and eminently creative moment necessary in order to interpret the whole of our self-reflexively generated reality. (p. 67)

Just as the reader must track at least three Dantes—the Pilgrim, the Poet he becomes, and the Poet who reflects on his experience of writing—so too, the viewer of Kubrick's (1968) film not only should reflect on Bowman's levels of transformation but also Kubrick's creative act in producing the film. So too, should the viewer of the film, like the reader of Dante, reflect on experiencing and participating in this creative, life-affirming act.

Finally, in what one could interpret as an apophatic omission, the audience of *2001* (1968) does not actually hear Bowman's final words as he approaches the massive monolith in space. Only in Clarke's original book (1968) and a recording played in *2010* (Hyams, 1984) do we learn what Bowman said. Realizing that the monolith is something of a portal or transdimensional—transhuman—gateway, as his small pod comes closer to it, Bowman's flattened affect breaks; he is startled—awakened—retrieved from his technological slumber through the dark expanses of space. He comes to himself at the crossroads of this life of ours and of human evolution itself—startled awake by the dark monolith. Full of wonder, his last recorded words before he enters the unknown are, "My God, it's full of stars."

References

Camarena, E. M. (2014, October 10). Why is this hard to get? *2001: A Space Odyssey Has Only THREE Sections*. [Blog post]. Retrieved from https://emcphd.wordpress.com/2014/10/10/why-is-this-hard-to-get-2001-a-space-odyssey-has-only-three-sections/
Clarke, A. C. (1968). *2001: A space odyssey*. New American Library.
Clarke, A. C. (1982). *2010: Odyssey two*. Ballentine Books.

Hyams, P. (producer & director) (1984). *2010: The year we make contact* [Motion Picture]. Metro-Goldwyn-Mayer Corp.

Kubrick, S., & Clarke, A. C. (producers) & Kubrick, S. (director) (1968). *2001: A space odyssey* [Motion Picture]. Metro-Goldwyn-Mayer Corp.

Lewis, C. S. (2013). *The space trilogy*. Harper Collins Publishers. (Original works published 1938, 1943, and 1945).

Pink Floyd (1971). *Meddle* [Audio album]. Harvest Capital.

Romanyshyn, R. (1989). *Technology as symptom & dream*. Routledge.

Chapter 4

Dante, Selfhood and Significant Journeying

John Took

It is right and proper, and indeed wholly desirable, that in the context of a 'Psychology and the Other' conference, we have a Dante slot, a Dante 'Salon,' for in Dante we have a Dasein analytic—an "all-embracing existentialist doctrine of man" as Paul Tillich (1980, pp. 128–129) put it—as highly developed in point both of conception and of articulation as anything in European letters. Tillich's exact words—the words of one who understood perfectly what was going on in Dante—are in fact worth recording here. For in one and the same breath, they confirm both the deep substance of the text—of the *Commedia*—and the means of its proposal:

> The greatest poetic expression of the Existentialist point of view in the Middle Ages is Dante's *Divina Commedia*. It remains, like the religious depth psychology of the monastics, within the framework of the scholastic ontology. But within these limits it enters the deepest places of human self-destruction and despair as well as the highest places of courage and salvation, and gives in poetic symbols an all-embracing existential doctrine of man. (p. 128)

Here, clearly, we have an entire agenda, enough to keep us busy for a whole series of dedicated conferences. For if on the one hand, we are invited by way of the 'Existentialist point of view' moment of the argument to ponder both the historical and the hermeneutical aspects of the text—both the circumstances of its coming about in the first place and the nature of its presence to us in the twenty-first century; then on the other, we are encouraged by way of the 'poetic symbols' moment of the argument to rejoice with Dante himself on what amounts to the triumph of the image as the means of ontological intelligence, on—over and against the proposition pure and simple—its unique adequacy to the matter in hand. So how much time have you got?

What, therefore, I propose to do in the few minutes at my disposal is to linger in the foothills and sketch out in a merely preliminary fashion the general shape and substance of Dante's 'all-embracing existentialist doctrine of man,' and this in its four main phases: by way, that is to say,

1) Of an anthropology turning upon the notion of, as Dante understands it, self and selfhood as the point-about-which of his meditation as a poet and philosopher.
2) Of an ethic—of, in truth, a love-ethic—as that whereby the individual seeks to negotiate and ideally to resolve the complex dimensionality and the ideal projectedness of his or her presence in the world as a creature both of accountability and of self-accountability.
3) Of—as in the *Commedia* especially a means of accessing and exploring this situation—a phenomenology of specifically human being, where it is a question of the *mood* of being as transparent to the *truth* of being.
4) And—by way of a gathering up of these things—of what in Dante amounts to a sense of what it is for man as man to be properly under way, of, in short, significant journeying.

Dante's, in each of these respects, is both an extraordinarily adult and extraordinarily sustained account of these things, all of which, alas, serves merely to underline the self-conscious inadequacy of what I am about to say to the business in hand. *Qui soprattutto quindi, Alighieri, La prego di accettare le mie profondissime scuse* [Here especially then, Alighieri, please accept my sincerest apologies].

A Basic Anthropology: Dante, Self, and Selfhood

Taking first, then, the anthropological moment of the argument, we may begin by saying this, that the notion of 'selfhood'—meaning by this the presence of self to self as a matter of concern (the Augustinian 'mihi quaestio factus sum')—is everywhere prominent in Dante and everywhere woven into his theology of creation. Now here we have to be careful since Dante's theology of creation is nothing if not a complex business. It is complex in its making room both for primary and for secondary causality, for a ceaseless opening out of the One who *is* as of the essence in ever-fresh channels of love-concern, and for the role of the Intelligences or separate substances in respect of the materialization and of the individualization of the idea as present from beforehand in the divine mind. But for all that, Dante, when it comes to man, in particular, has no doubt; for if the vegetative and the sensitive part of human nature comes about in and through the normal processes of procreation, then the rational soul, he thinks, is breathed immediately by God into the fetus, which makes of man an immediate product of divine intentionality and indeed the very pinnacle of divine creativity.

The passages in question, both in the *Convivio* as the great work of Dante's middle years and in the *Commedia* as the great work of his maturity, culminating as they do in a sense of man as—not unlike his maker—a creature circling steadily about the still center of his own existence (the exquisite "sé in sé rigira" of *Purgatorio* XXV:75), are in this respect as explicit as they are fulsome in their rejoicing in their sense of God's delighting in the first fruits of his handiwork. But what matters from our present point of view is his commitment to the notion of each and every individual as constituting in consequence of his or her status as an immediate product of divine willing a species, well-nigh, in his or her own right, a 'one-off,' unprecedented and unparalleled in the entire course of human history. The key passage here comes in the *De vulgari eloquentia* dating from much the same time as the *Convivio*—the "adeo ut fere quilibet sua propria specie videatur gaudere" [such that each individual might almost be said to constitute a species in his or her own right] moment of Book I, Chapter iii. This celebration of self, both in its actuality and in its specificity, is individualism on a grand scale, self, in the ideal emergence thereof, constituting at every point along the way both the first and the final cause of Dante's meditation as a poet and philosopher.

Structures of Consciousness and the Love-Imperative

But with this examination of the self, we are indeed only in the foothills when it comes to Dante's 'all-embracing existential doctrine of man.' For the human situation, he thinks, from whatever point of view you look at it—morally, intellectually, or psychologically—is unspeakably complex.

It is complex, first of all, by way of its manifold dimensionality. Man as man is present to himself by way of, in effect, the dialectics of that presence, of the kinds of polarity forever taxing him in conscience and, by way of their inherent difficulty, indeed of their endless intractability, making for the twofold agony and ecstasy of his *being-in-the-world*. Man as man, therefore, knows himself in the *temporality* of his being here and now, but in the selfsame instant, he is called out of *time* into *eternity* and thus to ponder the *height and depth* of the historical instant tending absolutely to transcend in point both of substance and intensity the mere *before and after* of that instant. Failure to resolve the polarity of time and eternity on the plane of properly human being is to deliver self, Dante thinks, to the most complete kind of ontological catastrophe, to the nothingness of which time as untouched by eternity is a first principle.

And what applies in respect of time and eternity applies too in respect of *locality* and *universality* as likewise to the fore among the polarities of specifically human being. Man as man, therefore, knows himself in the *locatedness* of his properly human presence in the world, but in the selfsame instant, he is called out of the *here* of that presence into the *here, there, and everywhere* thereof again tending absolutely to transcend in point of substance and intensity the mere whereabouts thereof. Failure to resolve the polarity of locality and universality on the plane of properly human being is once again to deliver self to the most complete kind of ontological catastrophe, to an over-wintering of the spirit in the region of unlikeness, in a *regio dissimilitudinis*.

And then, to complicate things still further, there is the call from *individuality* to *collectivity*, for rejoicing as he does in the specificity or one-offness of his presence in the world as a creature of moral and intellectual determination, the individual is called upon even so both to countenance and to rejoice in that of the next man, and this not merely in the alongsidedness thereof, but in the status of that man as a structure of one's own existence, as the in-and-through which—as Dante himself puts it in the ninth canto of the *Paradiso*—of the most complete kind of *in-youing* and *in-meing*, the most complete kind of mutual presencing. Here too, therefore, there is a note of urgency. Failure to resolve the polarity of *self* and the *other-than-self* on the plane of properly human being is to deliver self to the kind of solipsism of which the *Inferno* is the most sustained expression and exploration in the whole of European letters.

And then finally, when it comes to the nothing if not restive parameters of specifically human being in the positive living out thereof, there is the polarity of *freedom* and *destiny*, of knowing self as both *determining* and *determined*: as *determining* in the sense of empowered in respect of the *what might be* of self under the conditions of time and space, and as *determined* in the sense of standing even so under a summons, as, in the selfsame moment, constrained from out of the depths.

In all these senses, then, man as man is called upon to think through, to negotiate, and as far as may be to resolve the to-and-fro conflicting structures of his presence in the world as, in circumstances of the greatest ontological complexity, a creature of fundamental self-interpretation.

But as if that were not enough, we have, in addition to the complex dimensionality of specifically human being its proper projectedness, its forever *being-ahead-of-itself* in point of understanding and willing. Man as man, in other words, Dante thought, is forever called out of the *what is* of his presence in the world into the *what might be* and indeed into the *what must be* of that presence, and this in two senses: *proximately* or in respect of the calling proper to this or that individual man or woman as determined by the properties of personality, and *ultimately* in respect of what Dante speaks of as the kind of 'transhumanity' or transfigured humanity to which, irrespective of the properties of personality—but in a manner both countenancing and comprehending them all—each and every individual is called from beforehand.

Proximately, then, it is a question of—as Dante himself puts it towards the end of *Paradiso* VIII—the sword or the sermon. Just as, in other words, some are called to be apostles, some prophets, some evangelists, and some pastors and teachers, so some, Dante believes, are called to be paladins and some preachers. Selfhood, in the moment of positive implementation, is, in this sense, a matter of self-recognition, of knowing self in the proper vocation of self.

Ultimately, by contrast, it is a question of, as Dante understands it, the ecstatic character of specifically human being precisely as such, of—again as he himself understands it—the call in each and every individual to an ever-fresh re-shaping and re-substantiation of historical selfhood, a constant redrawing of the parameters of self on the planes both of knowing and of loving. No re-shaping and re-substantiation of historical selfhood, Dante thought, no properly human being in the unique fullness thereof but merely a delivery of self to the customary, the familiar, the routine contents of seeing, understanding, and choosing. Here, especially, then, Dante is at his most ecstatic, his precisely being a sense of human being properly understood as a matter of emergence-from-the-stillness (*ex-sistere*), of knowing self by way of the soaring substance of self.

At this point we come to the categorical imperative, to the love-imperative at the heart of Dante's ethic, of his meditation, that is to say, as one engaged at the point of man's proper well-being and proper happiness as man. To be brief, then—though here again, given the sublimity of Dante's discourse as *the* great love poet of European letters, brevity hereabouts borders on blasphemy—we may say this: that Dante's is an ethic turning quintessentially on the bringing home or the gathering in and harvesting of one love-impulse to another, on the kind of love-organization whereby, entirely without prejudice to its proper legitimacy, the occasional is taken up in the ontological on the plane of properly human loving.

To be more exact, man as man, for Dante, knows himself by way of two different kinds of loving, by way of:

1) The kind of love coeval and consubstantial with existence itself, a love, this, which, preceding as it does the moral moment proper of human experience—the moment either of consent or of dissent—Dante calls 'amore naturale'.
2) The kind of love generated by the sights and sounds of the world round about, a love which, presupposing as it does the moral moment proper of human experience—the moment either of consent or of dissent—Dante calls 'amore d'animo,' which we might translate as 'elective love.'

At every point along the way, Dante thinks, the latter ('amore d'animo') stands to be measured up against and to be regulated by the former ('amore naturale'), this alone ensuring its function as a principle not now of distraction but, by way of its proper legitimacy as but part and parcel of properly human living and loving in the totality thereof, serving, even so, the radiant finality of the whole. Only in the degree, then, to which the contingent is brought home to the connatural on the plane of properly human loving, the occasional to the ontic, does it set up a steady claim in conscience. Short of this, it shades off, Dante thinks, in something close to the demonic:

"Né creator né creatura mai",
cominciò el, "figliuol, fu sanza amore,
o naturale o d'animo; e tu 'l sai.

Lo naturale è sempre sanza errore,
ma l'altro puote errar per malo obietto
o per troppo o per poco di vigore.

Mentre ch'elli è nel primo ben diretto,
e ne' secondi sé stesso misura,
esser non può cagion di mal diletto;

ma quando al mal si torce, o con più cura
o con men che non dee corre nel bene,
contra 'l fattore adovra sua fattura."

[He began: "neither Creator nor creature, my son, was—as well you know—ever without love, either natural or elective. Natural love can never err, but the other may in respect either of an unworthy object or else by way either of excess or defect. So long as it is directed on the highest good and as regards all others is properly proportionate, it cannot be the cause of dubious pleasure. But bent upon evil or chasing the good with more or less zeal than it ought, against the Creator works his creature."] (*Purgatorio* XVII:91–102)

Dante's, then—and in truth at every point along the way, from the *Vita nova* as but his first systematic meditation on the love-problematic of specifically human being through to the love-encompassing resolution of the *Commedia*—the "love which moves the sun and the other stars" (*Paradiso* XXXIII:145) moment of the text with which it falls silent—is a matter of bringing home one thing to another on the plane of proper affectivity, anything short of or anything other than this making less for a building up than for a tearing down of whatever *is* in the world according to kind—in short, an offense against the primordial *let it be*.

A Phenomenology of Being

But there is more, for when it comes to what in Dante amounts to a Dasein analytic before ever such a thing was thought of, it is a question too of the phenomenology of specifically human being thus understood, of the mood or felt-sensation apt upon reflection to disclose the *how it stands and how it fares* with the individual—Heidegger's *wie einem ist und wird*—in the otherwise hidden recesses thereof. This is a phenomenology of the mood, again in Heidegger's sense of it, as 'never nothing,' as ontologically eloquent. Already, then, on the threshold of the *Inferno* it is a question of fear, of the kind of fear engendered not by mere happenstance or eventuality, but by being itself as astray in respect of its own innermost reasons, as forgetful, as somnambulant, as ranged over against itself at the point of fundamental willing and in the forum of conscience:

Nel mezzo del cammin di nostra vita
mi ritrovai per una selva oscura,
ché la diritta via era smarrita.

Ahi quanto a dir qual era è cosa dura
esta selva selvaggia e aspra e forte
che nel pensier rinova la paura!
...

> Io non so ben ridir com' i' v'intrai,
> tant' era pien di sonno a quel punto
> che la verace via abbandonai.
>
> [In the middle of the journey of our life, I came to myself within a dark wood where the straight way was lost. Ah, how hard a thing it is to tell of that wood, savage, harsh and dense, the very thought of which renews my fear ... I cannot rightly tell how I entered there, so full was I of sleep at the moment in which I forsook the true way.] (*Inferno* I:1–6 & 10–12)

—lines to which, as at once the point of arrival and the deep substance of this condition, we may add the "ch'io perdei la speranza dell'altezza" moment of line 54 [so much so that I despaired of the heights, of the sunlit upland]. It is, then, by way of fear thus understood, as a rhythm of anxiety operative from out of the depths, that the individual is alerted to and confirmed in a sense of existential crisis and thus of his imminent demise—Dante's "che poco è più morte" in line 7—as a creature of significant determination. But that is only the beginning, for knowing itself as it does in its far-wandering, the soul knows itself too in the anger, the restlessness, the paranoia, the renunciation, the inertia, the dissipation, and, again as the first and final cause of these things, in the despair engendered by and in turn serving to engender each and every self-consciously inauthentic inflection of the spirit.

No less eloquent, however, in respect of their status as ontological indicators, as bearing witness to the *how it stands and how it fares* with self in the innermost parts thereof, are the moods of being in its authenticity, of—as Dante puts it in the *Purgatorio* X:124–126—the 'butterfly' emergence of the individual into the fullness of his or her proper humanity. First, then, there is the peace whereby, having trodden the upward way, the purgatorial way of sorrowing and striving, the soul rejoices at last in the perfect stability and self-possession of its presence in the world. Its every love-impulse now perfectly gathered, winnowed and harvested, the spirit delights now in the 'wholeness' of its being—the "oh vita integra d'amore e di pace" of the Petrine canto *par excellence* of the *Commedia*, *Paradiso* XXVII—in, as Bernard of Clairvaux puts it, the "supreme tranquility, the most placid serenity" of the spirit in its homecoming. Peace, in short, is for Dante the mood of being in its stillness and self-transparency, in its gentle circling about the still center of its presence in the world. It is but the *static* mood of being in its authenticity.

Joy, by contrast, as all one with peace thus understood within the now sublime economy of the whole, is that whereby the spirit rejoices in the self-overflowingness of it all, in, as Dante understands it, the exhilaration of being in its actuality. So, then, taking his cue here from any number of emphases in, say, Richard of St. Victor or Bernard of Clairvaux—though, as is always the way with Dante, confirming their twofold truth and truthfulness from out of the recesses of his own passionate humanity—the "Oh gioia! oh ineffabile allegrezza!" on the threshold of *Paradiso* XXVII, or, at greater length and on the bliss of self as freed now for a more ample species of knowing and loving, the "more than myself" and the "streams of rejoicing" moment of Canto XVI:16–21:

> Io cominciai: 'Voi siete il padre mio;
> voi mi date a parlar tutta baldezza;
> voi mi levate sì, ch'i' son più ch'io.
>
> Per tanti rivi s'empie d'allegrezza
> la mente mia, che di sé fa letizia
> perché può sostener che non si spezza.'
>
> [I began: 'You are my father, you give me all boldness to speak, you uplift me so that I am more than myself; by so many streams my mind is filled with happiness that it rejoices in itself yet without bursting.']

Throughout, then, the pattern is the same: joy in its pure form being, for Dante, the joy contingent on the soul's coming forth from the stillness, on its knowing itself in the kind of transhumanity as but humanity itself in act. Joy, in short, is the mood of properly human being, not only now in its self-possession but, in the selfsame moment, its self-surpassing, its rapt exponentiality. It is but the *ecstatic* mood of being in its authenticity.

Dante and Significant Journeying

But given the components of what in Dante amounts to a Dasein analytic *avant la lettre*, to an account, that is to say, of the human situation in terms of the *being there* of self as the whereabouts of its contemplation, of the dialectics of that situation both in principle and in the positive living out thereof, and of a phenomenology of specifically human being in its self-losing and self-finding, we need now, in the final moments of our meditation, to gather up these things with a view to their integration one with another within the context of—as Dante understands it—man's proper journeying as man, of what it means for man as man to be properly under way. And here we are on firm ground, for what is the *Commedia* but a song of descents and of ascents on the part of one Dante Alighieri as pondering by way of what comes next—of hell, purgatory and paradise as 'states of the soul after death,' 'status animarum post mortem'—the notion of spiritual journeying here and now, this side of the bar: of *recognition* in the sense of witnessing in a now pure form the will to annihilation operative from out of the depths—the infernal phase of the journey; of *reconfiguration* in the sense of spiritual striving, of seeking by way of a fresh species of soul-sorrowing to affirm the *what might be* over the *what actually is* of self on the plane of properly human loving—the purgatorial phase of the journey; and of *transcendence* as rejoicing in the now revised substance of self and in this as but the coming home of self to its proper patrimony.

Taking, then, the first phase of Dante's 'altro viaggio' or alternative journey in the *Commedia* (there being no short cut to the sunlit uplands of the spirit)—the moment, that is, of recognition as always and everywhere preparatory to new life—we may say this: that hell, on the face of it, is indeed for Dante a matter of comeuppance. Any number of passages in the text bear witness both to the anger and to the artistry—to the *divine* anger and artistry—of it all, the *Inferno* having about it in this sense all the appearance of an essay in retribution. So, for example: the "quelli che muoion ne l'ira di Dio" [souls dying in the wrath of God] moment of Canto III, or the "dove si vede di giustizia orribil arte" [terrible art of divine justice] moment of Canto XIV. God's in this sense being a careful thinking through of how best to settle the score. This, then, whatever else it is, is retributive justice on a grand scale, justice as ample and intense in its conception as it is varied in its administration.

But were that type of justice all there is to it, you and I would probably say—and quite rightly—fine, but how in any properly adult and abiding sense of the term does this advance the act either of theological or of psycho-ontological intelligence for those of us still *in via*, as still on the way? And Dante, as more than ever mature in the ways and means both of theological and of psycho-ontological intelligence would indeed be all of a mind here; for hell, in Dante's sense of it, is a question not so much—and indeed in respect of what actually and ultimately matters about it not at all—of pain as inflicted *ab extra* or from beyond, but rather of the soul's entering into the recesses of its own existence there to ponder afresh the agony engendered by the leading but self-consciously inauthentic project, the agony, to be sure, but also the irony of its self-delivery. This, everywhere, is the situation in the *Inferno* and not only accounts for but constitutes the greatness of some of its greatest episodes.

Take, for example, the case of Francesca among the *lussuriosi* in Canto V, where by way of an exquisitely refined sense of what he is about in the *Inferno*, Dante, step by step, draws nigh in respect of the, in truth, devastating substance of his discourse hereabouts, in respect, that is to say, of hell as but a matter of knowing self in the catastrophe of self. First, then, comes the gracious encounter, the oh-so-courteous reception of the wayfaring spirit by Francesca as his chief interlocutor hereabouts—the "O animal grazioso e benigno/ che visitando vai per l'aere perso" [O gracious and kindly spirit visiting as you are our darkling air] moment of lines 88–96. But then, following on in the wake of the *captatio benevolentiae* and serving steadily to deepen and develop the argument, comes the moment of self-exoneration, the "more sinned against than sinning" strategy everywhere serving in circumstances of despair—of the despair generated again by the now consummate issuelessness of it all—to preserve a semblance of integrity and intelligibility—the "Amor che nullo amato amar perdona" moment of lines 100–108 with their insistence to the point of obsessive anaphora: "Love it was that lays hold of the noble spirit, Love which excuses no one from loving, Love it was, alas, that brought us to this pass." But then—ah then!—comes the devastating "Ma dimmi" of line 118, the pilgrim poet's "but tell me, Francesca how was it with you in the moment of sweet sighing?" at which point Francesca has nowhere to look but into the recesses of her own tragic existence, there to ponder yet again—and again and again—the forlorn substance of her being, the region from which there is now no return, no relief, no respite, no resurrection—the "Nessun maggior dolore" or "No greater sorrow" sequence beginning at line 121.

And what applies to Francesca by way of hell as but a matter of standing, at last, every high-level strategy of self-preservation notwithstanding, in the presence of the *eschatos* as for Dante dwelling deep within the historical instant and forever rising up Leviathan-like to tax and to torture the soul in conscience, applies *mutatis mutandis* to all Dante's larger-than-life but in truth everywhere tragic clientele hereabouts in the poem, to Farinata, Brunetto Latini, Ulysses, Guido da Montefeltro, and Ugolino; hell for each alike, every high-level strategy of self-preservation notwithstanding, is a matter of ultimate self-presencing, of knowing self in the now abiding substance of self.

This, then, is what it means to speak of human journeying under the aspect of *recognition*. To speak of human journeying under the aspect of *recognition* is to speak of the soul's standing withal in the fundamental truth of its existence as a creature of significant self-determination. But following on from the moment of *recognition* within the economy of the whole, and indeed in circumstances of sorrowing confirming it in its status as but the beginning of new life, is that of *reconfiguration*, of—by virtue of a commingling of nature and of grace at the still center of personality—the kind of love-harvesting making for its proper freedom, its proper coming forth on the plane of properly human being.

Now, typically Purgatory, for the old theologians, was a matter of satisfaction, of making good the debts incurred by sin as repented and as absolved but as yet less than fully redeemed or paid off. So, for example, Thomas, or rather Thomas's continuator in the *Summa theologiae*, where in the very last question of the *Pars tertia* it is a question, precisely, of the *reatus poenae*, of paying off the debt of punishment. And Dante too, as forever busy about honoring the traditions in which he stands, likewise registers this emphasis, passages from *Purgatorio*, such as those beginning "come Dio vuol che 'l debito si paghi" [how God wills that the debt be paid] (X:108) or the "cotal moneta rende/ a sodisfar" [such a sum to be paid for the sake of satisfaction] (XI:125), turning precisely upon the substance and spirit of, again, making good, of payments brought up to date. But—and this now is what matters—the transactional aspect of the *Purgatorio*, entering as it does into its overall interpretation, comes nowhere near exhausting the substance of this canticle, nowhere near touching upon what it is properly about. For at issue here is something morally, psychologically, and theologically wholly more significant than this, namely an embracing on the part of the one who says 'I' of the love-discipline making in Dante's sense of it for the soaring substance of historical selfhood, at which point the *transactional* gives way to the *transformative* as the first and final cause of his meditation hereabouts.

First, then, on the lower slopes of Mount Purgatory comes the ante-purgatorial moment of the argument, the moment of stasis, of recollection, of calling to mind how in truth, it stands with self in the recesses of self. This, in turn, gives way in Dante's proposal of it to purgatory proper, to the scarcely less than excruciating regime whereby the lesser is brought home to the greater on the plane of loving, the contingent to the connatural, the occasional to the ontological. And the outcome? For Dante, an emancipation of the spirit, a coming home to self in the now consummate autonomy of self, at which point—and in a manner fraught with every kind of socio-political and ecclesiological implication—episcopacy shades off into self-episcopacy and governance into self-governance—the "per ch'io te sovra te corono e mitrio" [wherefore I crown and miter you king and bishop over yourself] of Canto XXVII. Yet again, then—for this, always and everywhere, is the way of it with Dante—the dogmatic is taken up in the dialectical, in the dialectics of existence as, in keeping with the primordial *let it be* of Judeo-Christian sensibility, all that actually matters about it.

This, then, is what it means to speak of human journeying under the aspect of *reconfiguration*. To speak of human journeying under the aspect of *reconfiguration* is to speak of the soul's knowing itself in the manumission of self, in the setting free of self for the *still more than self*, the *still more than self* being but *self itself* at the point of emergence, in the now and forever more smiling substance of its *thereness* in the world. With this, therefore—this notion of the *more than self* as but *self itself* in its actuality—we come finally to the paradisal phase of Dante's meditation in the *Commedia*, where, to be sure, it is a question of grace as *elevating—gratia elevans*. Grace, that is to say, is that whereby the soul is raised up and confirmed in a fresh and properly speaking 'supernatural' order of awareness. Now, grace thus understood—as an incoming and thus extrinsic principle of elevation—indeed abounds in Dante's paradise, any number of passages bearing witness to his commitment and, beyond this, his gratitude hereabouts. So, for example, the "Ringrazia,/ ringrazia il Sol de li angeli, ch'a questo/ sensibil t'ha levato per sua grazia" [Thank oh thank the sun of the angels who to this sensible sight has by grace raised you] of *Paradiso* X:52–54 or the "Ben m'accors' io ch'io era più levato,/ per l'affocato riso de la stella" [Clear to me it was that I had been thus raised by the fiery smile of the star] of *Paradiso* XIV:85 or the "levarsi/ più alto verso l'ultima salute" [yet higher to raise himself towards his ultimate well-being] (XXXIII:26–27) of the final canto of the poem, passages one and all turning precisely upon the notion of *lifting* or *raising up*. Grace *lifting* or *raising up*, thus enters as of the essence into the overall interpretation of the text. But—and this, now, is what matters—grace, for all the incomingness of it, functions in Dante not only nor even primarily as a principle of extraordinary elevation or as that whereby, once again, the *natural* is taken up in the *supernatural* in all the strangeness and otherness thereof, but as an intrinsic principle of actualization, as that whereby man's proper power to be somewhat after the manner of his maker is quickened in its proper operation, its proper equality to the business in hand.

Epistemologically or on the plane of knowing, then, it is a question of grace as that whereby he is freshly enabled in respect of his proper leaping from one pinnacle of cognitive perfection to the next—the "di collo in collo" [from height to height] moment of, say, *Paradiso* IV:132—and as that whereby he is 'strengthened' in favor of an ultimate act of intellection—the "ma per la vista che s'avvalorava" [but through my sight, which as I gazed grew stronger] of *Paradiso* XXXIII:112. Nevertheless, affectively or on the plane of loving, it is a question precisely of love-intensification, of love-intensification to the point of love-intoxication—the "crescer l'ardor che di quella s'accende" [the ardor vision kindles to increase] of, say, *Paradiso* XIV:50. Indeed more than this—though this, alas, is matter for another day—grace, soteriologically, is that whereby, in consequence precisely of Christ's living and dying as man for man, the individual might be said in some sense to be made party to his own resurrection—the "per far l'uom sufficiente a rilevarsi" ['to make man able to uplift himself' as Longfellow has it] of *Paradiso* VII:116, where never in the entire corpus of ancient and modern letters has the reflexive particle—the 'si' of 'rilevarsi'—been so privileged in its power to theological elucidation. This, then, is what it means to speak of man's proper journeying as a matter of *transcendence*. What it means to speak of man's proper journeying as a matter of *transcendence* is to speak of—as Dante understands it—the call from out of the depths to the transhumanity proper to man as but humanity itself in act, as but a humanity operative at the far limits of its proper possibility.

Now were there time and enough to do so, we would embark on what in Dante amounts to a triumph, not merely of notional, but of expressive possibility, for the term 'transhumanity' appears in the context of a linguistic disclaimer, of Dante's reassuring us that where man's proper transhumanity is concerned, there are no words equal to the matter in hand. But do not be taken in here, for as Dante himself understood perfectly well, he is never at a loss for words, the *Paradiso*, the sublime *Paradiso*, at every point bearing witness by way both of its linguistic and of its imaginative strategies to its equality to the business in hand. But that too—the image, in Dante, as a matter of proper predication—is something for another day: the height, the depth, the power, and the precision of his 'all-embracing doctrine of man,' his Dasein analytic *avant la lettre*, is enough for the moment to be going on with. Height, depth, power, precision, clearsightedness, total commitment, and, withal, the image as uniquely adequate to the matter in hand. What more can we ask of an in this sense consummate companion, of, *secondo alcuna proporzione*, a fellow traveler along the road to Emmaeus. *Cosa quindi possiamo dire a proposito se non grazie Alighieri*. What more, then, can we say about all this other than thank you, Alighieri.

Reference

Tillich, P. (1980). *The courage to be*. Collins. (Original published in 1952).

Chapter 5

A Response to Took's "Dante, Selfhood, and Significant Journeying"

Dorothy Chang

Thank you, Professor Took, for bringing us along on such an in-depth journey into Dante's own understanding of self-journeying. I must admit that I am not a Dante scholar or a philosopher. So to that end, I will keep my response brief. I'll begin by first re-visiting some of Prof. Took's main points and end with some questions for further discussion.

In articulating Dante's 'all-encompassing existentialist doctrine of man,' Prof. Took's text itself takes us along on the journey, taking us deep into the mind of Dante, through the ebbs and flow and the ascents and the descents of Dante's *Commedia*. In Dante, the soul is depicted as one that is perpetually in the process of becoming, on a journey through the infernal recesses of Hell, up the mountain of sorrowful striving in Purgatory, and further higher to the spiritual ecstasies of Paradise. Not only are we swept up in the poetic journey in which Dante himself embarks, we are reminded also of the existential dimension inherent in his works. To do this, Prof. Took reads Dante through a Heideggerian lens. Heidegger, though writing for a 'modern' audience, is particularly apropos to this project specifically because he deals with the limits of modern subjectivity, and in exploring these limits, he looks backwards in time for a pre-modern self. Both Heidegger and Dante, therefore, are concerned with the 'not-yet but also the already-there' of being without dealing with being in absolutes. Ultimately, Prof. Took's project sees Dante as a poet-philosopher of being and the self and reminds us of the importance of uncovering the question of the existential in Dante's work.

The paper vividly sketches out what Prof. Took describes as the *Dasein* analytic in Dante. He, like Tillich, sees in Dante an understanding of the self and a process of becoming self that is always in-between, in process. The paper goes on to explore this existentialist doctrine of man in its four main phases: an anthropology, a love-ethic, a phenomenology of being human, and lastly, of 'significant journeying.'

The first phase of the journey, the anthropological moment in which the self becomes a question onto the self, as Prof. Took notes, is woven into Dante's complex theology of creation. The rational part of the soul, according to Dante, is given a divine spark through the breath of God. Through this breath of divine life, the soul/self becomes a one unlike any other and celebrates herself. This celebration of the self as a product of the divine will, in its specificity, is ultimately a pre-modern notion of individualism. But this emergence of the self as an individual only lands us at the very beginning of Dante's doctrine of the human, or as Prof. Took describes it, at the foothills of Dante's existential point of view.

Dante, as a poet-philosopher of being, was more than aware of the complexities and messiness of the human condition. The self, in her quest to selfhood, has to perpetually negotiate between the historical moment and eternity, locality and universality. The failure to resolve this paradox between time and eternity and locality and universality will result in nothing short of a catastrophe. Prof. Took notes that what further complicates this dichotomy between locality and universality and time and eternity is the call of collectivity and the negotiation between self-determination and self as being-determined. Dante describes the call from individuality to collectivity as something structured inherently within the self's own existence where the call to be as a being-with the other is constitutive of that self in her search for selfhood. In *Paradiso* specifically, Dante describes the indwelling of the other-than-self within the self. This mutual presencing of the self and the other-than-self is indicative of the collectivity of being, and it is in a dynamic of mutual presencing that Dante also sees a potential for catastrophe. As it was with time and place, the failure to reconcile the self and the other-than-self or the failure to reconcile the self as determining or being-determined results in disaster. Therefore, to be a human being requires one to perpetually negotiate the conflicting structures of her existence. Beyond this, the human person is always called out of the *what is* of her presence in the world into an uncertain future. Prof. Took writes that the first way of this calling is *proximately*, which is a calling proper to the properties of personality according to individual vocation, while the second way is *ultimately*, which seems to disregard individual personality and is a call that asks each person to reconfigure the self on the planes of knowing and loving.

This then points us to Dante's ethic of love, a love imperative as one who is engaged to the point of the human's proper happiness and her proper end. There are two types of love through which the human might know herself—natural love and elective love. Natural love, Dante suggests, can never err. This kind of love appears to go hand-in-hand with existence itself. Elective love, however, can err in its mode of loving—that is, it can choose to love the wrong thing, to not love enough, or to love too much. This elective love must always be governed by natural love, both of which must be part of proper human living. Love, as noted in *Purgatorio*, is the basis of all action, good or bad. The seven cardinal sins, purged on the mountain in *Purgatorio*, are the sins of improperly ordered love. Wrath, Envy, and Pride are loves for the wrong object. *Acedia*, or Sloth, is love of the right object with the lack of proper vigor. Lust, Gluttony, and Greed are then love of the right object with excessive vigor. For Dante, therefore, the two modes of loving must be brought together in order to make a claim of conscience, and anything short of this is nothing less than demonic, as Prof. Took writes. This reference to the demonic is a striking image of improperly ordered loves. As Dante traverses through Hell, the demons guard and torment their captives. The self is threatened on all sides by the violence of the demonic. I wonder if this demonic is constitutive of the pilgrim's journey. I wonder whether we might be able to think through the function of the demonic within the existentialist doctrine of the self and Dante's ethic of love, and the role of choice in this ethic of love.

But there is more in this. On the threshold of the *Inferno*, we come to the question of fear, the anxiety from the depths of existence where the human person becomes aware of her death. It is in and through this 'dark wood' that the individual person is notified of the self as constituted through her being-towards-death. However, this, too, is only a beginning, for the soul knows itself also in the despair and restlessness and the angst. But Prof. Took points out that through the purgatorial sorrow and striving, the self finds peace and experiences the wholeness of being-in-the-world. This peace is then transcended by joy, which is where the spirit rejoices in its overflowing. For Dante, as Prof. Took describes it, this is the ecstatic mood of being in authenticity.

Lastly, then, what is necessary is now a proper self-journeying. Through Hell, Purgatory, and Paradise, the soul journeys in this life. Recognition, for Dante, entails the acceptance of the angst and anxiety of annihilation. What's more is that this recognition is necessary and preparatory to a new life.

So the first phase of this journey to spiritual ecstasis appears ultimately to be a place of 'retributive justice' at first glance. The *Inferno* is a place in which the soul is condemned to experience Hell; yet, as Prof. Took notes, rather than being a retributive justice from outside the self, Hell is actually a reckoning with the deepest confines of a self that has lived inauthentically, a self that has not faced the question of its own existence. Hell is a matter of knowing a self that is self-determining, facing self-annihilation, and a constant threat of violence against being.

Following on from the moment of recognition, Prof. Took notes, is the moment of reconfiguration, or of purgation. The beginning of this reconfiguration seems, of course, to be transactional, a means of paying back what is owed. However, more significant than this recompense is transformation. Through reconfiguration, the human being is then restored to the self into the freedom of the self. The reconfiguration of the self is to free the self from slavery into self-transcendence. If Hell is a place of seeming 'retributive justice,' then purgatory appears to be a place of restorative justice. Dante's Purgatory is a mirror image of the life lived on earth or an inversion of life where the flames of purgation burn away the false self, the inauthentic self. In my understanding, the self, through the 'sorrows and self-striving,' is brought to a place of peace and joy through a series of repetitious acts. There appears to be an internal tension between transaction and restoration. In one sense, souls in purgatory are sentenced to perform their set of actions repeatedly until their time is up, but in another sense, the soul's repetitive actions are not pointless. They bring the self ever-upward.

This understanding of repetition reminds me of the thought of Søren Kierkegaard. Kierkegaard, too, describes the concept of repetition as something restorative. According to Kierkegaard, repetition is the bequeathing of freedom to the self. The task of repetition grants an individual freedom to the prospect of repetition in the face of overwhelming grief or loss. Repetition is an act of hope. It is the hope of a freedom that all shall be revived, that everything will be restored to the despairing soul. Therefore, one might suggest that, rather than being a prison where the soul must 'do the time' for their crime or a place where souls are forever doomed to a perpetual pointless repetition, repetition is actually part of a liturgical undertaking after which the soul ascends to the earthly paradise. This repetition is an important part of that restoration and purgatorial time figures prominently as well in this road of purgation. Dante keeps time meticulously in purgatory, noting each hour that he ascends the mountain toward earthly paradise. Time for the inhabitants is a precious commodity that cannot be squandered because time not spent working toward their penance is time wasted. To that end, I wonder about how purgatorial time and the concept of repetition factors into this understanding of self as undergoing the process of reconfiguration.

At this point, we finally come to the last leg of our journey: the stage of Paradise. It is in this phase that the human being is elevated up through supernatural grace. This supernatural grace is not something that brings the natural above and beyond to the supernatural. Rather, grace ultimately draws oneself to understand the self as a being which has within her the spark of the divine. The grace brings the self into her proper power. This is also what it means to speak of journeying as a matter of transcendence—that is, it is a call from out of the depths to go beyond itself and is always in the process of becoming a self.

This brings us to the end of Dante's journey and to the end of Prof. Took's reflection on Dante. I think that while we are brought out of this thought experiment on Dante, I am left with one last question. I am struck by this tension between collectivity and individuality that Prof. Took mentioned earlier on this journey of selfhood. Dante's journey throughout the *Commedia* appears to be a solitary and lonely one. The soul seemingly travels alone through the infernal recesses of hell, up the mountain of purgatory, and through the gates of paradise by herself until she reaches her ultimate goal. Everywhere in Dante, we see the emphasis on the self as being alone in this journey of selfhood. While there are guides along the way who are with Dante in this journey, the self is responsible for her own becoming and being. It is a private matter for the soul. The other-than-self seems merely an occasional encounter on the individual soul's ascent toward the divine and does not seem constitutive of the self-becoming self.

Nevertheless, the *telos* of this journey for Dante is ultimately participation in the divine community. At the end of Dante's journey, in the last Canto of *Paradiso*, Dante describes what can only be called the Beatific Vision of God. He writes that he can see the light of the divine Godhead as three intersecting rings of light, each ring a different color. Dante's eyes become filled with this three-ringed light, and not only do his eyes become filled with light, his eyes become light itself. This apprehension of the luminous light of the Godhead is not only a brief vision of the divine Other but a true participation in the divine Other. In this encounter with this divine Other, the self is transformed and becomes vulnerable to the incursion of the Divine Other. It is in this moment that the self becomes transformed as a being participating in the society of the Godhead, and in this transformation, the self must continue to negotiate this tension between the individual and mutual presencing of the Other. Applying a Heideggerian lens to Dante is a helpful way of exploring this existentialist point of view; but for Heidegger, there is no Absolute Being, no divine Being that is the *telos* or end of all human journeying. Does the Beatific in the here and now in Dante then complicate or even call for a thicker account of the *Dasein* analytic in the *Commedia*? Furthermore, is this journey of the soul a solitary one until the human person reaches a mystical union with divine society? Is the call to collectivity a constant call throughout the journey, or does it only see its end in becoming unified with that divine community?

Chapter 6

From Poetics to Phenomenology
Consciousness in Dante's *Divine Comedy*

Christian Y. Dupont

I feel a certain fear in beginning this essay with 'I.' But why should I? Dante introduces himself as author and actor from the very beginning of his *Commedia*, and progressively asserts his individual moral identity, as we shall see, in what will become a plurivocal song. Yet Dante also felt fear—the fear of death, and the fear of dying. He displayed cowardice and was reprimanded for it by Virgil, his guide, who then kindled courage in his heart and led him through the infernal realm and on to the heavenly kingdom. Many commentators down through the centuries have followed Dante on his journey, so I will borrow courage from them and do the same. Like them—and like you, fellow reader, to whom Dante occasionally addresses his thoughts directly—I will bring my own questions and sensibilities.

My questions here concern consciousness, its acts and its structures, as approached by methods developed by Edmund Husserl and elaborated by others who have been stimulated by aspects of his phenomenological philosophy. My method begins with a syntactical reading of the text of the poem as a poem—the 'thing itself' as given to my consciousness through the structures of grammar. Though my approach will appear to draw upon traditions of structural linguistics originating in Saussure, and to some extent does for its terminology, it depends even more on Husserl, particularly his *Logical Investigations* (1900–1901/1970), which Aurora (2015), Stawarska (2015), and others have shown to include a developed linguistic theory tied to and compatible with the ontological tendencies of his mereology and emergent phenomenology.

Emerging from this grammatical analysis, I will attempt to 'bracket' the poetic particularities in order to bring their 'intentional contents,' or meanings, into clearer view. Here it is worth mentioning that Husserl's conception and description of the methods of his phenomenological philosophy continually evolved through the stages of its development, yet they are chiefly characterized by his consistent approach to distinguishing subjective acts of consciousness, whereby phenomena are perceived, and objective acts, through which their intentional character and references are discerned and correlated—in other words, the distinction between subjective psychological processes and objective, or transcendental, logic. In the first elaborated presentation of his phenomenological philosophy, Husserl (1913/1967) introduces the phenomenological *epoché*, or reduction, as a method of 'bracketing,' or setting aside from consideration, assumptions concerning the existence of extra-mental reality so as to focus attention on the analysis of the intentional acts of consciousness whereby mental objects are constituted and ideal objects, or essences, are engaged by the mind (for a suggestion of how Husserl's 'bracketing' might be applied to the reading of Dante, see Franke, 1996, pp. 115–117).

To discern such 'essential' meanings in this English-language context will require some engagement with the problematics of translation. Yet in the spirit of 'pure phenomenology'—as Husserl (1913/1967) describes it—I will avoid turning to the copious historical-critical tradition of Dante commentary, which grounds interpretation of the *Commedia* upon analyses of Dante's allusions to other texts, including his other writings, and likewise those approaches, more common among early commentators, that involve speculation on presumed allegorical, numerological, or mystical meanings, each of which has its own degree of grounding and validity. Instead, I will proceed to examine what the intentional contents and relationships uncovered by the 'bracketed' poetical analyses might reveal about Dante's conceptions of the structures of conscious experience and how he may have wanted us to bring them to our reading of the *Commedia*.

At least that is my hope. And what prompts my fear at the outset. One may dismiss my approach as in keeping neither with structuralist poetics, nor phenomenology, nor Dante criticism: three beasts that threaten to chase me off the mountain. To be sure, my mention of 'structuralist poetics' is a conscious reference to the well-known work by Culler (1975), which has helped me to see that my approach bears some relation to French structuralism and its semiotic assumptions, although some may see in it more evidence of methods of 'close reading' characteristic of New Criticism. From the outset and in the end, I should and willingly do acknowledge that this essay merely represents an attempt—and a first one, at that—to write about how I read the *Commedia*, a process that has been informed by various sources but led mostly by own observations and questions, which is to say, the approach every reader inevitably takes. Thus, finding myself like Dante in a dark woodland, I will venture on, taking the opening lines of his *Inferno* as my guide.

"Nel mezzo del cammin di nostra vita."[1] With these seven words and eleven syllables opening Canto I of the *Inferno*, Dante announces and localizes his presence as he approaches his reader and prepares to recount what he witnessed during his journey through Hell, Purgatory, and Paradise. He also establishes the meter and sets up the alternating rhymes and interlocking tercets that propel his narrative through the 14,233 lines comprising the one hundred cantos disposed into the three canticles that mark the major topographical divisions of the *Commedia*.

The seven words in the first line of *Inferno* divide neatly into three syntactic units, each a prepositional phrase that seems designed to position Dante as both the protagonist and narrator of the poem in time, space, and what Husserl called 'lived experience'—*Erlebnis*. Husserl borrowed the term from Wilhelm Dilthey, Theodor Lipps, and others, but gave it his own more precise meanings in his

Logical Investigations (1900–1901/1970) and *Ideas* (1913/1967; see also Moran & Cohen's discussion of the term, 2012). Dante's choice of noun at the core of each, however, cannot be so neatly pinned down. Does the "mezzo" refer to a precise or merely approximate middle of a temporal sequence, or perhaps the midpoint of a geometrical line segment—a line made by walking?[2] "Cammin"— 'cammino' in modern Italian—can denote the act of walking as well as a path— or, figuratively speaking, a journey, or even one's moral conduct. Which sense or senses did Dante intend? Must we, can we even know?

The next noun, "vita" is rendered as 'life' by translators with more consistency than most other words in the poem. Most, but by no means all, choose to translate the accompanying possessive adjective "nostra," meaning 'our,' and thus offer 'our life' as the syntactical equivalent in contemporary English of "nostra vita." I prefer 'life of ours' as a means of calling attention to the common, shared, and therefore 'essential'—in a phenomenological sense—elements of 'lived experience' and the 'structures,' categorial and otherwise, that 'constitute' it. While I arrived at 'life of ours' independently, I subsequently found that it was used by Allan Gilbert in his translation of *Inferno* (Alighieri, 1314/1969). In a review, Needler (1973) judges Gilbert's effort harshly overall, calling it "a good example of the dangers of translating an interpretation, rather than the text" (p. 381). He does not, however, mention Gilbert's rendering of "nostra vita" by 'life of ours' in his lengthy catalog of infelicitous and erroneous translations. So although I fear some pushback against a relatively untried translation, I will invoke the Husserlian concepts of 'intersubjectivity' and the 'lifeworld'—*Lebenswelt*—against the solipsism that has haunted Western philosophy since Descartes and Berkeley, who, we may well note, came along long after Dante. Dante had no *a priori* reason not to see the world as inherently social, and indeed, the populated hierarchies of human and angelic beings witnessed by Dante in all three canticles of his poem would seem to presuppose a worldview—or rather, view of the cosmos—that is inherently intersubjective rather than solipsistic. If rendering "nostra vita" as 'life of ours' can bring us that much closer to what we may reasonably suppose to have constituted Dante's own lived experience, may I then be emboldened rather than fearful in offering it.

"Nostra vita" is the syntagm toward which the whole line tends, poetically and hermeneutically. In turn, it pushes back upon the preceding elements, shifting them toward more figurative than literal meanings. Thus, we might translate the opening line of *Inferno* 'Midway along the journey through this life of ours,' though doing so forfeits the prepositional triad observed earlier, a paradigmatic relationship in the original text that more readily invites phenomenological investigation than a contemporary idiomatic translation would invite.

Translation may likewise elicit or obscure phenomenological consideration of the second line of *Inferno*, which begins with a formulation that suggests numerous possibilities, once again both literal and figurative. "Mi ritrovai per una selva oscura," Dante writes, and we, shrouded in the darkness of our own veiled comprehension, are left to wonder just what he experienced and where and how. "Mi ritrovai" suggests most literally, and most fundamentally from a grammatical point of view, a 'finding of oneself' in a particular place—a 'here' as opposed to a 'there' or 'elsewhere.' More figuratively, and suggestively, it can imply a 'coming to awareness' of one's situation. The reflexive syntax does not lean toward one reading more than the other.

"Mi ritrovai," however, does prompt the question of whether the experience it indicates is indexed or structured with reference to a first-person subject, which is to say an 'I' or a 'self,' and from there whether that subject is turning a reflective mode of awareness back upon a more immediate awareness of having 'found himself.' Such questions are central to Western philosophy, particularly among philosophers in the phenomenological tradition, who have attempted to distinguish various modes of consciousness with respect to phenomenal experience on the one hand, and an ego, either personal and subjective, or transcendental, on the other.

For Husserl, awareness cannot be separated from the stream of phenomenal experience and examined as an object apart from it. As 'lived experience,' consciousness carries within itself an implicit appearing to itself. Its mode of existence, the 'as' of its 'appearing,' is 'for-itself'—"als für-sich-selbst-erscheinens" (Husserl, 1959, p. 189; for a discussion, see Moran, 2005, p. 205; for a helpful introduction to these concepts, see Gallagher & Zahavi, 2019). Awareness of awareness as an indirect mode of experience cannot be an object of perception as such, but only 'apperceived.' Kant (1781, 1787/1963, p. 136/A 107) recognized this problem as well, and so posited a "transcendental unity of apperception" as a condition for the possibility of a conscious subject perduring in time, which is to say an 'I.'

Although I cannot perceive my consciousness, I can reflect upon it. I can shift my attention from the manifold of sensory experience to consideration of the attentional state of awareness itself in its pure givenness. Might "mi ritrovai" signal that Dante as the protagonist or narrator of his poem, or perhaps both, has undergone such an attentional shift at the beginning of the second line of *Inferno* when he moves, grammatically and narratively, from an impersonal standpoint to an intersubjective one, and thence to a personal and subjective description of his situation and state of awareness: 'in the middle of the walk/walking (impersonal) through this life of ours (intersubjective), I found myself (personal and subjective)'?

The continuation of the line offers further possibilities for probing Dante's characterization of the attentional state he has just introduced. "Mi ritrovai per una selva oscura" briefly yet richly alludes to the perception that attended his coming to awareness—perhaps even the awareness of his awareness. "Selva oscura" is often translated as a 'dark' or 'gloomy' 'wood' or 'woods,' or as a 'shadowed' or 'darkened' 'forest.' Yet a 'selva' is neither a 'bosco' [small wooded area] nor a 'foresta' [forest]. In Dante's fourteenth-century Tuscan dialect, 'selva' would evoke the archaic Latin 'silva,' which denotes a woodland of unspecified proportion or growth, the lack of specificity owing perhaps to its etymological relation to the classical Greek ὕλη, which also gives rise to the figurative meanings of matter and substance based on the utility of wood for human purposes (for a discussion of the etymology of 'selva' in relation to Dante, see Tower, 2017, p. 19). Dante may well have had in mind the figurative meaning of raw, primal matter, if not matter conditioned for human use; but he more likely intended a literary allusion—to introduce just one in this investigation—to Virgil's *Aeneid* (VI.179): "itur in antiquam silvam, stabula alta ferarum" [he went into the ancient wood, the high stables of wild beasts] (see Bassanese, 2000, p. 287).[3] Still, we might allow both senses, if only as hypotheses. Likewise, we might let "oscura" be taken to refer not only to literal darkness but to more figurative obscurity, reflecting Dante's uncertainty about the precise qualities of his experience. In this regard, it may be worth noting that in terms of poetic structure, "selva oscura" appears at the end of the second line, shadowed beneath the intersubjective lifeworld—"nostra vita"—introduced at the end of the previous line.

The preposition "per" also suggests the possibility of a more figural interpretation of "selva oscura." The more natural diction choice might have been 'in' if Dante had wanted to indicate more clearly that he found himself in the midst of a dark woodland, echoing the 'nel' of "nel mezzo del cammin." In modern Italian, the preposition 'per' is generally used to indicate 'for' in an indirect object construction, as in 'I did this for you.' Such usage is rare, however, in the *Commedia*, apart from some notable passages, such as when Lucy implores Beatrice (*Inferno* II:105) to succor the one who loved her so, namely Dante, "ch' uscì per te de la volgare schiera" [who for your sake left the vulgar crowd]. 'Per' can also mean 'through' in a direct and literal sense, and is commonly used that way in the *Commedia*, most famously in the inscription over the gate to Hell: "Per me si va nella città dolente" [Through me one goes into the wailing city] (*Inferno* III:1). In addition, it can mean 'to' in the causal sense of 'in order to' when placed immediately before an infinitive, for example in a line that we will examine later: "ma per trattar del ben ch'i' vi trovai" [but in order to deal with the good I found there] (*Inferno* I:8). 'Per' can also take on the causal sense of 'for' or 'because' when it appears in a prepositional phrase that functions as an adverb. For instance, when Virgil informs Dante that he and others like him are in Limbo on account of their having lived before Christ and not having been baptized, he remarks that "per tai difetti, non per altro rio, semo perduti" [for such defects, and for no other fault, we are lost] (*Inferno* IV:40–41; here I follow the Hollander translation, Alighieri, 1314/2002, p. 63, rather than offering my own).

While some have suggested that interpreting "per una selva oscura" as an adverb phrase offers fruitful possibilities for both psychological and phenomenological readings of the *Commedia*,[4] doing so would strain the poetics of the passage beyond Dante's otherwise idiomatic usages. There is no compelling reason from a grammatical point of view to presume that "per una selva oscura" should be regarded as an adverb phrase modifying "mi ritrovai," resulting in a translation such as: 'I found myself by having experienced the dark woodland.' It is more natural and more faithful to Dante's use of language to interpret the line as indicating more plainly: 'I found myself within a dark woodland,' or even 'while walking within' a woodland, if one wants to capture something of the notion of movement 'through,' which 'per' conveys in other contexts in the poem, and thereby echo the sense of continual progression implied by "cammin" [walk/walking] in the preceding line and the rhythm of the poetic meter.

These plain readings of "per" are nevertheless pregnant with phenomenological possibilities insofar as they contribute to framing the perceptual data associated with the lived experience of the narrator of the poem, even with regard to the uncertainty surrounding their precise qualities, as noted above. Briefly, Dante's use of "per" rather than 'in' may reflect the ambiguity of his knowledge about where he is within the woodland, and even where the woodland is. 'Per' resists as definitive a localization as the preposition 'in.'

Yet does the statement thus understood indicate that Dante's "finding himself" denotes an act of reflective self-consciousness and not what Sartre, glossing Husserl, called 'pre-reflective self-consciousness' (see Sartre, 1936/1957; and Husserl, 1984, pp. 399, 424)? The latter can provide an implicit sense of oneself at the experiential level. The person living in what Husserl calls 'the natural attitude' employs the first-person pronoun, but primarily as a lexical index, that is, as the grammatical subject of a sentence whose meaning content does not depend on the subject having explicit awareness of his status as a subject, much less one actively engaged in reflection on the qualities of his or her attentional state. When Dante writes, "mi ritrovai per una selva oscura," does he simply mean to report the facts of an ordinary experience: 'I found myself within a dark woodland'? Or does he want the reader to understand that in and through that experience his attentional focus has shifted, and that he has begun to engage in a reflexive act of self-consciousness? For as much as we may want to bring our modern sensibilities and phenomenological attitude to the medieval poem, do we have a hermeneutical license to do so?

Perhaps not, or perhaps not yet. Let us continue reading and see in which direction further evidence leads.

"Ché la diritta via era smarrita." This third line of the first canto of *Inferno* does begin with an adverb of cause, "ché," which may be translated as 'because' or 'for' or an equivalent formulation signaling that what follows caused the condition described in the phrase preceding it, which, in Dante's case, means the condition of finding himself in a dark woodland. How did he end up there? "Ché ... la diritta via era smarrita": 'for' ... 'the right' or 'straight' or 'main' 'way' or 'road' 'had been lost.' Somehow while walking, Dante the protagonist had wandered off the path and gotten lost in the woods. These basic facts are related by Dante the narrator in seemingly plain fashion without any particular assertion of agency, at least for the moment. Yet the internal poetics of the line and their relationship to other elements do suggest that a fuller account with moral implications will follow.

The pairing of "diritta" with "smarrita" creates an internal rhyme that reinforces their contrasting meanings. 'Diritta,' from the Latin adjective 'directus,' denotes the qualities of straightness and directness, without curvature or divergence. The forms 'diritta,' 'dritta,' 'directa,' and other variations appear in various early manuscripts and printed editions, reflecting regional variations in linguistic usage, pronunciation, and spelling. Petrocchi (1966–1967) favors "diritta" on the basis of manuscript witnesses and for the fact that it preserves the basic hendecasyllabic meter. As such, however, it is a unique occurrence in the poem, whereas "dritta" occurs 15 times in his edition. Without contesting Petrocchi's choice, I might note that 'dritta' would create a stronger internal rhyme with "smarrita" than "diritta" does, and the consequent loss of a syllable would only emphasize the notion of loss described by the line.

By contrast, "smarrita" is an adjective signaling that its object has been lost, misplaced, mislaid, or, more figuratively, confused and no longer distinguishable. The particle 's' at the beginning of the word functions as a marker of negation in Italian. The opposition of "diritta" and "smarrita" therefore amplifies the sense that a reversal of fortune has taken place, that the right or main road indeed has been lost. "Smarrita" is furthermore positioned to rhyme against "vita" at the end of the opening line of the canto, thus prompting the reader to consider whether what Dante lost was not only the road he was following but participation in the intersubjective lifeworld—a sense reinforced by his evident aloneness in the dark woodland. The "via" that has been lost in the third line seems to echo the "vita" in the first. To the extent that such moral considerations are brought into view by virtue of the poetic structure, we are prompted to consider whether the poem is asserting that the quality of awareness experienced by Dante the protagonist was indeed self-conscious and reflective, or whether it reflects a shift in attentional state that has occurred on the part of Dante as narrator.

The next line, which begins the second tercet, explicitly shifts the frame of reference from the situation of the protagonist described in the poem to the narrator's situation as poet, thus adding another layer of awareness and another potential locus of reflection for us, as readers, to consider. "Ahi quanto a dir qual era è cosa dura." The line begins with an exclamation that disrupts the narration and creates both a temporal and perspectival disjunction. Dante's "ahi" is a cry of anguish that stems from the recognition that the mind suffers when the body suffers, and yet distinguishes the one from the other. The body feels pain, while the mind experiences distress over the pain, for the mind interprets the pain as an indication of a threat to the continuance of its embodied life. In this regard, the cry of anguish marks a primal moment of reflective self-consciousness, of being brought suddenly into the awareness of oneself as a self that possesses an individual existence that is threatened, even with non-existence, as we shall come to see in the case of Dante as the poem continues to unfold.

"Quanto a dir qual era è cosa dura" [as regards to telling what it was is a hard thing], Dante tells us, his readers. The telling, and the telling about the telling, explicitly stage acts of reflective self-consciousness on Dante's part as both protagonist and narrator, as well as at a third level as a meta-narrator reflecting on the problematics of narration. All three levels turn around the central element and syllable in this line—the "qual," the 'what'—which pushes the past tense of narrated action into the present quandary faced by the narrator. This begs the question: *What* was *it* that should make the *how* of the telling so hard?

The next line answers the implied query: "esta selva selvaggia e aspra e forte." The "selva selvaggia" is the culprit—"esta" [this one], the one in which Dante the protagonist, and perhaps also figuratively as narrator, found himself, namely the "selva oscura" [dark woodland], now referred to as the "selva selvaggia," a polyptotonic construction that emphasizes the 'wild' character of the woodland into which Dante wandered after straying from the main road. The wild, even savage nature of the woodland is reinforced by the adjectives "aspra" and "forte" that follow. Both can be translated in various ways. 'Aspra' can refer to the sourness of a lemon, the harshness of a screeching noise, the scathing quality of criticism, or the ruggedness of uneven terrain—the last being the most fitting in this instance given that woodlands, in general, have topographical features and because Dante will later refer to this particular woodland as a "valle" [valley] that leads to the foot of a hill (*Inferno* I:13–14). 'Forte' can refer to the strength of body or character, or forcefulness or fearsomeness in general. The series of three adjectives are coupled by the double use of "e" [and] as not merely a coordinating conjunction, but a correlative and compounding conjunction: "selva selvaggia e aspra e forte." Dante appears to be telling us that the cumulative effect of the wild, rugged, and fierce qualities of the woodland was so intimidating and overwhelming that it made it difficult for him to describe them with any precision.

The next line supports this interpretation and the notion of a third-level meta-narrative framework: "che nel pensier rinova la paura!" The "che" here is not the casual adverb 'ché' but another correlative conjunction that continues the series of adjectives describing the "selva": "che" [that one, or the one which] "nel pensier" [in the thought, or in the thinking of] "rinova" [renews or restores] "la paura" [the fear or dread]. The explicit mention of thought confirms that Dante, at least as narrator or meta-narrator if not also as protagonist, has entered into a state of reflective self-consciousness and wants to engage the reader in a similar act. As a reader, I—shifting to the first person to individuate and claim my responsibility as a phenomenological investigator, just as Dante at each level of narration asserts his authorial identity—will offer some further observations concerning these layered acts of reflection on the states of awareness which Dante experiences and communicates, especially in relation to the affective element he has now introduced, namely the fear or dread. But first, let me offer a summary translation of this second tercet so that we may conveniently refer back to it. As in previous instances, my translation is meant to be more literal than literary in order to facilitate poetic and phenomenological analyses, and therefore does not follow any one of the many published verse or prose translations, each of which has its respective merits along with inevitable shortcomings, as do my own: 'Ah, as regards the telling of what it was is a hard thing,/ That woodland so wild and rugged and fierce,/ The thought of which renews the dreadful fear.'

For "paura," I offer neither 'fear' nor 'dread,' but a combination of both, 'dreadful fear,' since the term in Italian comprehends both senses. In English, we may distinguish 'fear' as a response to a specific and immediate threat from 'dread,' a more generalized anxiety brought about by the anticipation of a negative experience. Monticelli (2019, pp. 111–116) argues on this same basis that the Heideggerian concept of *Angst* [anxiety or existential dread] is a more appropriate reference than 'phòbos' or 'Furcht' [fear]. Below I discuss Heidegger's concept of mood in relation to what Dante indicates by "paura," but for the moment, I wish to consider Dante's lexical options and decision to use "paura" in this context. 'Paura' occurs thirty times in the *Commedia*, and the adjectival form 'paurose' one additional time.[5] In most cases, it is used to indicate a general state of anxiety and distress as opposed to a reaction to a specific threat, and so includes an element of dread. Yet, there are some exceptions, notably another passage from this first canto of *Inferno*. In *Inferno* I:44–45, Dante's opportunity and ability to hope for the good is denied by the sudden appearance of a lion who interrupts his gaze and causes him to feel afraid in response to the possibility of immediate danger: "ma non sì che paura non mi desse/ la vista che m'apparve d'un leone." These clauses represent the second part of a complex double-negative construction framed by a pair of conjunctive adverbial phrases: "sì che ... ma non sì che." This formulation, which may be traced to the fourteenth century if not more precisely to this very passage of the *Commedia*, finds an equivalent in modern Italian in the adverbs 'sicché' or 'cosicché' or 'così che,' meaning 'such that' or 'so much that.' Inverting the clauses, the passage may be roughly translated: 'not so much that the sight of a lion would not give me fear' (see Franke, 1996, pp. 135–143 for a phenomenology of fear and anxiety in *Inferno* I, including remarks on this passage; see also Took, 2000, especially pp. 105–107).

Another common word in Italian that can denote both anticipatory anxiety and fear is 'timore' and its verbal form 'temere.' 'Timore' does not appear in the *Commedia*, but various conjugations of 'temere' occur more than a dozen times. Another noun, 'tema,' derived from 'temere,' occurs almost as frequently.[6] We might add that Dante does not employ 'terrore' [terror]—though he may have used 'orror' [horror] depending on the manuscript tradition one follows for *Inferno* III:31. For that line, Petrocchi (1966–1967) reads "E io ch'avea d'error la testa cinta," while other textual critics prefer 'orror' to 'error.' For a discussion and references, see Hollander's (2011) philological note on the verse.

Dante also used nominal and verbal forms of 'spavento' [fright] seven times, but the purpose of this digression is not to engage in deep semantic or etymological analysis, which would take us far beyond the scope of the present essay and my meager capabilities. Rather this accounting is meant to affirm that Dante is attuned to the nuances of language and experience, and perhaps even the notion that language structures experience both within and beyond its limits. Through prepositional triangulation and potent adjectives, Dante is able to tell us something about the experience of finding himself in the woodland, and at the same time indicate that the experience exceeds his linguistic competency, and possibly the capacity of language itself to describe.

This digression is also meant to call attention to Dante's awareness of the intrinsic connection between thought and emotion in reflective acts of consciousness. When Dante the narrator states that the thought of the wild, harsh, fierce, and dark woodland renewed or restored the dreadful fear that he, as protagonist, experienced, he seems to be asserting he could not think of the woodland without experiencing, at least to some degree, the associated emotional state. In other words, he claims that the bodily, lived experience of dreadful fear accompanies his attempt to cognize his experience through the application of reason and judgment; I would even add intrinsically and necessarily.

The foregoing analysis prompts me to invoke Heidegger's analytic of *Dasein*— the human condition of 'there-being' or 'being-there'—in *Being and Time* (1927/1962) in particular his observations concerning his specific use of what he calls 'Befindlichkeit' [state-of-mind] or a 'Stimmung' [mood] or 'Gestimmtsein' [being-attuned] (pp. 172–182, paragraphs 134–144). Of these, the first strikes me as especially suited to appreciating what Dante may have wished to convey by the locution "mi ritrovai" in relation to the feeling of "paura" that accompanied the original experience of finding himself—noting that 'Befindlichkeit' means quite literally 'the state in which one may be found'—in the dark woodland, as well as his attempt to tell about it in his poem. For Heidegger, being found in a particular state-of-mind or mood is a fundamental characteristic of human existence. The mood may be one of dreadful fear, or of hope, or some other attitude toward Being, but there is no 'being-there' without 'being-in-a-mood,' whether one is explicitly and thematically aware of the mood or not. In *Sketch for a Theory of the Emotions*, Sartre (1939/1962) elaborated on these notions as he engaged in his experiment in phenomenological psychology, and others have expanded on them more recently (see Solomon, 1976/1993, and Radcliffe (2009) for a critique of Solomon; see also Monticelli, 2019).

My purpose here is not to undertake such an experiment, nor to delve more deeply into phenomenological analyses of the particular emotional states that Dante describes, fruitful as doing so might be. I leave them for another time and perhaps another investigator, and instead present my preliminary observations as support for my contention that Dante as narrator, and more so as a meta-narrator, wanted his readers to engage in their own acts of reflective self-consciousness, and notice, as he did, the intrinsic relationship between thinking and embodied feeling, and between lived experience and language—perhaps especially poetic language.

Nevertheless, I must add that the components of anticipatory dread and a generalized anxiety contained in the "paura" that Dante experienced is further borne out by the next line, which continues the sequence of thought into the third tercet: "Tant' è amara che poco è più morte." "Tant' è amara" [So bitter is it (i.e., the fear)] "che" [that] "morte" [death] "poco è più" [is hardly more (so)]. The comparison is made in the present tense, the tense in which Dante the narrator writes, as when he remarks in the first line of the preceding tercet that 'as regards to telling what it was' (i.e., 'that woodland so wild and rugged and fierce') 'is a hard thing.' As self-conscious, reflective acts, telling and comparing are most naturally presented in the present tense not because they belong to the present but because they already transcend the experience of time as a continuous stream. They bracket the flow of lived experience and consider meanings as structured from phenomenal appearances rather than by their mere appearing, as they do in pre-reflective acts of consciousness. The comparison in this case to a presupposed experience of dying and death as the end and negation of experience fittingly recapitulates the elements of dread and fear comprised by the experience of "paura" they reference. The ultimately overpowering and limiting force of "morte" [death] is further reinforced by its placement at the end of the line, where it is rhymed against the description of the woodland as "forte" [fierce].

Yet Dante presses on, and so shall we. Reaching now a line we cited earlier, we hear our poet-narrator tell us: "ma per trattar del ben ch'i' vi trovai,/ dirò de l'altre cose ch'i' v'ho scorte" [but in order to deal with the good I found there,/ I will tell about the other things that I caught sight of there]. To me, the most evocative and richest word to examine poetically and phenomenologically in these lines is "scorte." 'Scorte' is the feminine plural form of the past participle of the verb 'scorgere,' referring to and standing in grammatical agreement with those "l'altre cose" [other things, feminine plural]. 'Scorgere' may be translated as 'to glimpse' or 'to catch sight of.' Synonyms include 'percepire' [to perceive] and 'intravedere' [to discern, especially visually]. A related reflexive verb, 'accorgersi,' is used more figuratively to signal 'becoming aware of' or 'realizing.' Recognizing the widespread regard that Dante has enjoyed as a poet, we should not assume that he chose 'scorgere' in this instance over the more common and direct 'vedere' [to see], which he employs elsewhere in the *Commedia*, simply in order to keep to his rigid rhyme scheme. Rather it would be more in keeping with his style and genius to construct a series of end rhymes in order to create semantic resonances that echo their verbal consonance and assonance. Consider the effects elicited by rhyming "vita" [life] with "smarrita" [lost], "oscura" [dark] with "dura" [hard] and "paura" [dreadful fear], and "forte" [fierce] with "morte" [death], as noted previously, and now "scorte" [caught sight of]. If we take Dante's use of 'scorte' as structurally intentional, the signification of 'glimpsing' as opposed to 'seeing' appears that much more fitting and appropriate. As a limit to all experience, death does not yield itself to direct perception; it can only be glimpsed indirectly, if at all. Similarly and more literally, the darkness of the dark woodland limits Dante's ability to discern objects clearly—a motif that recurs frequently in the *Commedia*, especially in *Inferno*, a "loco" [place] that Dante describes a few cantos later as being "d'ogne luce muto" [mute of all light] (*Inferno* V:28, following the Hollander translation, Alighieri, 1314/2002, p. 85).

So it is that in order to deal with the good that he found there in the dark woodland, and there again in Hell and along the rest of his journey, Dante the narrator must speak about those 'other things' that he only caught sight of on account of the darkness and any other limits that constrained his faculties of perception. Having introduced this problematic, he does not attempt immediately to name or describe those 'other things,' but instead turns back to the problem of telling how he lost the straight road and found himself in a dark woodland. He begins again, this time by employing the first-person pronoun in a manner that directly implicates self-conscious reflection: "Io" [I] "non so ben" [do not know well] "ridir" [to recount] "com'"(i.e., 'come') [how] "i' v'intrai" (i.e., 'io vi entrai') [I entered there]. The recounting, literally the re-telling, thus appears to signal a clearly conscious intention that Dante as narrator undertakes to attempt a fresh explanation of his changed circumstance—in other words, to come at it from another perspective and describe the new profile as it presents itself, if I were to translate my reading into a phenomenological register.

Yet it would be better to refrain from such hermeneutical leaps and allow Dante the chance to tell us what he will through the next two lines that round out this fourth tercet and what poetically may be called the first verse paragraph in the otherwise continuous stichic structure that constitutes the canto. For after this juncture, the narrative frame will shift to a new scene as Dante reaches the end of the dark valley and approaches the foot of the hill (*Inferno* I:13–14), where he will encounter the three beasts who threaten to turn him back.

"Tant' era pien di sonno a quel punto," Dante confesses, "che la verace via abbandonai": "Tant" [so] "pien di sonno" [full of sleep] "era"[7] [was I] "a quel punto" [at that point] "che" [at which] "abbandonai" [I abandoned] "la verace via" [the true way]. These lines refer back to the second and third lines of the first tercet: "mi ritrovai per una selva oscura,/ ché la diritta via era smarrita" [I found myself in a dark woodland,/ for the main road had been lost]. They are explicitly linked by the word "via" [way or road]. The adjectives Dante uses to describe the "via" in the respective passages play off of one another as if they were synonyms, which they nearly are: "diritta" [right or straight or main] and "verace" [true or real or genuine]. Both also can have literal and figurative meanings: a physical roadway can be straight or curved, while a moral pathway can be upright or misguided. And while the literal sense does not need to be abandoned in either context, the appearance of "abbandonai" [I abandoned] makes the moral dimension implicit in the first instance more explicit in the second. Whereas in the first case, Dante offers no explanation as to how the way had been lost, but merely reports it as an impersonal fact using a passive third-person verbal construction "era smarrita" [had been lost]; in the present context, Dante owns up to the responsibility of having abandoned it—for the most part. He in fact precedes his confession with a comment that might be intended to relieve him of some of the responsibility that he will claim: he says he was full of sleep at the point at which he abandoned the way. In the retelling, he tells more. But he also complicates the situation. Did Dante make a conscious decision to abandon the true way, or did he do so lazily and passively, on account of tiredness? Both imply a degree of guilt, but the former more so than the latter. The question may not be resolved and need not be in order for us to proceed with a phenomenological analysis of the poetical structures.

From a phenomenological perspective intent on uncovering the structures of the intentional acts at work in these verses, we recognize again that Dante has created a narrative that works simultaneously on three distinct levels. As the poet-narrator (second level), he relates what he as the protagonist (first level) could remember about his lived experience of falling into a sleep-filled torpor and consequently abandoning the straight and true way, while also pointing to the generalized meta-narrative problematic (third level) of recounting an experience from a memory that may have been tainted by loss even by the same torpor. We have observed how on the first level, what may be called the diegetic narrative is presented in the past tense, while the literary and meta-literary narratives representing the second and third levels of discourse are offered in the present tense (cf. Tower, 2017, pp. 30–31; and Monticelli, 2019). Binding these three levels together is the first-person singular pronoun at the beginning of the tercet: the "io" [I] that recognizes itself as the subject who has undergone the experiences described in the poem, and who is responsible for telling about them, and telling about the telling.

By this stage of the poem, Dante's 'I' has emerged as a consciousness that assuredly has moved beyond pre-reflective engagement with the world to reflective consideration directed at the structures of its experiencing. It recognizes that even though it is most immediately aware of the confused and solitary situation in which it finds itself at the outset, it nevertheless participates in an intersubjective lifeworld. Yet it also realizes that the darkness that impairs its visual perception and generally hinders its intentional acts consequently leaves those acts unfulfilled, disconnecting the 'I' from the lifeworld. It furthermore becomes aware that its state-of-mind, its mood, is conditioned by a dreadful fear that is provoked by both immediate threats and a generalized anxiety.

What we have only glimpsed, to play on Dante's formulation, without yet having had occasion to examine more fully, are the roles that memory plays in synthesizing perceptions, supporting their organization into a set of intentional relations and mental contents, and structuring modes of narration. These would be fruitful areas to explore phenomenologically, especially since Husserl, in his *Logical Investigations* (1900–1901/1970) and other writings, developed sophisticated analyses and theories regarding the acts of retention and protention that structure perception, memory, and imagination. They would also be fertile fields to survey poetically, as the *Commedia* contains numerous references to all three faculties, memory in particular.

Would time and space allow, I would turn from this study of the opening of the first canto of *Inferno* to the opening of the second, which in many respects represents a second, or new, or even true beginning to the poetic narrative. From there, I would proceed to the openings of *Purgatorio* and *Paradiso*. Like the second canto of *Inferno*, the initial verses of *Purgatorio* include an invocation to the Muses; in the case of *Paradiso*, to Apollo. Through his invocations, Dante appeals to their powers to aid his memory and strengthen his intelligence so that he might write what he saw, bearing proper and faithful witness to the extraordinary experiences he undergoes on his journey through the three eternal realms. In each case, as with the opening to the first canto of *Inferno*, these verse paragraphs also engage with the problematics of narrative and meta-narrative. And from investigations of their engagements with narrative, poetics, and the interplay of mental faculties, further and deeper insights into Dante's notions of consciousness would likely result.

What I hope this essay has accomplished is to have demonstrated what a poetical-phenomenological approach to reading the *Commedia*—and perhaps other poems—can yield in terms of such insights, and how it can do so apart from appeals to historical-critical analyses of the textual sources and intertextual allusions that make the *Commedia* such a rich and masterful work of poetry, as well as to allegorical and other approaches—not to invalidate or diminish their value but to complement them, even from the relatively independent standpoint attained by bracketing their presuppositions.

The most basic insight I believe that this methodology has achieved in this instance is to affirm that Dante, removed as he is from us by time and culture, was nevertheless aware of modes and structures of consciousness familiar to more recent thinkers like Husserl, and to ourselves as contemporary readers of his poetry, leaving aside or perhaps implicitly posing questions concerning whether they are not only transcendental but universal. If we can read and begin to understand the *Commedia*, I would assert, on the basis of my present investigation, that it is because the poem contains and evokes in us acts of reflective self-consciousness that may be directed at the intentionalities that constitute our own lived experience "nel mezzo del cammin" [in the middle of the walk] and our participation in the intersubjective lifeworld "di nostra vita" [of this life of ours]. And with this realization, the fear, the 'paura' that I felt at the outset is, to borrow Dante's phrasing in *Inferno* I:19, "un poco queta" [a little quieted].

Notes

1 Here and throughout, I follow the standardized text of the *Commedia* edited by Petrocchi (1966–1967), though I recognize that a vast and complex manuscript history stands behind it and other scholarly editions and their attempts to represent autograph texts that have not survived.
2 Writing this line evoked for me Richard Long's famous sculpture titled "A line made by walking" (1967), adopted by Sara Baume for the title of her 2017 novel, which I happened to be reading when I began to write this essay. It also brought to mind the converging lines that define the 'straight' path that the figure of Dante crosses in Salvador Dalí's illustration for the first canto of *Inferno*, as rendered by the woodblock artists who produced the portfolio of prints for Éditions d'art Les Heures Claires (Dalí, 1960).
3 In a similar vein, Hollander, in notes in his translation of *Inferno*, has noted that "many commentators have pointed out that the opening verse" of *Inferno* "echoes a biblical text, Isaiah's account of the words of Hezekiah, afflicted by the 'sickness unto death' (Isaiah 38:10): *in dimidio dierum meorum vadam ad portas inferi* ("in the midst of my days, I shall go to the gates of the nether region")" (Alighieri, 1314/2002, p. 12). But

again, in keeping with the methodology I sketched out in the beginning of this essay, I will refrain from combining a historical-critical approach with the poetical-phenomenological reading I am attempting in order to help the reader judge the merits of the latter.
4 See the opening of Aaron Daniels's introduction to this volume, where he credits Luke (2001, p. 10) with calling his attention to the possibilities opened by a causal interpretation of "per."
5 Readers interested in such analyses are referred to the Princeton Dante Project (Hollander, 2011) at http://etcweb.princeton.edu/dante/index.html, which includes a string search tool that readily allows one to retrieve passages containing given words or word roots and the number of occurrences in each canto and the poem overall.
6 'Tema,' [fear] is no longer used in modern Italian. It should not be confused with the homonym 'tema,' borrowed from Greek, meaning 'theme' or 'topic,' which does survive in modern Italian and also appears several times in the *Commedia*.
7 It is worth observing that although in modern Italian "era" is the third person singular conjugation of the imperfect tense of the verb "essere" [to be] and "ero" the first person singular, Dante uses "era" for the first as well as third person (e.g., *Inferno* XXII.4–6: "Io era già disposto" [I was already ready]). Given that the subsequent verb in the sentence, "abbandonai," is conjugated in the first person, it is more reasonable to assume that Dante intended "era" in this case to refer to a first person subject than to an implied third person or impersonal subject, which would require a more interpretative reading, such as 'my head' or 'that moment' 'was so full of sleep at that point that I abandoned the true way.' There being no grammatical reason to force such a reading, I agree with the majority of translators, who render "era" by 'I.'

References

Alighieri, D. (1969). *Inferno* (A. Gilbert, Trans.). Duke University Press. (Original work published 1314)
Alighieri, D. (2002). *Inferno* (R. Hollander & J. Hollander, Trans.). Anchor Books. (Original work published 1314)
Aurora, S. (2015). A forgotten source in the history of linguistics: Husserl's *Logical Investigations*. *Bulletin d'Analyse Phénoménologique, 11*(5), 1–19.
Bassanese, F. (2000). Dark wood. In R. Lansing (Ed.), *Dante encyclopedia* (pp. 287–289). Routledge.
Baume, S. (2017). *A line made by walking*. Houghton Mifflin Harcourt.
Culler, J. (1975). *Structuralist poetics: Structuralism, linguistics and the study of literature*. Cornell University Press.
Dalí, S. (1960). *Divine Comédie: illustrated with 100 woodcuts by Salvador Dalí*. Les Heures Claires.
Franke, W. (1996). *Dante's interpretative journey*. University of Chicago Press.
Gallagher, S. & Zahavi, D. (2019). Phenomenological approaches to self-consciousness. In E. N. Zalta (Ed.), *Stanford encyclopedia of philosophy*. Retrieved from https://plato.stanford.edu/archives/sum2019/entries/self-consciousness-phenomenological/
Heidegger, M. (1962). *Being and time. A translation of* Sein und Zeit (J. Macquarrie & E. Robinson, Trans.). Harper & Row. (Original work published 1927).
Hollander, R. (2011). *Princeton Dante project [website]*. Retrieved from http://etcweb.princeton.edu/dante/index.html
Husserl, E. (1959). *Erste Philosophie II 1923–24, Husserliana VIII*. Martinus Nijhoff.

Husserl, E. (1967). *Ideas: General introduction to pure phenomenology* (W. R. B. Gibson, Trans.). Allen & Unwin; Humanities Press. (Original work published 1913).

Husserl, E. (1970). *Logical investigations*. Routledge. (Original work published 1900–1901).

Husserl, E. (1984). *Einleitung in die Logik und Erkenntnistheorie, Husserliana XXIV*. Martinus Nijhoff.

Kant, I. (1963). *Critique of pure reason* (N. K. Smith, Trans.). Macmillan. (Original work published 1781 and 1787).

Long, R. (1967). *A line made by walking [sculpture & photograph]*. Wiltshire, UK & and various collections.

Luke, H. (2001). *Dark wood to white rose: Journey and transformation in Dante's Divine Comedy*. Parabola Books.

Monticelli, D. (2013). From living experience to poetic word. Frames and thresholds of Dante's *Divine Comedy*. *Interlitteraria, 18*(1), 238–257.

Monticelli, D. (2019). Fear in Dante's *Inferno*. Phenomenology, semiotics, aesthetics. In Z. Barański, A. Kablitz, & Ü. Ploom (Eds.), *I luoghi nostri. Dante's natural and cultural spaces* (pp. 106–128). Tallin University Press.

Moran, D. (2005). *Edmund Husserl: Founder of phenomenology*. Polity Press.

Moran, D., & Cohen, J. D. (Eds.) (2012). *The Husserl dictionary*. Continuum.

Needler, H. I. (1973). Translators' hell: Three recent versions of Dante's *Inferno*. *Italica, 50*(3), 375–399. doi:10.2307/478422

Petrocchi, G. (1966). *La Commedia secondo l'antica vulgata*. Mondadori.

Radcliffe, M. (2009). The phenomenology of mood and the meaning of life. In P. Goldie (Ed.), *The Oxford handbook of philosophy of emotion* (pp. 347–371). Oxford University Press. doi:10.1093/oxfordhb/9780199235018.003.0016

Sartre, J. P. (1957). *The transcendence of the ego: An existentialist theory of consciousness* (F. Williams & R. Kirkpatrick, Trans.). Noonday Press. (Original work published 1936).

Sartre, J. P. (1962). *Sketch for a theory of the emotions* (P. Mairet, Trans.). Methuen. (Original work published 1939).

Solomon, R. (1993). *The passions: Emotions and the meaning of life*. Hackett. (Original work published 1976).

Stawarska, B. (2015). *Saussure's philosophy of language as phenomenology. Undoing the doctrine of the* Course in General Linguistics. Oxford University Press.

Took, J. (2000). *Dante's phenomenology of being*. University of Glasgow Press.

Tower, T. (2017). *Natura narrans: Landscape as literature in early modern Italy* (Unpublished doctoral dissertation). Johns Hopkins University, Baltimore, MD.

Chapter 7

Gateways to the Ineffable
Dante's Poetry as Proto-Phenomenology

Aaron B. Daniels

Psychology practitioners and scholars who value integrating humanities perspectives into the social sciences should be particularly encouraged by Punzi and Hagen's recent call (2017) to integrate literature into clinical practice. This sort of postmodern classical revival, in which the human sciences draw upon core texts from across the globe to inspire, inform, and ensoul research and practice is not a new cry. This call is indigenous to Jung and his descendants. But when it comes to the post-World-War-II humanism, with its emphasis on growth and compassion, some literary sources make more frequent appearances. Mary Oliver's poems grace the pages and presentations of numerous humanities-minded psychologists. Dante Alighieri's? Less so.

Nevertheless, as this volume strives to show, Dante has vast riches to offer. If, for instance, psychotherapy is to avoid imposing clinical edicts on the patient, then it too must be a pilgrimage like Dante's, perpetually struggling with fidelity to the experiences of both parties in the room. Practitioner and patient will both find that their descriptions will always fall short of the unfolding edge of the presence for which both parties yearn. Bringing phenomenological sensibilities to Dante's work may yield many more clinical implications. This chapter aims to offer some touchpoints for those forays.

As researchers seek to understand their unfolding process in relation to their topic, Dante may also offer apt insights. Questions of reflexivity, smaller versus greater hermeneutic circles, as well as insight into the nature of phenomenology's project are just a few of the areas to which Dante's writings have contributions to make.

More globally, this volume seeks to establish linkages between fundamental ontological, epistemological, and hermeneutic stances bridging the first and second millennia that do not merely resonate with phenomenology but can be reclaimed as a provenance. Phenomenology cannot genuinely hope to compete with materialist human sciences if only the last 150 years of scientific developments count as evidence. For instance, if Wundt and Titchener are the fathers of psychology, phenomenology will always be marginalized. Yet a psychology that has, from its inception, disavowed, to the point of non-existence, theological, humanities-based, and philosophical discourses, cannot possibly hope to speak to whole human beings. The resulting psychologized husks may well warrant a pitiable place in Dante's Infernal landscape.

For now, this chapter offers some provisional observations, applications, and syntheses to provoke further conversations and scholarship. This chapter begins with a note on Radical Orthodoxy and its relationship to this volume's discourse. It then moves to some observations regarding Heidegger and poetic language. Next, dwelling with Dante's premodern position—if only just—the chapter looks at alchemy, Jung, and Romanyshyn's perspectives on modernity. The chapter then offers an extended application of the ideas contained herein to reflexivity in the clinical and qualitative research domains, by examining three gates in the *Commedia*: Hell, Dis, and Purgatory. Finally, some provisional conclusions emerge growing out of the ideas that weave throughout this volume.

Radical Orthodoxy

In his discussion of Duns Scotus as a—perhaps unwitting—father of modernity earlier in this volume, William Franke makes ongoing reference to the work of Milbank, noted for his advocacy of a movement labeled 'Radical Orthodoxy.' Franke's references are not surprising. As an emerging movement within contemporary theology, Radical Orthodoxy attempts to reclaim pieces of the pre-modern heritage of Christianity and critically examine elements of current belief, practice, and theology that bear the marks of modernity and the postmodern condition. Using postmodern philosophical tools and stances to critique modernity while stretching into the premodern, the movement gained its first widespread presentation in a 1999 collection of essays edited by Milbank, Pickstock, and Ward. As such, a re-examination of Dante's premodern status is in accord with the movement's intentions. Moreover, phenomenology could contribute to the epistemology of the movement by participating in this deeper provenance. It is this chain between the phenomenological, existential-phenomenological, and postmodern with the premodern for which this essay and several others in this volume seek to form a link.

More profoundly, if the human sciences want to truly re-member rather than dis-member whole humans, then the hard work of bridging sophisticated theological discourse and the human sciences must commence. Dante existed in an era where these divisions had not yet calcified; but, today, the rapprochement is awkward and halting due to the intervening 700 years of estrangement. This current collection of essays offers some local topography of zones that exist between disciplines and means to encourage future explorers to visit.

In his commentary on Paul's *Epistle to the Romans*, the third-century biblical scholar Origen comments that "The debt of love remains with us permanently and never leaves us; this is a debt which we both discharge every day and forever owe" (Barclay, 2002, p. 207). This ancient source provides apt justification for viewing Franke's works as consonant with Radical Orthodoxy, especially when seen in the light of his 2007 essay synthesizing Levinas—with his debt to the

Other at the heart of each person—and Dante, reviewed in the introduction to this volume.

Heidegger, Poetry, Philosophy, and Science

Heidegger is a key figure in many of the essays in this volume. His interrogations of *dasein* are essential for examining questions of presence, phenomena, and ontology. Applying these ideas, Heidegger also has extensive commentary on poetics. Thus, to help this current chapter serve as a resource for future researchers, the following extensive quotes serve to illustrate several key points of Heidegger's philosophy on questions critical to Dante. The material comes from "Letter on Humanism," originally written in 1946 and published in 1947.

Heidegger (1947/1993) begins his letter by noting the struggles of interrogating language and the inveigling ideas of subject and object embedded in grammatical analyses. Thus, he explains that,

> The liberation of language from grammar into a more original essential framework is reserved for thought and poetic creation. Thinking is not merely *l'engagement dans l'action* for and by beings, in the sense of the actuality of the present situation. Thinking is *l'engagement* by and for the truth of Being. The history of Being is never past but stands ever before; it sustains and defines every *condition et situation humaine*. (p. 218)

Therefore, a new discourse must emerge. He explains that this means that,

> In order to learn how to experience the aforementioned essence of thinking purely, and that means at the same time to carry through, we must free ourselves from the technical interpretation of thinking. The beginnings of that interpretation reach back to Plato and Aristotle. They take thinking itself to be a *techne*, a process of reflection in service to doing and making. But here reflection is already seen from the perspective of *praxis* and *poeisis*. For this reason thinking, when taken for itself, is not "practical." The characterization of thinking as *theoria* and the determination of knowing as "theoretical" behavior occur already within the "technical" interpretation of thinking. Such a characterization is a reactive attempt to rescue thinking and preserve its autonomy over against acting and doing. (p. 218)

And here, Heidegger introduces the crux of the current argument regarding the sciences, returning in some ways to his Husserlian tutelage.

> Since then "philosophy" has been in the constant predicament of having to justify its existence before the "sciences." It believes it can do that most effectively by elevating itself to the rank of a science. But such an effort is the abandonment of thinking. Philosophy is hounded by the fear that it loses

prestige and validity if it is not a science. Not to be a science is taken as a failing which is equivalent to being unscientific. Being, as the element of thinking, is abandoned by the technical interpretation of thinking. "Logic," beginning with the Sophists and Plato, sanctions this explanation. Thinking is judged by a standard that does not measure up to it. Such judgment may be compared to the procedure of trying to evaluate the nature and powers of a fish by seeing how long it can live on dry land. For a long time now, all too long, thinking has been stranded on dry land. Can then the effort to return thinking to its element be called "irrationalism"? (1947/1993, pp. 218–219)

Over six hundred years before Heidegger's "Letter" (1947/1993), Dante struggled with these very questions. The seduction of the Gentle Lady of natural philosophy—today's sciences—might have given Dante's efforts a seeming legitimacy and certainty; but, as Harrison (1988) explains, Dante notes a distortion and uncanny reflection—a "visual specularity" (p. 115)—as Dante seeks her consolations. The other—let alone the Other—is occluded by one's own agenda. In response to this realization, Dante not only returns to poetic discourse but raises it to an engaged and active philosophy of Being. The task falls to others to describe why Dante's poesis did not, until the second half of the twentieth century, merit consideration as a proto-phenomenology.

Perhaps Heidegger's (1947/1993) comment is a rebuke to those phenomenologists who seek to describe their efforts as a 'rigorous human science'; but, in their qualifications of the term, these phenomenologists clearly embed their critique of what other sciences achieve relative to the human condition. When Heidegger asserts that "thinking is judged by a standard that does not measure up to it" (p. 219), his critique of most of psychology's efforts is clear. Epistemologically mired in materialism, those psychologies cannot hermeneutically stand with any vantage on the thinking to which Heidegger speaks.

The conclusion of Heidegger's (1947/1993) passage creates the possibility for a link between Foucault's *folie*—madness—and Heidegger's 'irrationalism.' Since Dante's time, essential narratives of what is most human have become progressively marginalized to the point of non-existence. Concordantly, those same dominating narratives that ignore these irrational or mad elements have engaged in manic defenses against any challenge to their hegemony of reality. Dante's *Inferno* vividly explores worldviews of literalism, absolutism, and unassailable certitude. Simultaneously, these are landscapes of abject madness unacknowledged. The nihilism inherent in such concrete understandings devours the souls of those in its thrall, leading to their ultimate unspeakable entrapment.

The existential-phenomenological literature, especially Heidegger's works, deal with Augustine and Thomas as touchpoints for being, essence, and presence. However, Francis receives far less discussion, perhaps because his theology and spirituality are not the sort of overt responses to Greek thought that attracted the likes of Heidegger. Nevertheless, as authors, such as the Discalced Carmelite

Wallenfang (e.g., 2017a; 2017b) not only participate in the theological turn of phenomenology but reinforce his Carmelite ancestor Edith Stein's role as a key contributor to the tradition, the contemplative charism of these religious can easily take a turn toward a Franciscan phenomenology. This phenomenology would stretch even closer to the imaginal agenda in which the lived world is not simply 'animated' but is itself brimming over with Life—a return to the Garden, but also a new Creation. In the face of the often-perverse turns of postmodern philosophy, perhaps the tender sincerity of a spiritually-aware existential phenomenology would be a welcome relief. Without doubt, Edith Stein's role as martyr of the Holocaust could help to offset Heidegger's, at best, ambiguous record regarding German nationalism.

Alchemy, Jung, Romanyshyn, and Dante

Before commencing any discussion of alchemy in the context of Dante, the explorer of such territory should note that, in Canto XXIX of *Inferno*, Dante condemns alchemists to the tenth *bolgia*—trench—of the eighth circle of Hell. This position is quite deep within the pit. Dante reserves the eighth circle for fraud and its tenth, and deepest, *bolgia* is for falsifiers. Leprous scabs cover the condemned alchemists at which they endlessly claw. Literalizing alchemy with the promise of transforming lead into shining gold for one's credulous benefactors is clearly a dire sin in Dante's estimation. Generations later, however, philosophical alchemists will come to play with this tension of the literality of leaden matter and the symbolism of numinous spirit in new and essential ways.

Jung's Choice of Alchemy

Although not shy about controversial statements regarding religion, politics, and culture in general, Jung was careful about his choices of subject matter. Thus, in the first half of the twentieth century, Gnosticism and alchemy offered relatively obscure topics around which he could freely roam, unencumbered by expectations and previous commentary. Owing in no small part to Jung's influence, alchemy is no longer so obscure, certainly in popularized versions found in New Age bookstores and MacGuffins in Harry Potter plotlines. Serious alchemical scholarship is, nonetheless, still a vast minority in the literature.

Dante Predates Alchemy

Thus, in 2000, in an online message board, alchemy scholar Adam McLean decided to make an important clarification. A discussion thread had begun looking at precursors to European alchemy. One contributor noted the color of the steps leading to Dante's formal Purgatory—white, black, then red—and how they were, although out of alchemical order, the colors of the alchemical progression. Although alchemists earlier listed four stages—*nigredo, albedo, citrinitas,* and *rubedo;* that is, black, white, yellow, and red—many later alchemists subsumed the yellow into the red. Several other contributors to the online forum noted further parallels in Dante's and others' medieval works. McLean sagely responded:

> Could it not be that we should be looking for the influences of Dante, de Meung and the poets and authors of allegorical works during the 13th and 14th centuries, upon alchemical writers? Could it be that alchemical writers were responding to this material and recasting the way in which they communicated their ideas into similar allegorical forms? Thus the explosion of alchemical allegorical works in the 15th century. Perhaps we are reading the influences the wrong way round?

Pre- and Peri-Modernity

One of the reasons Jung chose European alchemy as a topic was because of its emergence in parallel to modernity. It was, in a sense, perimodern. Alchemy could hold in escrow the imaginal elements—actually the imagination itself—that an emerging modernity could not. Dante, however, is premodern, if only just. His perspectives rest on the sort of medieval assumptions that modernity so successfully unseated. Jungian authors would do well to reach back to this fertile territory to contrast Dante's perspectives to the isolating and nihilistic perspectives of modernity that Jung repeatedly sought to expose.

Talk of premodernity, perimodernity, modernity, and postmodernity can threaten to drift into sparkling abstractions on the complexity of multiple weltanschauungs across the last millennium. If by 'premodern' one intends pre-egoic, then one must reach into prehistory to find those sort of shifts in self-awareness. Surely, Dante wrestles with what it means to be entrapped in one's self-concept. His efforts across the *Commedia* speak to this abiding challenge of modernity that philosophical alchemists, in their perimodernity, also face.

But if by 'premodern' we mean to offer a critical narrative of the emergence of the supremacy of a materialist epistemology, then Dante surely grants a different perspective than his alchemical descendants. Alchemy already stands in a world leaden with its materialism. The complexities of the many nuanced stages of the alchemist's *Magnum Opus* bespeak how far into matter the alchemists' world had sunk, such that their eventually deeply symbolic procedures were necessary. As Robert Romanyshyn once summarized in lecture, modernity's divorce of spirit and matter leads to the halves longing for each other—'spirit wants to matter and matter wants to be inspired.' That does not describe Dante's lived world. Thus, his premodernity offers a different perspective on the problem of modernity. Dante's problem is solved through a devotion to the great work of poetry, not the alchemist's arcane symbolic transactions. Nevertheless, the alchemical imagination bears many traces of the poetic art.

Romanyshyn and Frankenstein's Monster

Romanyshyn's (2019a) 'poetic realism' brought to bear in listening to such daunting creatures as the *Diagnostic and Statistical Manual of Mental Disorders* (DSM) and Frankenstein's monster is surely alive in Dante and the alchemists. Romanyshyn notes that "the perturbations of soul fictionalizes the factual" (p. 7). Romanyshyn is not quibbling about the primacy of matter or perception. He is dealing with our lived reality, soaked in fictions. Many of these fictions are deadly serious and, if unacknowledged in their fictionality, can exact a horrible cost. Dante and alchemists alike struggle to gain a purchase on their lived worlds adequate to grant them this insight.

Romanyshyn (2019b) expands his insights in his latest book, *Victor Frankenstein, the Monster and the Shadows of Technology: The Frankenstein Prophecies*. Romanyshyn presents Victor Frankenstein's narcissism—and potentially malignant narcissism—as the modern gaze. This is the gaze that, though driven by the same longing that inspires Dante and the alchemists, cannot transform. At the risk of appropriating Romanyshyn's metaphor, Frankenstein's narcissistic alchemy yields a failed, monstrous creation. Yet the creation still screams out not merely an indictment but a call that Romanyshyn begs his readers to hear.

Dante's Alchemy

If the alchemists were, as McLean opines, inspired by Dante, what proto-alchemical insights might Dante offer in his *Commedia*? If these insights are to be phenomenological, then they must be about the process, the meaning-making, and the transformations of experience the journey effects. Here are two alchemical mottos and an ancient symbol to illustrate a deep gravity that may drive both Dante's great poem and the alchemists' Great Work.

'VITRIOL' is an archaic term for sulfur or its effects in the alchemical process. For alchemists, it is an acrostic of *Visita Interiora Terrae Rectificando Invenies Occultum Lapidem* [visit the interior of the earth to find the rectified hidden stone]. Although the Latin is a bit contrived, the implication is that, in the finding itself, one is actually rectifying the stone. The stone is, of course, the famous Philosopher's Stone, capable of effecting incredible transformations in elements, specifically turning lead into gold. Dante's journey through *Inferno* is such a vitriolic journey. Not only is it searing like sulfuric acid, but it strips away all the intellectual bad faith in which Dante had invested. In the abject silence of the deepest frozen pits, Dante must make his perilous turn on Lucifer's hip. Without this critical turn, he could not transform the momentum of this descent into the ascent, which leads him to the shores of the complementary Purgatory.

The stone, for Dante, was hidden in plain sight, as such mysteries typically are. Dante knew the philosophy and theology. Dante had tasted Divine Love. But the truth remained buried in his own quagmire of sin and vice. The descent liberated what was already there to be transformed and prepared for the ascent.

In Christian iconography, 'INRI' is popularly used as shorthand for the placard placed above the Crucified Jesus. In its Latin version, the inscription would read, *Iesus Nazarenus, Rex Iudaeorum* [Jesus of Nazareth, King of the Jews]. For alchemists, this inscription could contain another meaning of *Igne Natura Renovatur Integra* [Through fire, nature is wholly reborn]. Alchemically, it signifies the necessity of keeping the fires carefully banked beneath the alchemical flask, the alembic. Jungians eagerly embrace this motto for the carefully maintained analytic frame that creates the space for remarkable transformations in analysands. For them, it is not a neutral space, but one charged with the material the patient brings and the analyst stokes.

In Purgatory, Dante's last act on the slopes of the mountain is to leap into the searing flames that transform or liberate lust into Love. On the other side, he witnesses nature transformed. Not the Dark Woods of the beginning—illustrations frequently showing clutching vines and densely packed trees—but a return to the Garden of Eden. If one looks at a diagram of Dante's journey, one can see the Earthly Paradise at the summit of the mountain. This map may help the reader, but it deceives one about the process. Dante must go through the harrowing ascent in order to be able to leap through the flames. The powerfully symbolic dream of the eagle may have brought him to the Gate of formal Purgatory, but the taking on of the purgatorial labors and their ultimate flames were what renovated his phenomenology to be able to see the garden—whole nature.

Since Dante portrays the deepest level of his *Inferno* as nihilistically silent, offering the VITRIOL motto is arguably glib. Dante's descent was toward the unspeakable. Moreover, using INRI to represent the purgatorial transformation could also risk an experience-distant intellectualization. Beyond these sins, venturing any linguistic audacity in the face of the ultimate Beatific Vision of Paradise is potentially blasphemous. Thus, a symbol will have to suffice to point to this ascent to ineffability. One of the alchemical symbols for gold is the point within a circle: ⊙. It is also a symbol for the Sun.

With greed such a concern for Dante, a metaphor about gold would never have been appropriate to his journey of spiritual transcendence. This symbol, however, shows up much earlier in Dante's life. In the *Vita Nuova*, the Lord of Love mourns that Dante must dwell on the perimeter while He is at the center. One could view Dante's ascension through Heaven as an effort to obtain that center. However, a mystical paradox presents itself. In *Inferno*, Dante has gone to the center of the Earth, the center of the cosmos. He has then climbed to the highest peak to find the Earthly Paradise in *Purgatorio*. From there, in *Paradiso*, he begins an ascent to ever-expanding circles of the heavenly realms. When he gets to the farthest limit, the largest circle, he beholds his ultimate vision. Yet what he sees is not a portion of the largest circle imaginable. Instead, he witnesses a point.

Part of the mystical import of the point within the circle is that the point and the circle are synonymous. The deepest interior and the farthest extremes bring one to the same mystical reality. Moreover, phenomenologically, the whole process has been packed inside of itself, driven by the deepest of intentionalities to unfold into this epiphany. The tenacious pursuit of the phenomena has brought Dante to this moment. The reader can speculate about his inauthenticity, his sins and vices, and his self-deceptions; but these configurations were his phenomenology of that infernal or purgatorial moment. Only through the ongoing pursuit of those phenomenologies—the expression of the experience—could Dante fuel this epic journey. To Dante and his devotees, this is the only journey: the great work.

The Rhythm of Gates

The *Commedia* is a work of deep rhythms, echoes, and powerful structural parallels. Growing from the Thomistic structure of the transformation or perhaps refining of the passions, *Inferno*, *Purgatorio*, and *Paradiso* present unfolding insights into central potent emotional realities. Although gates and significant transitions abound through the *Commedia* and the entire work bears a profound liminality, in order to highlight these rhythms, one can profitably compare the Gates of Hell, Dis, and Purgatory. Each call upon the pilgrim to shift his understanding of his self, his task, his means of knowing and understanding, and his goal. So too must the therapist and client, as well as the researcher and mentor, continue to revise their understandings of their work dependent on the various epistemological, phenomenological, and hermeneutic shifts the journey entails and demands.

The Gates of Hell

Dante introduces the entire *Commedia* in the Dark Woods of Canto I of *Inferno*. This is the darkness that startles him into fearful awareness. Dante is not merely writing his own narrative and asking his readers to 'make of it what they will.' Dante speaks of "nostra vita"—this is midway on the journey of *our* lives. Dante intends his experience to speak to his reader, to life and the experience of life, and to those who would undertake such a harrowing journey because they must.

Therapy and research are both based on a problem and a problem that jars one awake to the necessity of doing something. Dante is no different. Awaking in the dark woods, he feels the need to get some perspective on his situation and seeks to climb the nearby hill to gain a sense of the landscape. Many clients—and therapists—as well as many researchers, seek to simply 'tweak' current knowledge. Clients may attempt to re-apply strategies that have seemed to work in the past, perhaps with redoubled effort. Researchers may simply build upon previous work, often by their mentor. For the many for whom these strategies work, the journey is a simpler one. This is not the case for Dante.

In attempting to climb the hill, Dante is confronted by the three beasts. Are the beasts a necessary objectification into some thing to fear that can move Dante out of his angst, as Monticelli (2015) would suggest? Are they, conversely, a sign of an inauthentic way of seeing and being that force Dante to traverse the horrors of Hell, as Franke (1996) suggests? Regardless, Dante is facing his own profound specific limitations that prevent him from gaining any perspective. This impasse demands a greater journey. What has worked before for Dante will work no more. The dark woods is the specific failure of Dante's way-of-being to carry him any further. The failed ascent of the hill is merely a confirmation of this impasse.

Jung mentions throughout his works that real problems are not solvable in their own terms. To a greater extent, for life's real deadlocks, what one thinks is the problem—and what one assumes to be its solution—is part of the problem. If the solution-focused strategies of 'counseling' fail to help clients on their way, then the more intensive process of psychotherapy is necessary. Here clients must come to challenge the way of understanding and seeing that define their problems. In successful psychotherapy, clients will come to know their lived epistemologies and phenomenologies. Jung explains that only growth, engaging with the forces of growth, a growing out of and beyond the confines and definitions of the problem, will free the patient—the one who suffers. Talking about the problem will not be enough. Psychotherapy must bring the problem into the room—in language, in embodiment, in imagery, and in relationship.

Researchers also reach impasses. The topic, the subjects, the problem—they may not yield to accustomed methods. Even if they do, the product may well be accustomed results. If new insights are to be achieved, previous understandings, assumptions, and methodologies must be abandoned; but this can be a terrifying process. The number of candidates who do not complete doctoral programs testifies to the daunting prospect of taking on a comprehensive examination of any subject, let alone attempting to make a substantive contribution. One cannot simply do more; one must do something new.

Dante runs down the hill in terror. He despairs. He sees a human shape and calls out in his despondency for this other to have pity on him. Enter Virgil, the mentor and guide. Akin to the first of the Twelve Steps, real change begins with admitting one cannot, as one knows oneself, solve this problem. 'I' am the problem—how I see, how I know, and how I define my predicament. The authentic experience of terror signifies a breakdown—a rock bottom, although that metaphor takes on different meanings once Dante and Virgil begin the true descent into Hell.

Virgil explains that a divine feminine hierarchy has sent him. The pity Dante sought from Virgil was already given to Dante by heavenly Beatrice, who saw him in the deepest of distress. She appealed via female saints to the Virgin Mary, who dispatched Virgil to Dante's Dark Woods. Thus, Virgil explains that Dante need not fear, for not only does Dante have friends in high places, but this process itself is ordained. Moreover, if he is able, if he fully engages with the process, it has the highest of goals.

Therapy, too, must not rely purely on the personality of the therapist. The therapeutic frame appeals to a faith in a process that will carry and transform the patient—and, depending on one's therapeutic alignment, the therapist as well.

Although few graduate programs will admit it, research can also be approached as a process of transformation for the researcher. This growth, however, can only happen if the mentor and the process's structure allow for the reflexivity of the investigator. The denial of this reality, as is the standard within most research institutions, imperils the researcher, but does remove an unwanted burden from those mentors unprepared to accompany their mentees on such harrowing journeys.

This brings Dante and Virgil to the Gates of Hell. The famous inscription opening Canto III:1–7 of *Inferno* ominously declares,

> THROUGH ME YOU ENTER INTO THE CITY OF WOES,
> THROUGH ME YOU ENTER INTO ETERNAL PAIN,
> THROUGH ME YOU ENTER THE POPULATION OF LOSS.
>
> JUSTICE MOVED MY HIGH MAKER, IN POWER DIVINE,
> WISDOM SUPREME, LOVE PRIMAL. NO THINGS WERE
> BEFORE ME NOT ETERNAL; ETERNAL I REMAIN.
>
> ABANDON ALL HOPE, YOU WHO ENTER HERE.
> (Alighieri, 1320/1994, Pinsky translation)

The gravity of the tone is not mere hyperbole. The darkest of material threatens to overwhelm one, but a greater gravity is at work. Will one recoil at the horror, retreating into an anxiety-laden inertia? Or will one keep putting one foot in front of the other to endure this harrowing process?

No one comes to therapy because things are going well. To examine oneself with the intention of transformation means encountering awful truths, abandoning cherished lies, and admitting, at very least, life-altering mistakes. Although therapy may contain laughter, forgiveness, grace, and joy, it can only get there because of a problem so severe that the distractions of an unexamined life must be abandoned.

So too, ought research to deal with real problems. Although some sort of curiosity would seem to motivate all researchers, the researcher occupies a position of real privilege, and the choice of research topic is always inherently one rife with ethical import. At its core, the ethical researcher must deal with a vexing social problem and set out, however distantly, to effect a change for the better. Moreover, the research process will not be easy. It will hurt. The number of relationships that fail during the course of graduate studies testifies to this painful reality.

But what of the hope these gates demand one abandon? How can therapy operate without hope, even necessitate the abandonment of hope? How can a researcher endure the rigors of a long-term research project without hope? For the one who is to journey through Hell—rather than take residence—the gates offer an essential but brutal truth. At this point in the journey, the 'hope' in question is a vain hope, a hope rooted in expectations that must be abandoned before anything new can emerge. Only the abandonment of this false hope can facilitate a true faith in the process. Patients in longer-term treatment frequently express a shift in their sense of what therapy is about and where it is going. They may have initially hoped for a quick fix to their problem. But a few years down the line, they discover that they have changed their sense of what is important, relativizing or completely redefining the initial problem.

A researcher, as well, cannot encompass the entirety of the process in some initial image. In fact, in qualitative research, these initial impressions and expectations are yet another piece of reflexive evidence. Clutching to some expected outcome is, in most cases, a form of bias that does not allow the project to unfold in its own authentic terms.

Throughout his writings, Husserl interrogates the idea of *adumbration*. For Husserl, adumbration is the ongoing prediction of the consistency of objects. Our current experience is constructed of micro-predictions. As we walk around a chair, for instance, we feel secure in our lived knowledge that a new perspective on it will not suddenly reveal a gaping cosmic maw. Artists of all types, of course, often play with these expectations. Nevertheless, the delight of the unexpected can only happen because every moment is rife with little unacknowledged adumbrations or teloi—miniature future predictions that are reassuringly, consistently fulfilled.

Thus, to extend Husserl's insight into the relational and life-course domains, people live with hopes, predictions, aspirations, and fears embedded in their relationships and lived worlds. Who I know myself to be, how I see, how I know, what I imagine, how I take up the other, and what I predict are all wrapped up into a future orientation that inheres from the smallest of my experiences to the largest of my life-course expectations. The abandonment of 'hope' could be taken up as an epoché of the veracity of this steady flow of teloi in order that, in becoming more obvious, one's expectations might be more fully interrogated.

Therefore, the Gates of Hell demand one let go into the process, trusting the guidance by the mentor. This mentor must necessarily be idealizable to some extent so that, later, the patient or neophyte researcher may re-introject these idealizations, much as Dante initially obsequiously defers to Virgil as a Great Poet, but will, by the end of *Paradiso*, have not only let go of Virgil at the end of Purgatory, but have become the Poet himself.

The Gates of Dis

Several authors reviewed in the introduction to this volume deal with Dante and Virgil at the Gates of Dis. An interrogation of 'seeming,' literalism, and the limits of rationality play a role in the essays from Shoaf (1989), Franke (1996), and De Monticelli (2000) when addressing this terrifying impasse, which is only overcome through angelic intervention. In order to highlight the import of this liminal moment for Dante, some context for these gates may prove helpful.

The shift in Hell is progressively toward sins of more intentionality and betrayal. Five of the nine circles of Hell precede Dis. Early in Dante's infernal journey, Paolo and Francesca, in Canto V of *Inferno*, gave in to the lust which now, in the Second Circle of Hell, whips them about in a tempest. The Stygian Swamp that Dante and Virgil traverse in Canto VIII to get to the City of Dis contains the actively wrathful and the sullen—seen as 'passively wrathful.' They occupy the Fifth Circle. The wrathful trample the depressed into the muck beneath the waters. The sins here are still a 'giving in to' but are more perverse and, if not agential, at least effortful.

Beyond these Gates of Dis, however, the sins involve a reinvestment in the sin, a doubling down that deepens the severity in Dante's ethical cosmology. Heresy gives way to violence to fraud to treachery and, at its heart, the deepest of betrayals as the trapped beast Lucifer endlessly gnaws on the frozen bodies of Brutus, Cassius, and Judas Iscariot.

Hell abounds with important shifts and impasses—cliffs too precipitous to scale down, beasts too fearsome to pass, but the Gates of Dis draw the attention of commentators with phenomenological sensibilities. So often, those condemned within that city's walls present complex justifications for their sins, belligerent defenses of their bestial choices, and are easily bribed with Dante's promise that his recounting of their stories will keep them from being forgotten among the living. Up to a point, these infernal denizens can twist logic to their perverse ends. However, even language will give out in the deepest of the pits. In Canto XXXI, in the Ninth Circle, Dante and Virgil encounter the giant Nimrod who can but babble. And, eventually, the deepest frozen center of Hell is blanketed in an eldritch silence.

Thus, the Gates of Dis represent the entrance into a nihilistic decay into utter, abject meaninglessness. Even the threads of pride tatter into worthless shreds. The ecstasy of mystical ineffability at the farthest reaches of Paradise is perversely twisted into vertiginous blather and wretched silence in the deepest pit of Hell. The unspeakable mocks and veils the ineffable.

Clinically, this is the most dire of territory. This is the land of the severe personality disorders, latent psychosis, the most insidious of traumas, severe dissociations, entrenched addictions, pervasive dangers to self and other, and the many species of full psychosis. It is a country through which patients may pass; but it is also the place where far too many become entangled or frozen. Like Lucifer flapping his wings to escape, but only freezing more solid his prison around him, most of the efforts of those in the clutches of deep pathology only further entangle them and, often, those around them. Too many patients at this level of suffering can only have their anguish lessened with the structures of case management and psychopharmacology. Others may avail of these services to gradually stabilize and make progress. For some, psychoeducation will provide a Virgilian commentary to help them understand their territory and take steps toward a change. Regardless, this is not a land of real insight.

At the Gates of Dis, as noted above, Dante must abandon the rationality and rationalizations onto which he has held thus far. From here on, the journey continues only as contained by the mentor and with the faith Dante has in this process. The purpose is to get through for its own sake. Although Dante catalogs his reactions, this is no time to take the material personally for long, lest he becomes enthralled and entrapped in a circle's cruel justice.

This territory can palpably alter the therapeutic space. The therapist may be dragged in many directions by countertransference. The patient may whip transferences about the consulting room like arterial spray. But at these darkest of depths, the temptation to elaborately interpret could prove deadly. The patient needs containment. Therapists need containment as well, in the form of their own personal therapy and clinically-oriented supervision. But efforts to explain away, justify, label, and otherwise dismiss the horrifying reality of this therapeutic landscape will likely prove as useful as Nimrod's prattle. The goal—the only goal—is to get through.

Research at this stage is about the work and only the work. One cannot constantly check in with the end goal, the conclusions, or one's future after the completion of the project. There is no future from here; there is only the labor. The mentor hopes to validate the individual pieces of the project and refer back to and potentially revise the schematics of the process. But the potential for the paralysis of becoming transfixed or overwhelmed is dangerously high. Intuitions of what the data may be insinuating can threaten one as well. This is no time to make major decisions, yet one may dimly sense that what drew one to this project has become distorted. Perhaps it has become not at all what one had imagined. Or, worse yet, one may intuit that one will have to do—intellectual—violence to one's original vision in order to keep moving.

At the very deepest point of Hell, Dante and Virgil must climb down the shaggy shanks of Lucifer in order to find a tunnel that will bring them to the other side of the world and to the shores of the Island of Purgatory. Dante, ever-vigilant to—medieval—astronomy and physics, writes that his pilgrims must turn end-for-end halfway down Satan since they are, after all, at the center of the earth. They are transforming their descent into an ascent without changing vectors.

The massive pit of hell is a cavern formed all the way to the center of the earth as it refused the falling abomination of Lucifer to touch it. As the earth created this horrified concavity, it simultaneously formed the complementary convexity of the Island of Purgatory on the opposite side of the planet. Dante is too informed by Franciscan spirituality to cast the earth and nature as fallen. This theme will develop more when Dante passes through the fiery curtain at the top of Purgatory to enter the Earthly Paradise.

The greater journey remains the same, in a sense; yet the perspective is entirely changed. Dante begins *Inferno* as an exile, filled with fear, bitterness, rage, wounded pride, and lust. For Dante, the other was, at best, an object of pity, or, at worst, an object of loathing. Only the Other of Beatrice receives greater regard, but this longing is strangled with grief, shame, lust, and nostalgia. The expedition of Hell has been *Dante's* Inferno—a guided tour of Dante's lived world. The inauthenticity of Dante's taking up of alterity is vividly illustrated throughout. The temptation to fall into the landscape has been great, and Virgil has had to frequently goad, chastise, and pull Dante along the way in order that the Florentine not become mired with his subjects.

Nevertheless, the profound hermeneutic reorientation on the devil's hip renders the infernal landscape as something new, but only upon having completed the arduous journey. By the time they exit the tunnel, Dante and Virgil will see the stars rather than the claustrophobic oppression of hell's disorienting miasma. Because of the preceding harrowing journey and because of the ultimate reorientation, openness and potential abound in this closing image.

The Gates of Dis marks an entrance into territory that destroys meaning; but by passing through Dis's interior and the rest of Hell, this meaninglessness becomes an indictment of inauthenticity's hidden nihilism. Heidegger declares that angst—the distant aching tone of inauthenticity—contains a call within it, but when we answer that call, we hear 'guilty!' Dante became so identified with his bitter exile that he scarcely realized how far he had fallen. The jarring awareness of awaking because of the darkness of the woods heralds the transformation as Dante and Virgil turn head-for-tail. Dante can now—and only now—see and reflect on what this first great journey has been.

'Keep your head down' is not a popular therapeutic aphorism, but perhaps it should be. Psychotherapy is not merely for the 'worried well.' This intensive practice exists for those clients for whom the life-shoring-up of counseling proves ineffectual. Though the romance of incisive insight and rich dream interpretation may lure both therapist and client, these tools can be dangerous seductions when the work is in an infernal phase. The experienced practitioner must, like Virgil, nudge, chastise, and sometimes outright challenge a patient who threatens to become frozen in self-justifying delusions. 'What does it all mean?' must wait for later. In hell, keeping one's head down and continuing the journey, the work, one step at a time, is the purpose. That is until the journey comes to that dizzying moment where a sudden, all-encompassing realization recasts the whole labor—that turn on the devil's hip. The verbal declaration will likely come far after the hermeneutic shift that enables the patient to see differently, take up the alterity of the other in the room—the therapist—more authentically, and come to know in new ways.

Keeping one's head down is far more of a common motto in the ranks of researchers. Gather the data, let the subjects speak, but keep moving. The possibility of becoming seduced into one subject's story is great but could misdirect the whole process. Only after completing the first great arc of the research work can one truly begin to guess what one has. The researcher, guided by the engaged mentor, ought to note his or her experiences and keep moving. In the infernal phase, to become lost in the reflexivity could pull one into the infinite regression of postmodernity's Petrarchan lyric nihilistic swoon.

The Gates of Purgatory

Once the reader becomes familiar with the rhythms of the *Commedia*, startling parallels emerge between the structure of Hell and that of Purgatory. This

Thomistic resonance offers another layer of commentary on the sorts of shifts and transformation necessitated by these landscapes.

Ante-Purgatory

The shores, plains, and foothills of Purgatory—so-called 'Ante-Purgatory'—turn out to be a lovely land. A large ascending swath of coast and Piedmont surround the official walls of formal Purgatory. Erudite and articulate people mill about. Singing abounds. Angels pass by. Here are those who could not, in life, commit in time to the intentional labors of rectifying their vices into virtues.

Perhaps the clearest therapeutic parallel to this benign region is that one ought not to enter therapy unless one absolutely must. Engaging in therapy out of curiosity, because it could be 'good for me,' or because someone said one should? These motivations will not carry the day. In addition to a simple stasis, several therapeutic contingencies might emerge in this ante-purgatorial territory. 'Therapy as toilet' is an expression to describe the client who comes to treatment, dumps all of his or her worries, stress, and problems, and leaves the session feeling remarkably better—week after week. The client is typically enamored of treatment; the dumped-upon therapist is typically not. This not-so-therapeutic pattern does not motivate the client to change; the client is far less burdened by what would otherwise be motivating problems. Another potential contingency is 'flight into heaven.' Here, the client distantly intuits that to go any deeper into the process will yield painful and possibly life-disrupting material. Thus, clients, after what they consider an appropriate amount of time on the couch, report being much better, and terminate treatment—with an unconscious sigh of relief. ('Flight into heaven' takes its name as a play on the more common 'flight into hell' where the client who has been outwardly nominally functioning comes to therapy and suddenly falls into an unexpectedly severe clinical decompensation, possibly necessitating hospitalization. Flight into hell, as the name implies, likely signifies a sudden acknowledgment of just how dark the woods have become and belongs much more to the infernal stage of the journey.) In any of these ante-purgatorial contingencies, the client maintains a basically functional life; but, perhaps for the sake of a relationship, a family configuration, financial obligations, or civic or employment demands, this person will mount elaborate defenses against altering what is, ostensibly, a functional life.

Ample testament to ante-purgatorial research can be found in the logorrhea abounding in 'scholarly journals.' The realities of 'publish or perish' within the academy create a system where a steady flow of publications, often in the format of a peer-reviewed journal article, are necessary for any career advancement. Are all of these works representative of life-altering moments of insight for the author? It seems scarcely possible. In reality, academics who are well-mentored for career advancement within the demands of a research and teaching appointment learn to collaborate with colleagues to produce a steady stream of conference presentations and papers. As much as this system may not encourage risk-taking, nor the unpredictability of personal engagement and growth, it does create the scholarship that gradually moves many academic disciplines forward.

Nevertheless, Ante-Purgatory holds up an uncomfortable mirror. Readers may find it easy to blame the inhabitants of Hell; but in Ante-Purgatory, readers witness how most of us spend most of our time. Thus, any indictment of these denizens is an impeachment of what 'stability' looks like in most relationships, cultures, and professions.

One could imagine that Dante has given a pleasant afterlife to those who were not gripped in the perversions and betrayals of Hell's sins but merely could not yet temper their desires. Yet what disrupts what could otherwise be an agreeable if not ecstatic here-after is the abiding desire for transformation. The achievement of the shores of Purgatory appears to demand a yearning for growth at the heart of an individual, something the denizens of hell cannot extricate from their crippling self-pity, self-justification, and perversion.

One might be forgiven for recalling the psychotherapist's joke, 'How many psychotherapists does it take to change a lightbulb?' The answer: 'One. But the lightbulb has to want to change.' If the patient is to move beyond the benign stasis of Ante-Purgatory, the work is going to become personal, intentional, and intensive. This shift is not because someone has foisted it upon the client, but because the client feels a deep call to these labors. At this stage, a mere solution-focused counseling 'fix' may actually exacerbate some symptom because this is a territory of deep symbolism and metaphor. Here, the symptom is a communication and a call. Any attempt to patch it over will lead to dissatisfaction at best.

In Purgatory, the role of the psychotherapist and research mentor will become more of a companion than a guide. Virgil, after all, has his afterlife in Limbo in the First Circle of Hell. Similar to Ante-Purgatory, Limbo is not horrific. It contains many virtuous pagans. It is a land of honorable ancient poets, scientists, philosophers, politicians, and military leaders. The landscape includes a vast, well-structured castle and is scarcely hellish. If one is to interpret Dante's Christian commentary metaphorically, then these individuals in Limbo, although stalwart and brilliant, were not driven by something adequately greater to extricate them from this rational territory. Once Dante takes on the toils of Purgatory, Virgil's role will be to reflect and witness. Virgil cannot draw upon his own experience except to ask questions and make observations. The structure of the process must carry the work. At the peak of the Mountain of Purgatory, Virgil will eventually make way for another—Beatrice: an other, *the* Other.

Researchers may find their studies awaken something deeper than curiosity. The research may even begin working them over. But without the necessary framework to support this process, their own transformation may become sidetracked or neglected. Although the interested reader is more likely to find commentary on reflexivity and researcher growth in texts on qualitative methods, mixed and purely quantitative methods do not necessarily defend the researcher against the vagaries of intentional subjectivity. To engage in any investigation into life is to invite life to transform. In Purgatory, reflexivity—taken up aright—can be trusted to drive the work.

Although Dante may faint in hell, he sleeps and dreams in *Purgatory*. Once he is within the walls of Purgatory itself, he will have waking visions. At one point, even the trees will seemingly speak. Souls only physically move and undertake Purgatory's labors during the day. But other tasks are apparently at work during the night. One can assume that, like Dante, these other penitent souls dream at night. Dante's first dream—always significant in psychotherapy—is of an eagle that carries him to the realm of fire. Startled awake by the scorching flames, Dante discovers he has been taken the rest of the way across Ante-Purgatory to the Gates of Purgatory. Dante informs us that dreams can have the power of prophecy now since this is a time when the flesh and earthly logic no longer weigh so heavily, "and when the mind, escaped from its submission/ to flesh and to the chains of waking thought,/ becomes almost prophetic in its vision" (Alighieri, 1320/2003, *Purgatory* Canto IX:16–18, Ciardi translation).

Hell was a landscape of brutal literality—a stuckness in the entrapping 'seeming.' The symptoms of hell cannot be interpreted away. A therapist might view a client's infernal dreams diagnostically but would scarcely invite 'dreamwork.' Purgatory, however, is a place of rich interconnected meanings—it is a place of meaning-making and, as such, invites, demands one engage in the work of dreams, visions, and the mythopoetic imagination. Dante abandoned rationality at the Gates of Dis. At the Gates of Purgatory, he can relinquish literalism and open himself to the mythopoetic imagination. At the top of the Mountain of Purgatory, Dante will pass through the great curtain of fire as he purges the vice of lust, transforming into love. This first therapeutic dream predicts the course of treatment. The process will bend to the gravity of love divine.

Researchers at this stage must now not only note their reactions but interrogate them. Observing one's shifting subjectivity becomes an exercise in the fullest sort of phenomenology. Not only does the qualitative researcher investigate the experience of the subjects—the subjectivity of the subjects—the engaged researcher gives voice to the experience of exploring this phenomenon. Investigators have fed themselves on a steady diet of the literature of the field. Conversations with colleagues challenge and deepen one's engagement and understanding. In qualitative work, researchers then obtain the primary data: the experience of the subjects. How can the researcher's lived world not come to be an essential source of evidence in the investigation?

This interrogation of the researcher's experience parallels the use of transference and countertransference in the clinical setting. The fantasies, dreams, and unvoiced tones of the therapeutic encounter become available not just for diagnostic purposes, but as primary means of advancing the therapeutic process. However, at this point, the containment must be absolutely hermetic in its integrity. The possibility of 'acting out'—falling into the literalizations of hell—is great. Thus, Dante and Virgil reach the Gates of a rigorously, liturgically structured Purgatory, its terraces full of rules, patterns, and rhythms—capable of containing these vital processes.

The Three Steps

As Dante approaches the gates, a seated angel bearing a sword greets and challenges the pilgrims. Dante sees three steps that presage the structure of the labors of Purgatory.

> We came to the first step: white marble gleaming
> so polished and so smooth that in its mirror
> I saw my true reflection past all seeming
>
> The second was stained darker than blue-black
> and of a rough-grained and fire flaked stone,
> its length and breadth crisscrossed by many a crack
>
> The third and topmost was of porphyry,
> or so it seemed, but of a red as flaming
> as blood that spurts out of an artery. (Alighieri, 1320/2003, *Purgatorio* IX:94–102, Ciardi translation)

By walking up these steps, Dante accepts these forthcoming labors by accepting the structure of the work. The steps can, among other symbolisms, be seen as an organization of the seven vices whose purgation the seven terraces promise.

Many patients and researchers know something of the territory they are entering. Perhaps they have even read accounts of others who have undergone the process. Openly declaring that one undertakes this process intentionally, however, bears a distinctly initiatory quality.

The first step is white and highly reflective. The mirror-like quality of the first step and Dante's observation of how he is reflected as he has never been before speaks to pride, envy, and wrath—the first three terraces of Purgatory. These vices involve a denial of one's faults and mask one's fundamental vulnerability. They are love directed to the wrong object, as Chang points out elsewhere in this volume: for self instead of the Other. They also involve an aggressive defense *against* reflection and the reintrojection of one's projections. The vulnerable narcissistic personality structure seems apt for these levels. The lived world of this configuration is one out of balance. Natural human brokenness is intolerable and is covered over with vainglorious inflation, acid resentment for the seemingly better—and unearned—fate of others, or annihilating rage at any encounter that reaches one's narcissistic wound. The reality of the other, their fundamental primacy in Levinas's formulation, is intolerable.

Few if any therapists think of the seven deadly sins in any clinical fashion. Yet any therapist who has worked with the personality disorders will recognize these patterns. Therapy cannot be advice-giving at this level. The process must involve intensive reflection—the ongoing course of handing back to clients what they could not or refuse to hold. It is also a deep process of the therapist witnessing and surviving what the patient finds intolerable. The therapist maintains a space where the seemingly unbearable can emerge; yet the space, the therapist, and the client survive. The unthinkable, the unspeakable, and, eventually, the ineffable can sit just beyond the therapeutic space for as long as necessary until the space is clear enough for their acknowledgment. The therapist will gradually reflect back to the client what the client could not previously hold, thus enabling the reintrojection of these elements.

In the reflexivity of research, certain reactions may be more welcome than others. A researcher will empathize with a subject's plight or feel rage at an injustice. Perhaps the mentor has created a space where the researcher can even feel anger at a subject's hateful actions and interrogate those feelings. Moreover, even the least reflexive programs often undermine the researcher's pride. But it is a very unusual program that allows the researcher to delve into the complex territory of resentment at a subject's victimization or envy of a subject's seemingly conscienceless violence. If there is not space for these complications, where will those issues next surface?

The next step is an eerie black, and its cracks seem to form a cross. This step can represent the turning point of Purgatory: popularly translated as 'sloth.' Perhaps notably, '*acedia*' is a term reserved for the study of the classics or theology. The temptation to turn sloth into mere depression is strong in a world in which oversimplified psychiatric language offers strange comfort. But Dante means here a listless failure to act on those highest impulses that, in his cosmology, drive us all. This is the anxious uncertainty that despairs, paralyzed by indecision.

A wide swath of clinical literature now acknowledges that various types of anxious depression—both syndromal and sub-syndromal—trouble far more people than was ever acknowledged throughout the twentieth century. Ours is an era of abject busy-ness, endless distractions, and a conspicuous avoidance of acknowledging the relevance of the big questions to daily life—no matter how many TED Talks one views, or how many podcasts on mindfulness one listens to as one 'gets in one's steps,' all carefully tracked for one with technology on one's wrist. Today, one can be quite active in one's acedia.

One of the great insights from the world of counseling and, particularly, cognitive behavioral therapy (CBT), is that clients are only in treatment for, at most, 45–50 minutes per week. For most clients, their activity in the remaining 125 waking hours of the week is what makes the difference in effecting change. CBT professionals assign their clients registers with scaled scores of symptom severity, journaling, relaxation exercises, and other homework assignments to make each day an opportunity for improvement. Apps for smartphones are becoming increasingly common as part of this battery of tools.

As stated previously, these solution-focused approaches will prove effective for many, if not most, clients. These tools are perfectly consonant with a culture focused on efficiency, efficacy, and improvement as modeled in corporate environments. Counselors utilizing CBT rarely ask their clients to examine dark territory and unfamiliar landscapes. They may invite clients to address their lived values, but only inasmuch as these ethics conflict with clients' treatment goals.

The disregard of what truly matters marks acedia; and a fervent pursuit of rational, socially-sanctioned goals can easily aid in this neglect. For those clients for whom short-term, solution-focused treatment proves ineffectual, the strange work of depth psychotherapy offers them a different type of vocation. This work may involve dream journaling, meditation, long walks, and consideration of both what attracts and repulses them. At times, this work may look like play, recreation, or self-care—activities that a CBT professional could easily endorse, but only as part of a treatment plan focused on very specific goals. Depth work may also include sitting with profound ambivalence and distress. Throughout treatment, the depth psychotherapist assures the patient that these states and the often disturbing dreams that accompany them are psyche doing its work—work that may have been neglected for a very long time.

Acedia, too easily labeled sloth, is neither about clinical depression nor laziness. At its heart, it is about a vice so ubiquitous in today's world as to be invisible. It is the willful neglecting of the work of soul- and meaning-making, neglecting the depths of our lives and of the world.

In research, the pressure to produce can be crushing. Qualitative researchers may find it far easier to address their subjective reactions to the material than to the process of research itself. Boredom, mental blocks, paralyzing anxiety, and other impasses, however, can be interrogated and interpreted once one reaches the purgatorial levels. Although it may be important to do *something* each working day on one's study, for some stretches, this something may be disappointingly little. Nevertheless, if one has purposefully engaged in the deep work of intentionality, one must grant these moments a respectful space. The soul-work of trusting greater processes to unfold is far from acedia. At these times, working in the garden, long walks, conversations with our hearts' friends, and other activities may prove crucial to advancing the Work.

Finally, the red step represents the vices of love-misdirected and, thus, restrained: greed, gluttony, and lust. In Dante's Thomistic theology, the entirety of Purgatory is driven by and about the liberation of Love. In the post-Darwinian and post-Freudian world, the idea that divine love is at the heart of all human motivation seems painfully naïve. The best one can hope for would seem to be 'enlightened self-interest.' The likes of Richard Dawkins mathematically explain away altruism as merely guaranteeing closer copies of one's own genes. Freudian phalli and mandorlas abound in the most mystical of imagery and offer proof that all of life is simply a sublimation of libido.

For the phenomenologist, the essential reframing occurs when one acknowledges that Freud and Dawkins—and everyone else—are themselves engaged in the process of meaning-making. Regardless of what meaning they make, they always already take up their lived worlds—even if it is to say that it is meaningless. Aided by the epoché, this realization is that the human kind of being is fundamentally phenomenological, not material. In the stronger forms of phenomenology, materialism is subordinate to the meaning-making that can yield a materialist epistemology—which subsequently structures the phenomenologies of so many people. That we all make meaning outflanks all the glib foreclosures of the post-Darwinian and post-Freudian worldview.

Nevertheless, this phenomenological epiphany is not enough to bring one to the fundamental gravity of love. The phenomenological realization is necessary but not adequate to take the next turn toward the primacy of alterity. Franke's 2007 essay bridging Dante and Levinas stands firmly in this new way-of-being. Purgatory is the necessary transformation from the literality of hell into the phenomenological and, thus, mythopoetic imagination that can become available to its incalculable debt to the Other. This is the Other to whom the most authentic orientation is wonder, awe, and love. This is also the Other against whom, for far too many, their lives, cultures, and relationships are a monumental defense.

In a sense, this ideology profoundly resonates with twentieth-century humanism. Carl Rogers's (1902–1987) therapeutic 'unconditional positive regard' is the very *agapé* of which he learned in seminary. His faith that this type of love can liberate people into growth and to express further this same type of love is the core of his theory of psychotherapy. This deceptively simple humanism rapidly gives way to a transhumanism.

Most therapists who may mobilize Rogers's 'unconditional positive regard' are, nonetheless, loathe to discuss their use of 'love' in psychotherapy. The reluctance to address love directly is understandable. Love becomes too easily countertransferential and threatens to exacerbate transferences from the patient. The potential for 'acting out' would seem to only be heightened by even allowing love to be discussed, let alone becoming a central focus of treatment. As understandable as this verbal dodge may be, some central questions may put the lie to this avoidance. What drives the psychotherapist? What does the patient truly seek? Why is relationality the central means of treatment in this therapeutic setting?

Most patients—that is to say, most people—wrestle with what love means and how to love—which entails, of course, how to be loved. Questions of sexuality, intimacy, gender, acceptance, embodiment, and a host of other issues can carry the question for the entire course of treatment. But are any one of these topics the fullness of love? Does a drive to have love burst its parochial sequestration not drive Dante and the Christianity to which he speaks? Although it will only be within the expanding circles of Paradise that Dante will transcend any definitions, Purgatory is the process to prepare for such apotheosis.

Patients can learn to love more fully. Patients may also learn to give selflessly. For instance, volunteering has been a critical component of recovery and treatment for many. For some patients, liberating love may at first seem like disillusionment. Love may not be able to save them from pain. It may not give them the acceptance they cannot give themselves. The reintrojection of projections within the first three terraces of Purgatory speaks to this necessity. Love, in its biggest sense, also demands an acknowledgment and commitment. Overcoming acedia in the fourth terrace can lead to letting go of the false and temporary loves that keep one busy, but uncommitted. In these final three terraces, love comes to the forefront. Greed, gluttony, and lust all may contain the call to a fuller and more mature love; but unto themselves, they are, for Dante, a misdirection and a foreshortening. The dissatisfaction felt by those trapped in these vices typically and sadly leads to a further investment in them to greater extremes—a doubling down on a failed investment. But, if properly redirected, Dante promises that these vices can yield to something magnificent and world-transforming.

Love in the domain of research is even less well discussed in the literature. Falling in love with a subject would seem to be even more of a misunderstanding of the nature of the work. Yet, why would one take on qualitative work if not a love for the humanity of the subject as opposed to their quantitative parameters. Action research that seeks to effect change while gathering data speaks to a love that drives the work. Social justice and transformation drive so many researchers, but to admit that love drives these undertakings seems a rare event. Perhaps the academy's culture struggles with the confined definitions of love and reserves nobility for less troublesome words, such as 'compassion.'

The key with Dante is that love is transformative. To engage with it is to invite it to pull one along a cosmic journey. Rather than the occasional pity he expressed in hell, Dante experiences a loving compassion for those he encounters in *Purgatory*. Although much remains to be said, this section on the three steps can conclude with a brief summary: The three steps, and thus the entirety of the terraces of Purgatory, could be glossed as 'reflect and withdrawal one's projections,' 'invest in and trust the process,' and 'learn to love more fully.'

Dante Takes on the Responsibility for the Process and, Thus, Avoids the Seduction of Mere Allegory

Because Purgatory is a place of such rich references, initiatory experiences, and transformation, a danger exists, perhaps most strongly for depth psychologists, to fall into the excessive symbolism. If the patient's imagery becomes a mere invitation to apply some Jungian secret decoder ring, then the vital experience can become easily lost. This cipher-like approach to Dante shows up most strongly in the Singletonian camp, where the *Commedia* is a cryptograph for elements of Christian theology.

Even if psychotherapy dwells with the imagery, the images do not merely represent something else. The images bring with them embodiment, relationality, select memories, teloi, and many other elements of a lived world. As a, perhaps neglected, psyche finally finds a space for its voice, the torrent of imagery can easily overwhelm both parties in the consulting room. Again, a containing structure becomes essential. Jung and his successors discuss many of these struggles in the literature on active imagination. In all cases, the hard work is to keep the imagery vital.

A flood of data can quickly make the qualitative researcher long for quantitative methods. Moreover, anxiety may emerge as one attempts to cast a new light on, for instance, shifts in tone, fine nuances of changing subjectivity, or striking syntactical breaks in subjects' narratives. This discomfort can motivate a researcher to apply a kind of jargon-filled coding to the subjects' descriptions. These postmodern-neologistic results can quickly homogenize what has been unique to each subject. In research, one way to avoid the foreclosure caused by interpretive certainty is to conclude with new questions. Often a perfunctory addition at the end of an article, genuine further questions can engage in a rhizomic process where new questions initiate new investigations that come to new questions and so forth. Research that attempts to answer more than it asks will participate in a dangerous appropriation of Truth. As Dante and Augustine express, longing for this Truth ought to drive the process, but Truth will never be the outcome in this world.

Although Dante engages in florid symbolism, the poetry always outpaces the allegory. True to his proto-phenomenology, Dante achieves this by taking on the process itself, rather than sitting in a dispassionate recounting. As several commentators note, even in his recounting, the power of the experience still moves Dante. As Dante comes to the Gate of Purgatory, he does not knock on the door. Rather, he approaches the angel, "Devoutly prostrate at his holy feet,/ I begged in mercy's name to be let in,/ but first three times upon my breast I beat" (Alighieri, 1320/2003, *Purgatorio* IX:109–111, Ciardi translation). Dante enacts the traditional gesture during the 'mea culpa, mea culpa, mea máxima culpa' [through my fault, through my fault, through my most grievous fault] of the Penitential Act of the Mass. Thus, Dante ritually renounces the equivocations and defensive dodges of hell, clearing the ethical way for the angel to carve the letter 'P' onto Dante's forehead seven times, instructing him, "Once entered here, be sure you cleanse away these wounds" (Alighieri, 1320/1981, 113–114, Musa translation). These are the seven *peccata*—'sins'—that the labors of the seven terraces of Purgatory will wash away.

To complete the tone of this liminal gate, the angel holds up two keys to unlock the door. One is gold; the other is silver. The angel applies the silver key first and then the gold. The angel explains,

> "Whenever either one of these two keys
> fails to turn properly inside the lock,"
> the angel said, "the road ahead stays closed.
>
> One is more precious, but the other needs
> wisdom and skill before it will unlock,
> for it is that one which unties the knot.
>
> I hold these keys from Peter, who advised:
> 'Admit too many, rather than too few,
> if they but cast themselves before your feet'." (Alighieri, 1321/1981, *Purgatorio* IX:121–129, Musa translation)

The symbolism of the keys goes to the 'Office of the Keys' relating to the forgiveness of sins. But Dante does not fall into a derivative meaning of the keys to Heaven and Hell. The angel explains that the precious gold one turns easily, but the silver, not so much. At the risk of drifting into a Singletonian Christian symbolist essay, the gold can be seen as solar and, thus, God's Grace; but the silver, lunar, key is psyche. This is soul's work. All of this symbolism still points back to the experience Dante seeks to convey. These are personal and intimate encounters. Just as Dante had to abandon, in abject terror, his rationality in order for the Gates of Dis to be opened by the intervening angel, he must also make a major transition away from his Infernal inventory to a deep personal investment in his transformation through labor with this angel at the Gates of Purgatory.

What could only be known to be true in retrospect about hell is now an intentional 'taking up' in Purgatory. The 'getting through' that carried much of the infernal journey, now must become an intensely personal opening up and owning up. When Dante knocks on his chest, rather than the Gates of Purgatory, he is asking the silver key to open his heart and soul. Although the natural sciences' Gentle Lady once seduced him, Dante knows that no study is purely objective nor subjective—the truth transcends those terms into the objective truth of subjective experience. Only now can Dante live into this truth. In Purgatory, the rationality abandoned at the Gates of Dis returns transformed. The Gates of Hell, Dis, and Purgatory each demand an abandonment of previous assumptions and habitual paradigms. At Hell's Gates, Dante had to let go of his expectations and abandon the strategies that brought him to that dire place. At Dis, Dante realized the profound and nihilistic limits of rationalism. At Purgatory's gates, the transformation is far more intimate. The logic of these gates is not self-justification, defensiveness, or self-deception. This purgatorial rationality renders explanations of how the world works physically, psychologically, and ethically in concert. The logic is now consonant with life and is life-affirming. If Heidegger must remind readers that *dasein* is always my *dasein*, then Dante must realize that this is Dante's Purgatory and not merely a wonder-filled cosmological vision. This will become clearer as Dante personally undertakes the purgations in this self-chosen penitentiary. The shift is not the Dis gate's abandonment of the vanity of reason uninspired by Grace. In this case, it is a shift toward one's own existential responsibility. Meaning-making—that is, the phenomenon—is always *my* meaning-making for which I am, typically unwittingly, responsible. Purgatory offers its residents an opportunity to take up this responsibility authentically.

Teaching the idea of existential responsibility to students of any level can be challenging. The idea that each person is responsible for their life can quickly twist into blaming the victim, jingoistic bootstrappism, or a host of other inauthentic stances. 'Responsibility' carries copious baggage, and the word may not really convey the existential meaning intended without extensive explanation. Furthermore, existential responsibility requires even more clarification if it is to be utilized in a Christian context, with contentious and central doctrinal issues such as grace, predestination, total depravity, free will, and salvation unavoidably emerging.

As psychotherapy enters a more purgatorial phase, it frequently must wrestle with existential responsibility. Patients who have struggled with a history of trauma may be able to get past the worst of the crippling symptoms but will subsequently face the challenge of how to move on with their lives. Many therapists find themselves uttering a statement akin to, 'What happened to you was not your fault; and what you do now is your choice.' No amount of therapy can change the reality of a traumatic event, although it may create a space to change the meaning. Trauma and its aftermath can leave patients feeling out of control. Can patients learn to take back whatever agency is real? This is part of the process of also taking responsibility for the choices one has made and makes. As the 12 Steps explain, real change involves a real inventory of the effects of one's choices—neither guilt-wallowing nor blithe disavowal. Dante provides a powerful illustration that this process must be intentional and ongoing.

If research is to move beyond mere curiosity and safe discoveries—if it is to be transformative—then researchers will have to move beyond being retrospectively surprised at changes in themselves. Moving to a stage of the work where one interrogates one's own experience and turns to close colleagues and friends to have conversations about this process must be intentional. Here, the mentor cannot lead. The process, the container of the transformation, must provide the rigorous structure that allows the transformations to unfold.

Much more remains to be said about the ethical, hermeneutic, epistemological, and phenomenological shifts Dante experiences in his *Commedia* and how they may cast new light on the phenomenology of psychotherapy and reflexive research. To complete this section, the achievement of the summit of Mount Purgatory provides a potent description for the goal of these transformations. Dante passes through a great sheet of fire—a final purgation that allows the Love that drives this process to emerge unfettered by lust. Dante finds himself in the Earthly Paradise. This is the phenomena unburdened by Dante's infernal clutching or the distorting vices that Purgatory released. This paradise is the Garden of Eden. The entirety of history has collapsed as Dante returns to the garden. Dante sees Creation rather than some derivative 'world' of human making. He meets a woman, Matilda, who he perhaps knew in life. She gently guides him to witness a barrage of the highest of symbolism. All of this is, nevertheless, so that he may finally truly see Beatrice—the Other. Dante has encountered a beloved other, Matilda, in order that he may come to the Other, the Beloved, Beatrice. The Cantos in the Earthly Paradise repeatedly refer to vision, the eyes, and light. At first, Dante cannot truly look at Beatrice. He sees reflections of a griffon—a lion and eagle combined, and thus a symbol for Christ being both human and divine—in Beatrice's veiled eyes. Thus, this embodiment of the obligation to the Other, for the Christian, announces itself to him. But when she unveils herself to him, Dante must turn away at the brilliance and is briefly blinded.

As the entirety of the *Commedia*, perhaps ironically, illustrates: phenomena in their fullest exceed our expressive capacity. As Franke mentions at various points, phenomena are, however, that very drive of expression. Heidegger reminds us that phenomenology is this very language—*logos*—of appearing—*phaenomenon*. It may prove tempting to say that Dante was not present to the phenomena in *Inferno*, and gradually prepared himself for this revelation in *Purgatory*. That would demean the reality of the process. The Dark Woods, the Gates of Hell, the hellish suffering—all of these were the real phenomena as, wrapped up in his struggles, his changing hermeneutic stances, his expressive capacity, his epistemologies, Dante strove to give these realities voice. In the voicing, the phenomena shift. These phenomena have been intentional. They have, through his deepest and sincerest engagement with them, driven Dante to this new lived world. Is this a fuller phenomenon? For Dante, undoubtedly. But could Dante somehow have simply come to some heartfelt transformation halfway down the noxious slopes of Hell and suddenly seen the Earthly Paradise? Clearly not. The expression, the engaged mythopoesis, has driven Dante through the process to come to this blistering moment of clarity on the summit of Purgatory.

Beyond here, in Paradise, these therapeutic and investigative insights cannot go. Heaven is a place of overflowing, effulgent sublimities. *Paradiso* is a transpersonal, transhuman, and mystical poem. Franke offers the Levinasian 'ultraphenomenology' for this realm. Yet, even the claustrophobic terrors of *Inferno* were driven by this ultraphenomenology. Though the Presence Dante will encounter at the farthest reaches of Paradise was incomprehensibly inaccessible in Hell, its reality still drove the pilgrim. If psychotherapy and research can acknowledge that such transcendent powers drive the process, then a wholesale transformation of mental health treatment and scholarly investigation could occur.

A Provisional Conclusion

Dante is, through his poetics, striving to give the truest, most authentic voice to his experiences. He came to reject rigid formalities and developed, quite literally, a language to better give his journey voice. Rather than the pat aphorisms of philosophizing, Dante's poetics begin and end on the precipice of ineffability. Thus, Dante's poetic method is a phenomenology. Dante is also criticizing the detachments of asceticism, the self-annihilation of mysticism, and the confined rationalism of a purely natural scientific approach to the lived world. He is thus a progenitor of philosophical phenomenology. Furthermore, his approach transcends the division of human inquiry into disciplines. He was present at the inception of the Western European dismemberment of *philosophia* into discrete disciplines, yet ultimately offered another far more integrative and fulsome path. He is thus a paragon for those phenomenologists who cannot abide remaining confined within the artificial limits of the divorced disciplines. True to Augustine, Francis, and Aquinas, Dante also transcends the habitual divisions of spirit/matter and fundamental dichotomies of good—spirit—and evil—matter. His is a profoundly incarnational, lived spirituality in which the pull of sin is nothing less than divine passion misunderstood and poorly pursued. A phenomenological sensibility is, therefore, critical for the reader of Dante's works. Textual analyses that rest entirely on tradition or symbolism will yield a pedantic deadness. Readers must bring themselves in their fullness to the experience of the texts. Readers thus ought to approach Dante phenomenologically, both examining their own experience of reading and reflecting on how he calls them to interpret and voice their own experience. Dante's *Commedia* offers descriptions that are phenomenologies of the experiences of stuckness in *Inferno*, the labors of liberation in *Purgatorio*, and the sublime visions of transcendence in *Paradiso*. The clinical implications for diagnostic and process commentary are, arguably, epic. So too are the implications for the researcher willing to admit the entirely reflexive nature of all research. And, ultimately, one can place the provenance for phenomenology long before the twentieth century. Scholars can look to a line beginning with Augustine, through Francis and Aquinas, to Dante and eventually reaching to Brentano, Husserl, Heidegger, and Merleau-Ponty.

Readers too often remain stuck in trying to solve the epic medieval references crossword puzzle when approaching Dante. The rewards of resolute explorations of the Florentine's work may seem reserved for a pocket of arcane scholars. Nevertheless, Dante's writings trace a path of liberation, not doctrinaire certainties. Thus, this chapter and the entirety of this volume come with the sincere hope that it may help readers, scholars, and practitioners chart a course to where they may have new eyes to see, to use Dante's metaphor, the stars.

References

Alighieri, D. (1981). *Dante's purgatory* (M. Musa, Trans.). Indiana University Press. (Original work published 1320).

Alighieri, D. (1994). *Inferno* (R. Pinsky Trans). Farrar, Straus and Giroux. (Original work published 1320).

Alighieri, D. (2003). *The divine comedy* (J. Ciardi, Trans.). New York: New American Library. (Original work published 1320).

Barclay, W. (2002). *The new daily study Bible: The letter to the Romans*. Westminster John Knox Press.

De Monticelli, R. (2000). Dante's *Inferno*: Phenomenology of a strange passion. *Psychopathology, 33*(4), 182–191.

Franke, W. (1996). *Dante's interpretive journey*. University of Chicago Press.

Franke, W. (2007). The ethical vision of Dante's *Paradiso* in light of Levinas. *Comparative Literature, 59*(3), 209–227.

Harrison, R. P. (1988). *The body of Beatrice*. Johns Hopkins University Press.

Heidegger, M. (1947/1993). Letter on humanism. In D. F. Krell (Ed.), *Martin Heidegger: Basic writings: Nine key essays, plus the introduction to being and time* (pp. 213–265). Harper.

McLean, A. (2000, October 9). *ACADEMY: Dante, Lully, de Meung and alchemy*. [Online Discussion Group]. Retrieved from www.thealchemywebsite.com

Milbank, J., Pickstock, C., & Ward, G. (Eds.) (1999). *Radical orthodoxy: A new theology*. Routledge.

Monticelli, D. (2015). Fear in Dante's Inferno: Phenomenology, semiotics, aesthetics. In Z. G. Barański, A. Kablitz, & Ü. Ploom (Eds.), *I luoghi nostri: Dante's natural and cultural spaces* (pp. 106–128). Tallin University Press.

Punzi, E., & Hagen, N. (2017). The incorporation of literature into clinical practice. *The Humanistic Psychologist, 45*(1), 49–61.

Romanyshyn, R. D. (2019a). Diagnostic fictions. *Journal of Humanistic Psychology, 59*(1), 107–120.

Romanyshyn, R. D. (2019b). *Victor Frankenstein, the monster and the shadows of technology: The Frankenstein prophecies*. Routledge.

Shoaf, R. A. (1989). Medieval studies after Derrida after Heidegger. In J. N. Wasserman & L. Roney (Eds.), *Sign, sentence, discourse: language in medieval thought and literature*. (pp. 9–30). Syracuse University Press.

Wallenfang, D. (2017a). *Dialectical anatomy of the eucharist: An étude in phenomenology*. Cascade Books.

Wallenfang, D. (2017b). *Human and divine being: A study on the theological anthropology of Edith Stein*. Cascade Books.

Part II

Dante: Yesterday, Today, and Forever

Chapter 8

When Bici Said Come

When Bici came and tapped me on the shoulder, and said "come" in that imperious tone, she said I had no choice and neither did she.

Of course I worried I didn't know where I was going. I had never been out of the beatific garden of the comfortably damned. I am not the one to guide your besotten lover, I turned to tell her but she was gone.

The next day I hid myself from the warm trespasser. I knew he would be as smitten of me as he had been of Bici in the world they once shared. I needed to let him come to the recognition of who I was slowly so he would be all in. It would take time.

Everybody said that he was an ambitious copycat and oh so competitive. What I did on earth—he would do in heaven. Take the world from here to there. But that's not true. He picked me because he didn't want to be alone. He knew I would stick with him. He didn't realize, didn't count on the fact, that I would bail half way through.

I once had a dream that I was a figment of his imagination. That I wasn't real. That he had created me because he needed someone to hold the flashlight behind him to light his way to the next circle. Then I turned into a bird and flew to a tree and watched him go without noticing I was gone.

Sometimes I wonder if he thought perhaps I knew more than I really did. That I had been on this trip before as we made our way from circle to circle. Sometimes I wondered if I carried all the fear for him.

Bici always said get used to it V. He did the same shit to me on earth. Wherever he was he was writing stupid poems, mooning over my refusal to acknowledge him, and then mooning over my death. Really he was turnip of a boy in life and now he is a turnip of a pilgrim in the afterlife. Get used to it V. she told me. It's not you, it's him.

I left him right before things got good and before he even knew I was gone. I will go back to the Elysian Fields and he will look back at the blinding scene of earth and sky below him and only then realize I am gone.

Now I am where I started and ended with Homer and Statius and Lucian and Aristotle and Plato. All the dropped names. The frat boys sitting under the leafy tree drinking watered wine and talking talking talking and I talk with them but not about this. Not because they wouldn't believe me, but because they wouldn't care.

Hattie Myers

Chapter 9

Dante and the Medieval 'Other'[1]

Peter S. Hawkins

By the time Dante set quill to the *Commedia*'s parchment, probably around 1308, he was a Florentine exile whose only resources were the force of his convictions and his brilliance as a writer. Wandering from one place to another across central and northern Italy, he took in the whole of his world—took in the cosmos, in fact—and presented it as God might judge it in eternity.

His three-part afterlife tells the tale. In a mash-up of history that mixes the 'modern' world with the ancient, high culture with low, he gives the reader a brilliantly coherent vision of divine justice that cuts through the subterfuge of human lies and illusions. In his imagined Paradise, moreover, he repeatedly celebrates "l'uno e l'altro," the one and the other, "più e meno," more and less, with the Three Persons of the Trinity serving as the ultimate model of diversity in unity. Beyond this, Teodolinda Barolini (2006) has argued that the entire *Commedia* is an exemplar of medieval multiculturalism. She speaks convincingly of Dante's "extraordinary and purposeful eclecticism, the voracious syncretism with which he embraces and makes his own a veritable cornucopia of cultural traditions" (p. 103).

Since Dante's death in 1321, many of his rough places have been made plain through the slow process of veneration. The outsider Florentine exile with contested, even heterodox, theology has become Father of the Italian Nation, Defender of the Faith, the consummate Insider. Over the last hundred years, in particular, the papacy has embraced him as the archetype of orthodoxy, either forgiving or forgetting his withering diatribes against the popes and hierarchy of his time. In 1921, on the sixth centenary of the poet's death, Benedict XV—and apparently without irony—referred to "the intimate union of Dante with the see of Peter." At the conclusion of Vatican II, Paul VI acclaimed, "Dante is ours!" In 2006, Benedict XVI, in his first encyclical, *Deus Caritas Est*, credited Dante not only with teaching him about the meaning of love but with revealing a continuity between the pre-Christian world of Aristotle and Christian revelation. In this spirit of inclusivity, and in 2015, on the 750th anniversary of the poet's birth, Pope Francis recommended the *Commedia* as a spiritual guide for all Catholics, calling Dante "a prophet of hope, herald of the possibility of redemption, of liberation, of the profound transformation of every man and woman, of all humanity"

(Vatican Information Service, 2015, p. 1; Esteves, 2015, offers further discussion of Pope Francis's comments on Dante's standing in the eyes of the Holy See). Note the open embrace of *every* man and woman, of *all* humanity. Remember, too, Francis's impromptu aside to reporters on a July 2013 return flight to the Vatican from Brazil, "If a person is gay and seeks God and has good will, who am I to judge?" (Staff Reporter, *Catholic Herald*, 2013, p. 1).

"Who am I to judge?" This is not a question that Dante seems to have asked very often. Nor is it a customary question for those who embrace the poet as a bulwark against change, the paragon of values that are the same "yesterday, today, and forever" (*Hebrews* 13:8). Take, for example, the politicians who have expressed an affinity for him. Mussolini was an avid reader and declaimer of the poet. Allegedly, he started each day with a canto. *Il Duce* celebrated him as a fascist *avant la lettre*, planned a *Commedia* theater or Danteum for Rome, and in the first year of his regime, had a bust of the poet placed in every Italian embassy and legation as a symbol of the Mother Country (Bosworth, 2002). More recently, former Prime Minister Giulio Andreotti, long tarnished by charges of political corruption and dealings with the Mafia, invoked Dante in 2007 when rebuking his opponents in a debate over same-sex unions. Forgoing the familiar condemnations of homosexuality in Leviticus and St. Paul, Andreotti appealed instead to the native son whose poem may well have even more cachet than the Bible among his countrymen. Acceding to Dante's quasi-scriptural authority, he found in the *Inferno* the evidence needed to nail the argument against same-sex unions: "It would be a good thing... if everyone were to reread Dante: *i sodomiti nella 'Divina Commedia' finiscono all'inferno*," [the Sodomites in the *Divina Commedia* end up in hell] (see Calabrò, 2007 as cited in Barolini, 2011, p. 184).

Instead of positioning the poet as one inclined to "Just Say No," Teodolinda Barolini, whom I cited before on the matter of Dante's medieval multiculturalism, takes a different tack in a study whose title reveals her approach, "Dante's Sympathy for the Other" (2011). She argues that the "embrace of difference" that is evident in the metaphysical domain of the poem—what I have spoken of above as *Paradiso*'s emphasis on the one and the other, the more and the less, the Trinity's diversity in unity—is also paralleled in "Dante's many startling non-normative postures in the social and historical sphere" (p. 177). Contrasting the *Commedia* with standard medieval representations of the Other, she highlights Dante's atypical openness to those customarily impugned or even placed beyond the pale: the sexually suspect—women and homosexuals; non-Christians—Jews and Muslims; Ethiopians and Indians—contemporary pagans like "the man born on the banks of the Indus" (*Paradiso* XIX:70–71), and of course the estimable pagans of antiquity—those living at a temporal rather than a spatial distance from Christianity. To be sure, Barolini does not dismiss contrary evidence to inclusivity, of which there is fair share. The *Commedia* has 'triggers' that easily disturb those hoping for a confirmation of our present-day notions of diversity. The poem is upsetting to the tender hearted, often wildly censorious, and always challenging; it is an 'unprotected text,' as New Testament scholar Jennifer Knust (2012) has recently termed the Bible. Anyone who teaches the poem knows this to be the case.

Here I ask your indulgence as I draw upon my own experience in the classroom. At Boston University, I remember a Muslim fasting during Ramadan, who reported being sick when he encountered the Prophet and his son-in-law Ali disemboweling themselves in *Inferno* XXVIII. Another case in point: Coming fresh from their Holocaust studies lecture to my Dante class, two Jewish students were understandably offended to discover that the arch-hypocrites in *Inferno* XXIII, crucified on the floor of their *bolgia* and trampled upon for eternity, were none other than the New Testament Temple hierarchy who, like the students themselves, rejected Jesus as the Messiah. But that occasion for offense was nothing compared to their outrage when they later found that the deicide charge crops up not only in Hell (XXIII:122–123) but also in Purgatory (XXI:82–84) and Paradise (VI:92–93)—as if to ensure that no Jew who reads the poem should ever forget the reported cry of the Jerusalem crowd in Matthew 25:27, "His blood be on us and on our children!"

At Yale Divinity School, where students are overwhelmingly Christian, albeit of various kinds and degrees of fervor, it is the exclusion of the unbaptized from salvation—and Virgil in particular—that most regularly raises hackles. It is no comfort to them that virtuous pagans are given 'preferred seating' in Limbo, the first circle of hell, which—with its verdant flowery lawn and beautiful stream—corresponds to what Virgil in *Aeneid* 6 imagined the blissful Elysian Fields to be. It does not make anything better that the guardian of Purgatory is none other than Cato, a pagan anti-imperial suicide who, on so many counts, should not be among the redeemed at all. The last straw, however, is when they discover that the Trojan Ripheus, a very minor character in the *Aeneid*, should appear high in Paradise (XX) in the company of King David and other just rulers who came before as well as after Christ. The poet, in fact, stages the reader's shock at this point with an authorial aside: "Chi crederebbe?"—who would believe it? And yet there he is, Ripheus, shining brightly, redeemed by virtue of a special intervention of divine grace and through the inscrutable workings of predestination. Rather than rejoice in the rescue of the one lost sheep, however, students deplore the loss of the ninety-and-nine virtuous pagans who were not given special treatment. More to the point, none of these exceptions to the rule mitigate the loss of Virgil. How can *he* not be saved?

Student 'issues' regarding Dante's judgments have not been ignored by contemporary scholars. Along with Barolini (2011), there are others who have struggled to come to terms with the complexity of Dante's treatment of the medieval Other—treatment that is far subtler, more at odds with cultural norms, than may appear at first glance. On the matter of crusades, Islam, and "the man on the banks of the Indus," there is Brenda Schildgen (2002, pp. 66–91) in *Dante and the Orient*; on Dante and the Jews, there is both Rachel Jacoff (2004) and Jay Ruud (2013). Catherine Cox (2005) and Sylvia Tomasch (1988) are much less supportive of Dante as an exception to the anti-Semitic rule (see also, Ziolkowski's *Dante and Islam*, 2014; and Kleinhenz, 2015). No one argues that Dante is a poster child for our official embrace of difference, or that he is 'just like us.' Yet he is also surprisingly out of line with what Barolini (2011) calls the "stereotyping imagination" of the Middle Ages. If different from us, he is not entirely at one with his own world either.

True, Muslims are denounced as a "gente turpa," [base folk] (*Paradiso* XV:145) by Dante's great-great-grandfather, Cacciaguida—who died fighting them in the Second Crusade—just as contemporary popes are condemned for warring on fellow Christians rather than against the Infidel. Nonetheless, we find three eminent Muslims in Limbo—Averroes, Avicenna, and Saladin—among the esteemed poets and philosophers of antiquity.

It is irrefutable that the Jewish Temple hierarchy of Jesus's day, not to mention Judas, is all among the damned. On the other hand, no contemporary Jew appears anywhere in the poem, whereas an anti-Semite—or an ordinary medieval Christian—might easily have made them languish in a variety of hellish locations. The *Inferno*'s usurers, for instance, are all scions of Catholic banking families, not the "traitorous" Jews reviled by the Lateran Council (canon 67). It should be noted as well that ancient Hebrews fill the City of God along with those who, like John the Baptist and the Virgin Mary, bridge the Testaments. Eve and Mary are neighbors; the matriarch Rachel sits next to Beatrice in the celestial rose. Indeed, Hebrews occupy precisely *half* of the celestial rose.

Many Dante scholars, therefore, on the one hand, look for a balanced sense of what cultural norms the poet follows and, on the other hand, what norms he feels free to nuance, skirt, or challenge. That said, there can be no doubt that when Dante wrote the *Commedia*, he surely knew he would be stepping on toes, making his readers squirm. He clearly aimed to disturb the peace. And if people do not like it, as Cacciaguida says in *Paradiso* XVII:129, then "let them scratch where the itch is."

Dante's avatar within the narrative—the pilgrim—often does so. He meets sinners in hell who elicit strong identifications and reactions from him. Whenever he does, we are alerted to his vulnerabilities: There but for the grace of God goes he. But as is evident in my students' response to Dante's presentation of Muslims or Jews, readers react negatively not necessarily because they are brought under conviction of the truth but because they resent the imposition of alien judgments or find their own identity or values castigated from on high. They resent it when they find themselves, or someone they love, in hell.

So, too, in my case, does their teacher. Although there are a number of places where I personally find the poet's pointed finger too close for comfort, there is nothing for me quite like *Inferno* XV–XVI, the burning sand that recalls the biblical Cities of the Plain, where the poet impounds clergy, 'literati grandi,' and many right-thinking Florentine worthies on account of their sexual "violence against nature." This is the particular population Giulio Andreotti was thinking of when he reminded his countrymen that "*i sodomiti nella 'Divina Commedia' finiscono all'inferno.*" And yet, although forever on the move, their features burned almost beyond recognition, they nonetheless transcend their suffering. Indeed, they are far more gracious and appealing than anyone else in hell outside of Limbo. These are moreover, *my* people.

But who exactly are they? Before there was the present-day array of difference collected in the aggregate of LGBTQI, there were 'Sodomites.' The "sin against nature" could refer to a dazzling number of deviancies but most commonly was taken to mean men who had sex, especially intercourse, with men or boys. Some were married with children, like all the named Florentine figures Dante speaks to within this pocket of hell, others—the monks and clergy we hear about but never meet—were not.

It was thought that such unspeakably sinful behavior could be treated successfully. For instance, Thomas Aquinas's teacher, Albertus Magnus, recommended that "hairs from a hyena's neck, burnt into ashes and mixed with pitch and smeared on the anus of a sodomite who practices anal intercourse, will cure him of this vice" (as cited in Camille, 2001, p. 74). Those apprehended in the act could be killed, often by being castrated and burned alive; according to the *Fuero real*, a Spanish legal code of Dante's day, a Sodomite should be hanged by the legs until dead, with the corpse kept in public view as a warning about the fate of those straying from the sexual *vera via* (see Boswell, 1994; Peqigney, 1991; Holsinger, 1996; Cestaro, 2003; Camille, 2001; and Hawkins, 2004).

In some of the many visions of the afterlife that precede the *Commedia*, these legislated means of dispatch come off as humane: At least at death, their torment ended. The late twelfth-century Monk of Evesham reports that the most loathsome and severe of afterlife punishments are reserved for those guilty of that wickedness "unmentionable by a Christian, or even by a heathen or a pagan." Huge fiery monsters relentlessly sodomize the Sodomites: "Their cries were horrid until they apparently fainted dead, and then were revived to be exposed to fresh torments" (as discussed in Gardiner, 1989, p. 210). The visual arts bear a similar witness. A figure labeled 'Sodomitto' in Giotto's Last Judgment fresco in Padua's Scrovegni Chapel is "skewered from mouth to rear by a pole" (as cited by Barolini, 2011, p. 183).

What we find in *Inferno* XV and XVI stands in vivid contrast to these horrific scenarios. Neither their constant motion, the continuous rain of brimstone, nor the "wounds that the flames seared in" (*Inferno* XVI:10–11) compromise the courtesy and *gentilezza* of Dante's encounters with the Sodomites (see Hollander, 1996). Unlike the majority of the self-preoccupied damned, these figures are openly, genuinely interested in Dante; they also share the condemnations of present-day Florentine turpitude that are later voiced by the blessed in heaven. There is an abundance of mutual affection and respect, which Virgil actively encourages rather than reproves, as he does elsewhere when the pilgrim is too 'involved' with those he meets. Yes, Dante's beloved former mentor, Brunetto Latini, talks about fortune rather than grace; he is remembered by the pilgrim for having taught him how a man can make himself eternal through secular achievement—genius, glory, fame, honor—rather than receiving the eternal gift of life from God. But what does any of this have to do with sodomy? And if, as Giulio Andreotti reminds us, "the Sodomites end up in hell," why is their reason for being there—which Latini speaks of as the stain of "one same sin upon the earth" ("un peccato medesmo al mondo lerci," XV:108)—why is it completely buried within high-minded conversation about politics and literature? Why is the *Inferno*'s condemnation so oblique?

And, to keep the questions coming, why does Dante not, in fact, leave the Sodomites in hell and simply have done with them? Because he does not, *pace* Andreotti, make that predictable choice. Instead, the poet arranges for at least some Sodomites to have a second coming in the *Commedia*. Rather than running in perpetual circles, "lamenting their eternal sorrows" ("piangendo i suoi etterni danni," *Inferno* XV:42), this group actually gets somewhere: They are all on their way to heaven.

We find them on Mount Purgatory's terrace of lust—just outside the Garden of Eden, in the realm of the seventh and least pernicious of the 'deadly sins.' Within a wall of fire, on a "burning road" ("cammino accesso," *Purgatorio* XXVI:28), Dante sees two distinct groups rushing toward each other. "There on both sides I see each soul make haste, and each one kiss another, without stopping, contented with brief welcomes" (31–33). Who are they? According to Dante's interlocutor, the love poet Guido Guinizelli, one group of penitents offended in the manner of Julius Caesar, whose sexual submission to the conquered king of Bythnia caused his Roman soldiers to greet him with the salutation "Regina" [Queen] (78). Guinizelli says that these souls reprove themselves in the fire: "they help the burning with their shame." But as they do so, they join the other group of carnal sinners who equally stoke opprobrium upon themselves by recalling Pasiphae, "who made herself a beast" (87) through heterosexual lust. Guinizelli identifies himself as belonging to this latter group who, in their compulsive drive toward the opposite sex, warrant the term "ermafrudito" (82).

Astonishingly, in *Purgatorio* XXVI, Sodomites it would seem make up *half* of Purgatory's lustful penitents. (Who knew?) In apparently equal number to their heterosexual counterparts, they gradually move their way to God through the refining fires of chastity, with Eden's earthly paradise already on the horizon and heaven "further up and higher in." Moving clockwise and counterclockwise, the two sexual 'orientations'—the normative 'one' and the marginalized 'other'—are presented as equivalent. It is impossible to say which is worse, the succinct cry of the "Queens"—"Sodom and Gomorrah"—or the hermaphrodites' more detailed "That the bull may hurry toward her lust, Pasiphae hides in the cow" (40–42). Nor does the poet show interest in exploring how each group is "unnatural," whether man with man or man with woman. Instead, the emphasis is on the purgation of excess, on the proper ordering of Eros. What matters is that lust becomes love.

It is impossible to know exactly what Dante intended by reversing the categorical condemnation of *Inferno*. Those Sodomites damned in hell—those clerics, mentors, *literati*, civic leaders—were they all unrepentantly guilty of coercing the young and therefore of perpetuating violence against the vulnerable youth in their charge? (Had the youthful Dante in some way been suborned by Brunetto Latini? If so, why is he so surprised to find him *here*, and why is he so full of veneration?) Are the Sodomites in Purgatory there because they repented their homosexual ways before their death? (Probably not, unless the "hermaphrodites" running past them also repented their heterosexuality.) Did the poet change his mind about homosexuals between writing the first canticle and the second, somehow convinced that Sodomites can enter the kingdom of heaven like their heterosexual counterparts as long as they become good, loving, God-oriented lovers?

This latter possibility seems far-fetched for the fourteenth century, and even a stretch for the twenty-first, as we see in the on-going controversy over homosexual legitimacy that continues to roil churches and, even after the Supreme Court's decision on gay marriage, disturb many a legislator and county clerk. Not to mention what we find presently in Russia, Poland, Hungary, and Brazil from clerics as well as politicians.

Nonetheless, the surprise factor of Dante's poem is such that "who would believe it?" is often the most appropriate response. Although the *Commedia* may not provide the altogether "safe, positive, and nurturing environment" that some would like liberal arts education to be all about (e.g., http://www.qcc.cuny.edu/diversity/definition.html), what it has to offer is much more valuable: an unsettling world of contradictory judgments, in which complexity militates against resolution and some issues remain open-ended. The poem may be a massive monument to the One—but not at the expense of the Other.

Note

1 An earlier version of this work appeared in *Medieval Perspectives*, Journal of the South Eastern Medieval Association, ed. Daniel O'Sullivan, 2017.

References

Barolini, T. (2006). *Dante and the origins of Italian literary culture*. Fordham University Press.

Barolini, T. (2011). Dante's sympathy for the other, or the non-stereotyping imagination: Sexual and racialized others in the *Commedia*. *Critica del testo*, *XIV*/1, 177–206.

Boswell, J. (1994). Dante and the sodomites. *Dante Studies*, *112*, 63–75.

Bosworth, R. J. B. (2002). *Mussolini*. Bloomsbury.

Calabrò, A. (2007, February 14). *Andreotti: non posso dire sì a unione dello stesso sesso*. Corriere della Sera.

Camille, M. (2001). The pose of the Queer. Dante's Gaze, Brunetto Latini's body. In G. Burger & S. F. Kruger (Eds.), *Queering the middle ages* (pp. 57–86). University of Minnesota Press.

Cestaro, G. P. (2003). Queering nature, queering gender: Dante and Sodomy. In T. Barolini & H. Wayne Storey (Eds.), *Dante for the new millennium* (pp. 90–103). Fordham University Press.

Cox, C. S. (2005). *The Judaic other in Dante, the Gawain poet, and Chaucer*. University Press of Florida.

Esteves, J. A. (2015, May 4). *Pope commemorates the 750th anniversary of Dante Alighieri's birth: Highlights union between famed Italian poet and the see of St. Peter*. Retrieved from http://www.zenit.org/en/articles/pope-commemorates-the-750th-anniversary-of-dante-alighieri-s-birth.

Gardiner, E. (Ed.) (1989). *Visions of Heaven and Hell before Dante*. Italica.

Hawkins, P. (2004). Tough love: Dante and the sodomites. *Yale Review, 92*(3), 55–67.

Hollander, R. (1996). Dante's harmonious homosexuals. *Electronic Bulletin of the Dante Society of America*. Retrieved from http://www.princeton.edu/~dante/ebdsa/index.html

Holsinger, B. (1996). Sodomy and resurrection: The homoerotic subject of the *Divine Comedy*. In L. Fradenburg & C. Freccero (Eds.), *Premodern sexualities* (pp. 243–274). Routledge.

Jacoff, R. (2004). *Dante and the Jewish question*. Bernardo Lecture Series, No. 13, Center for Medieval & Renaissance Studies. Sate University of New York, Binghamton.

Kleinhenz, C. (2015). *Dante Intertestuale e Interdisciplinare* (pp. 81–96). Aracne.

Knust, J. (2012). *Unprotected texts: The Bible's surprising contradictions about sex and desire*. HarperOne.

Peqigney, J. (1991). Sodomy in Dante's *Inferno* and *Purgatorio*. *Representations, 36*, 22–42.

Ruud, J. (2013). Dante and the Jews. In K. T. Utterback & M. Llewelyn Price (Eds.), *Jews in Medieval Christendom* (pp. 147–162). Brill.

Schildgen, B. D. (2002). *Dante and the orient*. University of Illinois Press.

Staff Reporter. *Catholic Herald*. (2013, July 29). If a gay person seeks God, who am I to judge him? says *Pope Francis*. Retrieved from https://catholicherald.co.uk/if-a-gay-person-seeks-god-who-am-i-to-judge-him-says-pope/

Tomasch, S. (1988). Judecca, Dante's Satan, and the Dis-placed Jew. In S. Tomasch & S. Gilles (Eds.), *Text and territory: Geographical imagination in the European middle ages* (pp. 247–266). University of Pennsylvania Press.

Vatican Information Service (2015, May 4). *"Dante, prophet of hope", Pope's message for the 750th anniversary of the birth of Dante*. Retrieved from http://www.cssr.news/oldnews-en/?p=1359

Ziolkowski, J. M. (Ed.) (2014). *Dante and Islam*. Fordham University Press.

Chapter 10

Surprised by Grace: Hermeneutic Reflections on Dante's Judgments

A Response to Hawkins

James M. Kee

In a deeply learned, thought-provoking paper recently presented at 2019's Psychology and the Other conference, Peter S. Hawkins addressed the matter of Dante's relationship to the medieval 'other.' As presented in the preceding chapter, this relationship, Hawkins argued, is a complex one. On the one hand, Dante's understanding of divine justice predictably leads him to locate Jews, Muslims, and other non-Christians in various circles of his *Inferno*. The same holds for 'sexually suspect' persons such as the sodomites. It is true that, measured against the cultural norms of his day, Dante's treatment of these figures is, at times, relatively sympathetic. Nevertheless, he does consider them to be condemned to Hell, and within the cosmic scope of the poem's vision, such an eternal fate is finally what matters. On the other hand, Dante the pilgrim also encounters souls that one would expect to be in Hell but are not. The pagan Cato, who opposed the Roman empire and committed suicide, is the guardian of Purgatory. The Trojan Ripheus, a minor character in Virgil's *Aeneid*, is encountered in the sixth sphere of Paradise, leading Dante to exclaim, "Chi crederebbe?"—that is, "Who would believe it?" (*Paradiso* XX:67). And despite the presence of sodomites in *Inferno* XV–XVI, others guilty of the same sin are purged of their lust, along with heterosexuals, on the seventh terrace of Purgatory. They are thus assured, eventually, of a place in Paradise.

Complexities such as these pose serious challenges for contemporary readers of the *Commedia*—especially when one teaches the poem to first-time students of it. Hawkins movingly recalled having to teach canto XXVIII of the *Inferno*—a canto in which Mohammed and Ali disembowel themselves—to a class that included a Muslim student fasting during Ramadan. Also in the class were Jewish students who learned that on three different occasions, Dante repeats the charge of deicide against the Jews: *Inferno* XXIII:122–123; *Purgatorio* XXI:82–84; and *Paradiso* VI:92–93. What are we to do? In the face of such consequential blind spots, it is not sufficient to call for detached, historical objectivity. At the same time, one does not want such moments to leave readers radically alienated from the *Commedia* as a whole, closed off from the disclosive powers that the great poem may have even today.

Given that these issues were raised in the context of a conference on psychology and the other, I have to presume that the conference's organizers think Dante can help the discipline enlarge its focus beyond the individual self. Professor Hawkins's presentation on Dante's relationship to the medieval 'other' certainly suggests that their hopes are well placed. In reflecting further upon these matters, I will present a two-fold argument:

1) That the tradition of hermeneutic phenomenology contains resources for dealing responsibly with Dante's alienating judgments while still being open to the poem's vision of human destiny.
2) That the surprises encountered are indices of Dante's remarkable, and growing, sensitivity to the workings of divine grace.

How are we to engage Dante's poem in a manner that seeks both to read him responsibly within his historical context and argue with him about judgments that we today find deeply problematic? To do so, we must first avoid supposedly enlightened aesthetic or historicist perspectives that assign his epoch to a superseded past. It will not do simply to reconstruct the poem as an aesthetic or historical object while bracketing off any challenges it might address to our own lives. Gadamer (1989) has demonstrated that such existentially detached methods are an impediment to full understanding (pp. 42–100 & 173–242). In earlier work, I wrestled with questions such as these while trying to make sense of William Langland's great fourteenth-century English poem, *Piers Plowman* (1370–1390/1995). I found a pathway through the difficulties with the help of the hermeneutic reflections of Gadamer and, among others, Heidegger, Ricœur (1976), Bruns (1992), and Marion (2002, 2012). Notably, this hermeneutic tradition was first brought to bear upon the study of the *Commedia* by William Franke (1996), who appears elsewhere in this volume. What lessons can we draw from hermeneutic phenomenology that can help us to engage the contradictory tensions we encounter in the poem?

Hermeneutics is concerned with understanding. A successful effort of interpretation discloses the lived experiences, or possible forms of life or modes of being, that texts articulate. Contemporary hermeneutics—as opposed to the Kantian-inspired hermeneutics of an earlier era—does not approach understanding as an epistemological matter, as a transaction between a subject and an object. As Gadamer (1989) argues, understanding is here conceived on analogy with the Aristotelian virtue *phronesis*, as a matter of practical insight and judgment (pp. 312–324). Thus contemporary hermeneutics designates not a theory or a method, but a family of reflective insights intended to assist our efforts to understand.

Let me highlight some of these practical insights. In his reflections on the origin of the work of art, Heidegger (1971/2001) seeks to clear a space for encountering works of art on their own terms—on terms not prejudiced by metaphysical categories. He argues that the work of art is one of the few essential ways in which truth happens (p. 54). He thereby calls attention to the fact that works of art must be carried out. There are, he insists, two different ways to carry out the work of art: by creating and by preserving. The latter term includes the work of interpretation. Intriguingly, Heidegger (1950/1994) describes the activities of creating and preserving in almost identical language. Both involve a 'letting be'—German verbs with the root -*lassen*: guided by the subject matter of the work, both the creator and the preserver make the work happen in a way that allows the subject matter to appear in its truth (pp. 48 & 54). We can better imagine what is being said here if we think of a work of music rather than a framed painting on a wall. The painting too readily leads us to think of the work as an object; the musical composition clearly must be performed. The work's mode of existence in time requires a preserver as much as a creator. The German verb translated as 'to preserve' is *bewahren*, which is etymologically related to *Wahrheit*, the German for 'truth' (p. 54). One might say, therefore, that the interpreter's task is to 'keep faith with the truth of the work,' to enable it to happen again in some new situation.

Creating the work and interpreting it are thus parallel, complementary activities. Both are carried out in service of disclosing some subject matter in its truth. 'Truth' here does not mean the correspondence of a statement to some fact. More primordially, it refers to an event in which some subject matter is brought forth, unconcealed—what Heidegger (1971/2001) hears when he meditates on *aletheia*, the Greek word for 'truth' (p. 57). In both creating and interpreting, the subject matter must lead. What I am calling the 'subject matter' is usually thought of as a possible mode of existence, or form of life, or way of finding oneself in a world. Moreover, in visionary literature such as the *Commedia*, this bringing forth is not a re-presentation of some subject matter that was somehow already present. The subject matter that the work brings forth is one that otherwise would have remained hidden. As Heidegger (1971/2001) has pointed out, however, events of disclosure are also occasions in which something is concealed (p. 58). This is inherent in their historical character. There can be no events of total disclosure, no absolute knowledge, within the process of history.

These insights have consequences for how we should conceive both the language of an interpretation and the character of the person who does the interpreting. First, language here is not primarily an instrument of thought. It precedes thought even if it ultimately serves it. It is the medium to which we must submit if the subject matter of the work is to be brought forth in its truth. It is not fundamentally expressive of psychic states; nor is it fundamentally conceptual, taking hold of the work's subject matter as scientific definitions take hold of their objects. Along with Donald Marshall (1976), we might rather think of it as indexical (pp. 287–291). The classic example of an indexical sign is the smoke that indicates fire. As indexical, the language of a literary work does not possess within itself the truth of its subject matter. Rather, it points thinking toward the work's subject matter. It is evocative: It calls forth from the interpreter an imaginative response that would apprehend the work's subject matter in a fresh intuition. It requires that the interpreter's own language be a living language, responsive not just to the work's historical context but to the time and place in which the interpreter lives. This latter requirement is implied by Gadamer's insight (1989) that "Understanding is, essentially, an historically effected event" (p. 300). Paradoxically, if we understand at all, "we understand in a *different* way" (p. 297).

The interpreter of works like Dante's is not fundamentally a subject standing over against an object of inquiry. The work of interpretation, therefore, is not, at its most basic, a matter of applying objectifying methods. To be sure, there is a place for objectifying methods in developing insights and correcting oversights. Paul Ricœur's analysis (1981) of the constructive role played by 'distanciation' in hermeneutic experience is helpful here (pp. 131–144). But my concern is with what remains concealed in our intellectual activities when we consider only such methods. If interpreters of a visionary work of literature are to enable the work to disclose its subject matter afresh, they must first be openly attentive and receptive, not detached and suspicious. They must be willing to let the work's language affect them evocatively. This involves the serious play of a disciplined imagination—one that is assertive in coming up with possible notions of the work's wholeness but not willfully aggressive in a manner that would seize the work and make it serve one's own projects. This imaginative play must always seek to keep faith with the truth of the work.

Hermeneutic reflections such as these can help us to address the alienation that we feel when we encounter certain harsh judgments in Dante's poem. They indicate that we should neither simply bracket our response as anachronistic nor dismiss the poem from a standpoint of enlightened superiority. As I said earlier, the truth of a work of art happens as an interplay of showing and concealing that functions indexically. As the creation of a historical being, the *Commedia* is marked by both its disclosures and its blind spots. In interpreting the poem, we must labor to articulate its disclosures evocatively while criticizing honestly its moments of blindness. Because of developments in our understanding of nature and history, Dante's blind spots are often associated with those two subject matters. At places, his understanding of nature reflects metaphysical positions not based adequately upon empirical inquiry. Consider, for example, his use in *Purgatorio* XXV:40–48 of Aristotle's theory of human generation, whereby the father contributes the active principle and the mother only passive matter. His historical horizon, in turn, is comparatively limited in space and time—problematically, for example, when he interprets the destruction of Jerusalem in 70 CE as God's vengeance upon the Jews for the death of Christ (*Purgatorio* XXI:82–84). Still, his conviction that human existence is conditioned by given natural structures of some sort and his vision of history as a process of eschatological transfiguration are matters that we would do well to engage seriously, with existential openness.

Let me now turn to my second topic—those surprising moments in Dante's poem when we react by saying, "Who would believe it?" To begin, I want to draw upon the work of the contemporary theologian Robert Sokolowski (1995) and argue that the *Commedia*'s vision finally rests upon what Sokolowski has named 'the Christian distinction.' By doing so, I am seeking to act upon Gadamer's (1989) insight, mentioned earlier, that to understand at all, we must 'understand in a different way.' This insight is a consequence of his "principle of the history of effect (*Wirkungsgeschichte*)" (p. 300). Sokolowski (1995), in developing his notion of the 'Christian distinction,' re-thinks the subject matter that Thomas Aquinas (1252–1256/1968) articulated as the distinction between *esse* and *essentia*, but Sokolowski (1995) does so as a phenomenologist. He thereby implicitly acts upon Gadamer's principle, acknowledging that if Aquinas's distinction is to be understood today in its truth, we must take seriously the historical continuities and discontinuities that both connect us to and separate us from the saint's thought.

The Christian distinction concerns how we conceive of God, the world, and their relationship. The notion is a subtle one—indeed, Sokolowski argues (2006) that intellectual confusion has reigned among both Christian thinkers and their critics because of the failure of both to recognize it and appreciate its significance (p. 48). He introduces this unique distinction (1995) by contrasting it with a philosophical understanding such as Aristotle's (pp. 15–17). For Aristotle, the world is the cosmos, the comprehensively ordered totality. The divine is the highest substance or kind of being, but it remains within the world—as a kind, an essence, to be distinguished from all other kinds of beings within the totality. In the symbols of the Creator and Creation, however—which emerge from events of revelation—God and the world are radically reconfigured. The created world is everything that is not God. It exists, but Christians acknowledge that it need not be, that its existence is radically contingent. Moreover, if the world did not exist, God would still be and would not be diminished in any way. Nor does the world add anything to God's being.

The world exists and is sustained because of a mysteriously free act of love on God's part. It continues to be the matrix within which human living and dying unfold, and reason continues to seek, discover, and come to understand essential structures in the world. But reason acknowledges that consciousness, in faith, is also called to be open to a Creator who is radically beyond all cosmic contents. And this Creator cannot be conceived as a being with a divine essence, an essence that would simply distinguish the divine from the human in the way that the human essence distinguishes humans from horses. Here we can see the equivalence between Sokolowski's analysis (1995, pp. 41–42) and that of Thomas Aquinas (1265–1273/1947), who names God as *ipsum esse subsistens*, as the self-subsistent act of existing, and who understands finite beings as existing according to their respective essences by participating in the *esse* of God.

This Christian distinction has implications for the ways in which we talk about God and the world. Because God is Creator and the world is created, everything we say about God must be understood figuratively and as uttered against a background of silent mystery. Our language is derived from our experience of 'things' in the world. God is not one of those 'things,' nor is God a thing of any kind. But if we are not to remain silent about God, we must say that God is *like* something in the world of our experience. If we are not reflectively aware of the nature of such statements, however, we will unconsciously fall into thinking about God as if God were one of the 'things' in the totality, even when we think of God as the *Supreme*

Being. At places, Sokolowski's cautionary assertions remind one of Wittgenstein (1958): much confusion results when "language goes on holiday," and we forget the deep grammar that conditions the discourses of Christian theology (p. 19e).

In its figurative strategies and structures, Dante's *Commedia* displays the poet's profound understanding of and respect for what I have been calling the Christian distinction. Moreover, the poem suggests ways in which we might re-think matters concerning 'the Other' and alterity generally. Let me first outline what I mean by the poem's relevant strategies and structures; I will then conclude by drawing out some of the terms suggested by Dante's poem for thinking otherness.

I want first to call attention to the eventful character of the *Commedia*, how its subject matter emerges in its truth. A. C. Charity's book on Dante's relationship to the Bible entitled *Events and Their Afterlife* (1966) is helpful here. Charity takes the exegetical notion of 'typology' and discerns in it a poetic strategy used by biblical writers and Dante to interpret their experience historically. Biblical writers understand Israel's present and future in light of patterns that emerge from God's actions in the past. Typology, thus understood, articulates a vision of history as a divine–human dialogue. God acts and human beings respond. In the *Commedia*, typology is not simply present when the poem alludes to biblical events like the Exodus. It names a comprehensive poetic strategy whereby Dante composes his *Commedia* in the hope that the poem might disclose just how, within the context of the early fourteenth century, he and his contemporaries could recognize, respond to, and thereby participate in God's ongoing saving initiatives.

Dante's particular version of the Bible's saving narrative is shaped, not just by his understanding of the Exodus type and its fulfillment in the death and resurrection of Christ, but by this type as interpreted through the lens of Christianity's metaphysical theologies. In order to indicate how this strategy saturates the *Commedia* with Dante's awareness of the Christian distinction, I will describe how its most basic structures—the canticles of *Inferno*, *Purgatorio*, and *Paradiso*—reflect that distinction.

Sokolowski (1995) argues that the Christian distinction, despite what might seem like its demotion of the world, in fact, "preserve[s] the integrity of nature" (p. 22). Indeed, because the natural world is created by God out of love, its status is elevated beyond its just being there. In Dante's presentations of Hell and Purgatory, we can discern his respect for the dignity of created nature and, in particular, of human nature. He draws upon an Aristotelian-Thomistic understanding of human nature, of the human character. Human beings are called to actualize the potential excellences that are theirs by nature. The pilgrim Dante's journey through Hell is a study of the ways in which human beings can de-form those potencies. In Purgatory, Dante sees—and participates in—the process whereby deformed habits are undone, and the excellences proper to human nature are made actual. Because human nature has been wounded by sin, the refining purgatorial journey requires divine grace and the soul's response to such grace. At the end of the journey, the pilgrim soul achieves the autonomy—and a correspondent freedom—proper to its nature (*Purgatorio* XXVII:139–142).

The matter is different, however, when we get to the heavenly Paradise. The virtues proper to human nature have already been fully actualized when a soul enters the Earthly Paradise on the top of Mount Purgatory. The soul has been delivered from the dark wood of sin and death. But when viewed in light of the Christian distinction, the worldly Paradise at the peak of Purgatory's mountain, for all its created dignity and integrity, is not the ultimate locus of human destiny. There is more to human destiny than the actualization of the virtues proper to human nature. Eschatological existence exceeds any such conceivable form of natural teleology. Hence Dante's vision of Paradise articulates the meaning for human destiny of a divine grace that superabounds. The realm is primarily structured, not in terms of the vices and virtues of the human character, but according to the mysterious ways in which divine grace is communicated to human beings, gifting them with their destinies (*Paradiso* II:112–148). Grace is the supernatural means by which the human heart is brought to the fullness of rest in the beatific vision.

To articulate these ultimate truths of revelation, Dante must move beyond representation to a process of signification freed from the demands of mimesis, as Rachel Jacoff (2007, p. 109) has put it. In the world of experience, we are all familiar with the realities represented in Hell and Purgatory. Thus, the natural excellences and deformities of the human character can be represented. But Paradise is concerned, finally, with what lies beyond all forms that human nature might take—with what Dante named *trasumanar* (*Paradiso* I:70), the human life *trans*-formed. The letter of *Paradiso*'s text is finally more evocative than representational. Instances of the inexpressibility *topos* are common even as the language in which Dante would "show the shadow of the blessed realm" (I:23–24) becomes more and more articulate. As Christian Moevs (2005) has analyzed in rich detail, the forms in which the heavenly realms appear themselves undergo a transformation: The created, visible cosmos, we learn, is simply a copy of a model (*Paradiso* XXVIII:52–57). And given the poet's reflective awareness of the distance between his intuitions and the signs through which he seeks to disclose them, we might read his account of the model as itself a shadowy form of figuration. The backbone of *Paradiso*'s narrative movement is the ongoing process of self-transcendence that, by the grace of God, the pilgrim-poet undergoes. He reaches a point at which he wishes to share what he has glimpsed concerning the ultimate destiny of human beings, the beatific vision. But to do so faithfully, Dante's narrative must leap over the moment in the narrative present and recollect it from the past (XXXIII:55–66). Perhaps more than any other part of the *Commedia*, *Paradiso* insists upon the ongoing *eventfulness* of revelation—not just its afterlife in structures of verbal meaning. We become aware, through the shifting of tenses between past and present, that the writing of the poem, as well as the interpreting of it, are themselves repetitions of the journey, and that only through such repetition can the eternal happen, as Augustine (397–398/1992) might have put it, amidst the soul's temporal distention (p. 240).

The structure of Dante's *Commedia*, therefore, is not merely symmetrical—a vision of the afterlife in which a hell is set off against a paradise with a realm that mediates between them. The integrity of the created natural world, so respected in Dante's presentation of Hell and Purgatory, is transcended in Paradise. Human destiny lies beyond all finite form. It is found in the worldly creature's unimaginable relationship to its Creator, in the human being's participation in divinity as such, in a divinization of the human, if you will. There is otherness here, the otherness of a Creator who must first be acknowledged as Wholly Other. But we discover in the end that the Wholly Other's love of its creation makes a relationship between Creator and creation possible. This is nowhere seen more clearly than in the divine person who became human so that humans might participate in the divine (*Paradiso* XXXIII:124–141). As for the status of selves and others within the world, there can be no radical otherness between them. Most primordially, they all exist as creatures because of their participation in the self-subsistent *esse* of their Creator. To be sure, there are differences among creatures that result from the differences among their finite forms. But none of these differences justifies the objectification of another as *radically other*. For Dante, human beings are finally persons created in the image of a personal God, not just individual selves. That means they are primordially in relation—to each other, to the world, and to their Creator.

Dante's poem is indeed full of surprises when measured against orthodox or conventional Christian teachings—surprises that arouse wonder within us. I am arguing that these surprises are indices of Dante's astonishing consciousness of how divine grace is at work in the created world. The pilgrim who finds sodomites in Hell is one preoccupied with the reality of sin; the poet who puts them there is limited by a metaphysically rigid conception of human nature. By the time we get to the seventh terrace of Purgatory, the poet is primarily concerned with how grace can transfigure disordered erotic desire into agapic love—whether one is heterosexual or homosexual. He has learned from his pilgrim's grace-filled journey. Perhaps *we* can learn something of value about the psyche from such a poet's self-transcending journey in response to his Creator's grace.

References

Aquinas, T. (1947). *The summa theologica*. Benziger Brothers Edition (Fathers of the English Dominican Province, Trans.). Retrieved from https://dhspriory.org/thomas/summa/FP/FP004.html#FPQ4OUTP1. (Original work 1265–1273).

Aquinas, T. (1968). *On being and essence* (A. Maurer, Trans.). Pontifical Institute of Mediaeval Studies. (original published 1949, based on original 1252–1256).

Augustine (1992). *Confessions* (H. Chadwick, Trans.). Oxford University Press. (Original work 397–398).

Bruns, G. (1992). *Hermeneutics ancient and modern*. Yale University Press.

Charity, A. C. (1966). *Events and their afterlife: The dialectics of Christian typology in the Bible and Dante*. Cambridge University Press.

Franke, W. (1996). *Dante's interpretive journey*. University of Chicago Press.

Gadamer, H.-G. (1989). *Truth and method* (2nd Rev. ed.) (J. Weinsheimer & D. G. Marshall, Trans. & Rev.). Crossroad.

Hawkins, P. (2019, October 4). Dante and the medieval "Other". In *The Dante Salon at the psychology and the other conference*. Boston College, Chestnut Hill, MA, [Lecture].

Heidegger, M. (1994). Der Ursprung des Kunstwerkes. In M. Heidegger, *Holzwege* (7th ed., pp. 7–74). Vittorio Klostermann. (Original work published 1950).

Heidegger, M. (2001). The origin of the work of art. In *Poetry, language, thought* (A. Hofstadter, Trans.). (pp. 17–87). Harper Collins. (original 1971).

Jacoff, R. (2007). Introduction to Paradiso. In R. Jacoff (Ed.), *The Cambridge companion to Dante* (2nd ed., pp. 107–124). Cambridge University Press.

Langland, W. (1995). *The vision of Piers Plowman* (2nd ed.) (A. V. C. Schmidt & J. M. Dent, Ed.). (original 1978 based on 1370–1390 original).

Marion, J.-L. (2002). *In excess: Studies of saturated phenomena* (R. Horner & V. Berraud, Trans.). Fordham University Press.

Marion, J.-L. (2012). *Givenness and hermeneutics* (J.-P. Lafouge, Trans.). Marquette University Press.

Marshall, D. (1976). The ontology of the literary sign: Notes toward a Heideggerian revision of semiology. In W. V. Spanos (Ed.), *Martin Heidegger and the question of literature: Toward a postmodern literary hermeneutics. Boundary* 2 (pp. 271–294). Indiana University Press.

Moevs, C. (2005). *The metaphysics of Dante's Comedy*. Oxford University Press.

Ricœur, P. (1976). *Interpretation theory: Discourse and the surplus of meaning*. Texas Christian University Press.

Ricœur, P. (1981). *Hermeneutics and the human sciences* (J. B. Thompson, Ed. & Trans.). Cambridge University Press.

Sokolowski, R. (1995). *The God of faith and reason: Foundations of Christian theology*. The Catholic University Press of America. (original 1982).

Sokolowski, R. (2006). *Christian faith and human understanding: Studies on the eucharist, trinity, and the human person*. The Catholic University Press of America.

Wittgenstein, L. (1958). *Philosophical investigations* (G. E. M. Anscombe, Trans.). Macmillan Company. (original 1953).

Chapter 11

Purgatorio
A Liturgy of Forgiveness and Restoration

Dominic Aquila

The liturgical character of *Purgatorio* is well established in Dante scholarship (Hawkins, 2006; Mandelbaum's translation of Alighieri, 1320/1982; Tucker, 1960; Webb, 2013). In Mandelbaum's translation (1320/1982), he sees *Purgatorio*'s structure as a *line of rite* that frames and controls the poem's action, rhetoric, and rhythm, and invests them with seriousness and focus. Its chants, hymns, visual art, poetry, gestures, processions, postures, and movements combine to create for its readers and hearers a synesthetic experience imitative, or at least suggestive, of the Church's liturgy: the Mass, the Liturgy of the Hours (the Divine Office), and the administration of sacraments—Baptism, Confession, Confirmation, Eucharist, Marriage, Holy Orders, and the Anointing of the Sick.

Liturgy is the public prayer of the Church with deep roots in pre-Christian synagogue rites. Its form and content have been comparatively stable. Changes or reform to the liturgy are carefully thought through and, for the most part, have developed organically over centuries, spiritually uniting communities of the living and the dead (Ratzinger, 1986). An essential mark of liturgy, writes Hildebrand (1943), is "its character of communion-prayer" (p. 41), which is a hallmark of *Purgatorio*. In *Purgatorio*, penitents have been forgiven their transgressions and strive in common to purify any remaining desire for that which falls short of the unalloyed love of God and others.

The common life of *Purgatorio* contrasts sharply with the isolated, self-absorption that marks the sufferers in *Inferno*. Early on in *Inferno*, the figure of Francesca da Rimini establishes this typology of egocentric self-pity. She does not name Paolo, with whom she committed the sin that damned her; she refers to him coldly and dispassionately as "this man." Then in a parody of the marriage vow—the high sacrament of human community, she adds, he "who never shall be parted from me" (*Inferno* V:134–135).[1]

Inferno and *Purgatorio* each establish and present an anthropology and ontology of the human person. *Inferno*'s characters present themselves to Dante and Virgil fundamentally as self-involved, atomized selves. By way of contrast, in *Purgatorio*, persons implicitly or explicitly acknowledge their essential identity as relational beings. For Dante, this relationality—to God and to other persons—is imitative of the relationality of persons in the Holy Trinity, and constitutive of what it means to be human. Having been forgiven of their transgressions, the aim of souls' progression up Mount Purgatory is the restoration of the self and the human community through a covenant of friendship, aided successively and signified by the elements of Christian liturgical practice.

Liturgy: A School of Community

'The spirit of communion' is integral to liturgy, according to Dietrich Von Hildebrand. In *Liturgy and Personality* (1943), he argues that liturgy is a corrective to distorted notions of individualism. "An isolated man," writes Von Hildebrand, "one who has not become conscious of the ultimate objective link binding him to all other men [and women] before God, is unawakened, immature and even a mutilated [person]" (p. 53). Without compromising each person's uniqueness, the communal and supra-individual character of the liturgy develops in its participants a profound understanding of the primacy of the 'I-Thou' bond that is at the center of each person's authentic nature. Liturgical prayer, in the words of Von Hildebrand (1943), "possesses an incomparable; communion-forming power" (p. 42). Drawing on response-to-value theory, he sees liturgy as embodying the highest of values. Values, in general, and the liturgy, in particular, "possess a unifying power; and the higher the value in question, the greater this power" (p. 42). Liturgical texts and actions draw their participants out of the world of distraction and lift the barriers that isolate them one from another.

Emphatically, the 'I-Thou' communion is not a peripheral aspect of authentic personhood; rather, it is the ground of one's being. It is falsified by a voluntaristic attitude toward one's relation to others. In a voluntaristic view of human nature, one decides and controls his or her relation to the other, the world, and to God. For Von Hildebrand, such voluntarism in human relations is a mark of egotism, "which exists secretly even in the most jovial joiner of clubs" (p. 42). It exemplifies "narrowness and limitation" (p. 42). This voluntaristic conception of the human person is on full display in *Inferno* and corrected in *Purgatorio*. Dante presents the central figures of *Inferno* in tableaus where their propinquity to others suggests some sort of perversion of communal existence. Defiantly egocentric figures such as Francesca da Rimini, Farinata, and Ugolino appear linked together for eternity in close quarters with other figures whom they ignore, disdain, and ultimately devour—Paolo, Cavalcante, and Ruggieri.

Liturgy's communal character is also central to Romano Guardini's classic work, *The Spirit of the Liturgy* (1997). Guardini, like his contemporary, Von Hildebrand, was keenly aware of the powerful nineteenth- and twentieth-century ideological and political forces affecting liturgical thought and practice. Besides the desacralizing tendencies of these forces, they also confused the relation of the individual to the community by either promoting an excessively self-determining individualism on the one hand or, on the other, a collectivism that smothered individualism. As a response to these forces infiltrating discussions on Christian liturgy, Guardini argued that liturgy is a public space for proper human formation *in conspectu Domini* [in the sight of the Lord]. Liturgy invites those of individualistic bent to suspend their dispositions toward self-concern and self-sufficiency for the sake of the community. Guardini (1997) proposes that those more disposed toward the primacy of the community would submit themselves to the rigor of inherited liturgical forms and thereby reorient their collectivist sensibilities toward valuing the human person *qua* person.

The received tradition of liturgical forms is essentially and "above all a system of actions" (1957, p. 216). In Guardini's words:

> [The liturgy] is not a sum of individuals but a wholeness: the Church. It exists even when one or the other, or many, have divorced themselves from its body; for it does not have its origin in the desire of the individual for community, but in the creative will of God, which embraces the whole of mankind ... Through the Liturgy man steps out of his separateness and becomes a part of the whole; a living organ through which the total message of the Church is expressed and enacted. (p. 217)

The liturgical "system of actions" unveils "matters of deepest import" hidden beneath ordinary movements, gestures, objects, and words, such as light, time, space, bread, wine, walking, standing, steps, and kneeling (Guardini, 1979, p. 10). Liturgy transforms the workaday into poetry. For "true liturgy is at root poetry," which heightens "our essential connection with all things and the fundamental communion of all being" (1979, p. 10). By sacralizing the ordinary through signs, types, symbols, metaphors, and similes, liturgy forms "the fundamental Christian temper" writes Guardini (1997, p. 86). "By it men [and women] are to be induced to determine correctly their essential relation to God, and to put themselves right in regards to reverence for God, love and faith, atonement and the desire for sacrifice" (Guardini, 1997, p. 86).

Reading *Purgatorio* in the light of Guardini's theory of liturgy, we see exactly the determination mentioned by Guardini in the behavior of the penitents in Purgatory. The first request made of Dante and Virgil by the new arrivals to the shores of Mount Purgatory is "show us, if you know, the way by which we can ascend this slope" (*Purgatorio* II:59–60). Faith, one of the aims of liturgy, according to Guardini, is no longer necessary in eternity. What persists in Purgatory is the soul's single-minded desire to undo the harm of sin and restore its pre-fallen relation to God, which is done so by removing from their souls desires that hinder achieving it. Mount Purgatory, as Dante puts it, "delivers man from sin" (*Purgatorio* XIII:3). Anthony Esolen (1320/2004) translates this line, "lo monte che salendo atrui dismal," more literally as "the mountain that dis-evils those who climb."

Study and discussion of liturgy have been largely the interest of theologians. Recently, philosophers, such as Nicholas Wolterstorff, have entered the conversation. His account of liturgy shares much in common with Guardini's. Like Guardini, he sees liturgy as active and performative, which for a time, mitigate against the forces of distraction and isolation from the world and God. Liturgy, for Wolterstorff (2018) is, first of all, "an enactment." Its participants together perform

> scripted verbal, gestural, and auditory actions, the prescribed purpose of their doing so being both to engage God directly in acts of learning and acknowledging the excellence of who God is and what God has done, and to be engaged by God. The liturgy itself is that type of sequence of act-types that is enacted when the participants do what the script prescribes. An extant liturgy offers to us a certain type of sequence of act-types for directly engaging God in worship and for being engaged by God. Rather than having to devise such a sequence for ourselves, we can join with others and follow the script. In following the script we suspend *for a time* the exercise of our own autonomy with respect to the matters prescribed by the script and together submit to the script. (Wolterstorff, 2018, pp. 17–18; my emphasis)

The temporary submission to a script, as Wolterstorff puts it, echoes Guardini's interest in the liturgy as a remedy for excessive individualism and an undisciplined collectivism. Liturgy *qua* liturgy encourages men and women from individualistic and collectivist extremes to submit themselves to the formal, scripted actions of the liturgy. In doing so, they are led to discern the right relation of the individual to the community and to God.

The Purgatorian Liturgy: Verbal Scripts and Symbolic Actions

The transformative and revivifying power of liturgy discussed by Von Hildebrand, Guardini, and Wolterstorff are announced immediately in *Purgatorio*. Its opening lines gesture toward the *Genesis* creation narrative, invoking the generativity of liturgy. The *Genesis* story of creation is liturgical in its literary form—"a solemn, stately, ordered symmetrical text that is more like a liturgical antiphon than it is a narrative" (Brueggman, 2003, p. 34). God's repeated affirmation of the goodness of His creation is "something like a congregational response to a priestly litany," that crescendos to the intensified phrase "very good" on the sixth day as God judges all He has created (Brueggman, 2003, p. 34).

As Hawkins (2006) notes, following an immersion in the dank darkness of *Inferno*, "light... is the first thing we notice in Purgatory" (p. 47). The gently hued and serene sky, with stars "not seen since the first people," hangs over the "more kindly waters" washing the shores of Mount Purgatory. Darkness, water, light, and the first people rehearse the signal elements of the creation of the universe. On the first day of creation, "There was darkness over the deep, and God's spirit hovered over the water. God said, 'Let there be light,' and there was light" (*Genesis* 1:1–3). On the sixth day of creation, "God said, 'let us make man in our own image, in the likeness of ourselves'" (*Genesis* 1:26).² The plural form of God—Elohim—is the basis for the Trinitarian doctrine of God and thereby the intrinsic nature of the persons made in His image.

The allusion to the *Genesis* creation narrative invites a comparison between the old creation and the new creation in Christ. Hawkins (2006) points out that the pilgrim Dante's descent into Hell beginning on Good Friday and his ascent to Purgatory on Easter morning imitates the movements of Christ, movements that are memorialized in the Church's Sacred Triduum liturgy—the liturgies of Holy Thursday evening, Good Friday, and the Vigil Mass of Easter. The resurrected Christ, and Dante in imitation of Him, signify a new creation.

The world created anew in Christ is a persistent theme in the letters of St. Paul (Wright, 1988). Often the themes of the *Genesis* creation and new creation are contrasted, as, for example, in Chapter 1 of St. Paul's *Letter to the Colossians*, which compares the old creation and new creation in Christ (*Colossians* 1:15–23). St. Paul tells the Corinthians: "for anyone who is in Christ, there is a new creation; the old creation has gone and now the new one is here" (*2 Corinthians* 5:17). Under the old dispensation, according to St. Paul, men and women existed in the state of bondage. In the new dispensation, they are elected to the adopted sons and daughters of God (*Romans 8*; *Ephesians 1*; *Galatians 4*).

As Anthony Esolen suggests in his 2004 translation, the theme of Divine filiation deeply informs the liturgical elements in *Purgatorio*'s first canto. "The Lord wants sons [and daughters], not slaves" (Alighieri, 1320/2004, p. 410). Purgatory is not a prison. As Esolen explains, it is a place wherein those formerly held in the bondage of sin are made heirs through adoption. Canto I strikes a paradoxical relation between the dignity of Divine filiation in the new order of creation and the persistent need for humility. Dante depicts this tension through a series of liturgical actions. Following the directive of Cato, the guardian of Purgatory, Virgil vests and purifies Dante for the ascent up Mount Purgatory: "Go then, but first wind a smooth rush around his waist and bathe his face, to wash away all of Hell's stains" (*Purgatorio* I:94–96).

Commentators on these lines interpret the girding with a smooth rush as a cincturing, imitative of the priest's vesting for various liturgical celebrations, but especially the Mass (see Hollander & Hollander's commentary in their translation of *Purgatorio*, 2003). As the priest ties the cincture around his waist he recites, "Gird me, O Lord, with the girdle of purity." The act of cincturing, together with Virgil's ablutionary act of cleansing Dante's face—suggestive of Baptism and the washing of the priest's hands in preparation for consecrating bread and wine—signify the virtue of chastity (Hollander & Hollander, 2003; Thurston, 1908). It also calls to mind St. Paul's spur to the Ephesians: "So stand your ground, with truth buckled round your waist" (*Ephesians* 6:14). The posture of standing—"stand your ground"—accords with the dignity of a child of God. It is the posture of resurrection. The rush or reed signifies humility (Esolen's translation of Alighieri, 1320/2004; or the Hollander & Hollander translation, Alighieri, 1320/2003). Through these liturgical actions, postures, and objects,

Dante conveys the dynamic tension between the high calling of divinized humanity, effected by the Resurrection, and humbleness.

Dante emphasizes the importance of *Purgatorio*'s resurrection theme by recapitulating it as the act of plucking a reed. "Oh wonder! Where he (Virgil) plucked the humble plant... there that plant sprang up again, identical, immediately" (*Purgatorio* I: 134–136). Dante scholars agree that this scene echoes the scene from the Aeneid when Aeneas plucks a golden fruit from the sacred wood, after which another fruit is reborn. But this action also presents, as Esolen notes, "a small mysterious resurrection" (Alighieri, 1320/2004, p. 413).

The Purgatorian Liturgy: Music and the Common Life

Canto II of *Purgatorio* is the cantica of music. Souls enter Purgatory with song, writes Dante, and in hell "with savage lamentations" (*Purgatorio* XII:112–114). The music of Canto II completes the trio of elements that Wolterstorff (2018) assigns to liturgy: "scripted verbal, gestural, and auditory actions" (p. 17). The first two permeate Canto I, the third, Canto II. The new penitents to the Isle of Purgatory arrive chanting Psalm 113—the first instance of audible music in the *Commedia*—in celebration of their forgiveness. The chanting and hymn-singing in *Purgatorio*'s terraces is a common action that signifies penitents' concern for directing each toward God.

The new penitents chant Psalm 113 in unison ("ad una voce") as they step off the angel-powered boat onto the beach of Mount Purgatory. Dante writes:

> "*In exitu Israel de Aegypto,*"
> with what is written after of that psalm,
> all of those spirits sang as with one voice.
>
> Then over them he [the angel] made the holy cross
> as sign; they flung themselves down on the shore,
> and he moved off as he had come—swiftly (*Purgatorio* II:46–51)

Williams (1994) sees in these lines the fusing of community, individual souls, and liturgy or ritual. He writes:

> There slides across the sea a ship of felicity. There are in it the souls who are determined to undergo redemption; they are singing *In exitu Israel*, and in one general movement they leap from the ship to the beach. The movement is common, as is the song; their individuality is here understood better in the whole organic body. The psalms sung in Purgatory are part of the Church's ritual, but here is better to say that the ritual is part of them. (p. 149)

The union of pilgrimage and liturgical action signaled by the *In exitu Israel* underlines the musical mode historically reserved for chanting *Psalm* 113: the *tonus peregrinus*, literally 'pilgrim's tone' as noted by Lundberg (2011). In the first exchange with the souls coming ashore, Dante, the poet, puns on the idea of the pilgrim, choosing "peregrin" rather than 'pellegrini,' a more familiar term for pilgrim. When they ask Dante, the pilgrim, and Virgil: "Do show us, if you know, the way by which we can ascend this slope," Virgil responds: "You may be convinced that we are quite familiar with this shore; but we are pilgrims [peregrin] here just as you are" (*Purgatorio* II:59–63).

Psalm 113, *In exitu Israel de Aegypto*, is one of five liturgical texts sung by the penitents in ante-purgatory (*Purgatorio* I–IX). In Canto V, the late repentants chant *The Miserere—Psalm* 51, "Have Mercy on me, O God." In Canto VII, the souls of earthly luminaries in the Valley of the Princes sing the *Salve Regina*—Hail Holy Queen: a plea to the Virgin Mary to turn her eyes toward their "mourning and weeping in [their] valley of tears." In Canto VIII, we hear the *Te Lucis Ante*—To Thee Before the Close of Day—typically sung at Compline, the last hour of the day. And, finally, the *Te Deum Laudamus*—We Praise Thee, O God—in Canto IX: a hymn in praise of the Holy Trinity, typically sung on occasions of thanksgiving.

Each of these five chanted texts highlights a particular event in ante-purgatory. But, taken together, they signify the sanctification of time and the reestablishment of an ordered reality in ante-purgatory, in contrast to the disorder and chaos of *Inferno*. *Psalm* 113, *In exitu*, is the last of the *Psalms* sung for Holy Saturday vespers. It marks the beginning of the day on Easter Sunday, when Dante, Virgil, and the pilgrims arrive on the shores of Mount Purgatory. The *Te Lucis Ante*, chanted at Compline, ends the day. The *Te Deum Laudamus*—a hymn of thanksgiving—celebrates the entrance to Purgatory proper, a new beginning, and the painful process of purgation, expiation, and atonement.

The Liturgy of *Psalm* 113: Exodus and Liberation

As Holloway (1993), Singleton (2000), and Tucker (1960) have shown, *Psalm* 113 signals the importance of the Exodus story as the controlling allegory and image of ante-purgatory and, indeed, the entire *Commedia*. Accordingly, given its importance, Dante, the poet, introduces and envelopes *Psalm* 113 with elaborate and deeply symbolic liturgical images. Canto II opens by first orienting the reader to Jerusalem, the center of Jewish life, and the premiere pilgrimage destination for Jews and Christians. Jerusalem was, in the words of Wright (1994), "the focal point of everything that the Jews were and did" (p. 53). As Wright describes it:

> The great majority of Jews went up to Jerusalem for the festivals singing the psalms en route; the great majority of Jews heard scripture read regularly in their synagogues. In these ways they acted out, and thereby demonstrated to themselves, their belief that Jerusalem, and its Temple, were the center of the created order, the place where the creator of the world, who had entered into special covenant with them as a nation, had chosen to place his "name." (pp. 53–54)

Having set the relation of Purgatory to Jerusalem, Dante, the poet, established the geographical and physical context for the liturgy to follow in Canto II. The next phase in the unfolding of this liturgy is metaphysical, focusing on the phenomenon of light and alluding to the phenomenon of sound. Dante, as pilgrim, sees an approaching light:

> And just as Mars, when it is overcome
> By the invading mists of dawn, glows red
> above the waters' plain, low in the west,
>
> so there appeared to me—and may I see it
> again—a light that crossed the sea: so swift,
> there is no flight of bird to equal it. (*Purgatorio* II:13–18)

The comparison of the approaching light with the glow of Mars suggests a synesthetic experience of sight and sound and implicates the properties of order and relationality signified by each. In *Convivio*, Dante understands light as the ordering principle of the universe, and music as the ordering principle of relationships. As discussed earlier, the light of the Easter dawn in Canto I of *Purgatorio* alludes to the creation of light on the first day of the *Genesis* narrative by which God brings order to the universe. In *Paradiso*, Dante poeticizes the ordering power of light by associating it with the Heaven of the Sun (*Paradiso* X–XII) and the relational properties of music with the heaven of Mars (*Paradiso* XV–XVII). In Dante's schema of *Paradiso*, each planet represents a liberal art. The heaven of the Sun signifies arithmetic, the heaven of Mars, music. These two sciences are integrally linked in the quadrivium of the liberal arts curriculum, which also shapes the ordering of *Paradiso* (Mazzotta, 1993). Arithmetic is the theory of number, music its application.

In *Convivio*, Dante compares the Heaven of the Sun to arithmetic because as the Sun illumines all heavenly bodies, so too does arithmetic illumine all the sciences. For, as Dante states in Book II, Chapter 13, the sciences are "considered under some numerical aspect, and in considering them we always proceed by number" (Alighieri, 1304–1307/1990). A little further in the same section of *Convivio*, Dante associates music with the planet Mars. Leaning on Boethius's understanding of music. Dante writes in the same section:

> Music, which consists entirely of relations, as we see in harmonized words and in songs, whose harmony is so much the sweeter the more the relation is beautiful, which relation is the principal beauty in this science, because it is its principal aim. (Alighieri, 1304–1307/1990)

Mastrobuono's (1979) reading of Canto II of *Purgatorio* provides another liturgical association for "the light that crossed the sea." He sees it as a reference to the rite of the Paschal Candle, which begins the Easter vigil liturgy, an event that would be occurring in Jerusalem at the moment of Dante's sighting of the light in Canto II. The Easter candle signifies the column of fire that preceded the Hebrews to the Red Sea during their exodus from Egypt, and then at night moved around to their rear to keep apart the rival camps of the Egyptians and the Israelites.

The final and most suggestive connection between ante-purgatory and the Easter vigil is a musical one. *In exitu Israel de Aegypto*, in which the arriving souls chant as they approach the isle of Mount Purgatory, alludes to the Easter Proclamation or the *Exultet*, in which the Deacon, Priest, or lay cantor chants: "This is the night on which you brought our forefathers the Children of Israel, dry-shod through the Red Sea in the flight from Egypt." Mastrobuono (1979) points out that which is being commemorated during the Vigil Night of the year 1300—the year of Dante's pilgrimage through the afterlife, is the second Exodus, that is,

> our redemption wrought by Christ, and it is for this reason, that even as the angel of God comes symbolizing the historical event of the Exodus from Egypt he [Dante, as poet,] will now have to send the souls to the Mountain [of Purgatory] in the name of "the New Covenant of the Cross." (Mastrobuono, 1979, p. 117)

Prayer and Forgiveness

This new covenant is the setting and energy for the repair of the social bonds weakened or destroyed by sin. As Omberto Aldobrandeschi tells Dante, the pilgrim, in Canto XI on the terrace of the prideful, "my arrogance has not harmed me alone for it has drawn all my kin into calamity" (*Purgatorio* XI:67–69). In his conversation with Aldobrandeschi, Dante, as pilgrim, models the penitential steps necessary for social generation. In a gesture of solidarity, Dante adopts the bent-over posture of Aldobrandeschi and others, who make reparation for their sin of pride by carrying heavy boulders on their backs as they walk around the terrace of the prideful. To be sure, Dante, the pilgrim, is learning something about his own pridefulness as he mimics the contrapasso of the prideful. But, in part, he is also sharing in their suffering, and participating in the new covenant of the cross by symbolically bearing the burdens of another, in effect, helping him to carry his cross.

Besides this gesture of empathy toward the penitents—a symbolic participation in their reparatory sentence—Dante, the pilgrim, also mitigates the suffering of the penitents through his role as the Purgatorians' envoy to the living, carrying back to the living their requests for prayers, prayers that will shorten the term of their correction and regeneration, whether communal or personal, and bind the community of the living and the community of souls in Purgatory. The occupants of ante-purgatory press him with special earnestness because of the extended wait they must endure before they can even begin to expiate their sins on the terraces of Purgatory proper. The frenzied opening of Canto VI captures vividly the determined urgency of the ante-purgatorians. The "pressing throng" and "persistent pack" of one-time earthly notables swarm Dante, "always pray[ing] for others' prayers for them" (*Purgatorio* VI:26). In earlier ante-purgatory canti, Manfred, Belaqua, Jacopo del Cassero, Buonconte da Montefeltro, and Pia de Tolomei petition Dante to remind their living relatives and friends to pray for them. The structure of the autobiographies of the latter three in *Purgatorio* V—those of Cassero, Montefeltro, and Pia de Tolomei—are liturgical icons in the sense that they form a sort of triptych of prayer requests.

Prayer is two-way communication in *Purgatorio*: the living pray for the Purgatorians and the Purgatorians pray for the living. Mandelbaum (Alighieri, 1320/2004) writes in his commentary that since the rulers in the Valley of the Princes in Canto VIII are already saved, they chant the compline prayer *Te Lucis Ante*, "not for themselves, but out of compassion for the living" (Alighieri, 1320/2004, p. 334). The *Te Lucis Ante* prayer asks God, the Creator of the world, for protection against all nightmares, from the fears and terrors of the night, and temptation from sin, which no longer troubles the souls in Purgatory, but endangers the living.

Dante, as poet, gives prominence to the prayer of the Purgatorians for the living in the final petition of his version of the Lord's Prayer in Canto XI, the only complete prayer in *Purgatorio*. The penitents on the terrace of the prideful in communion pray:

> Even, as we forgive all who have done
> us injury, may You, benevolent,
> forgive, and do not judge us by our worth.
>
> Try not our strength, so easily subdued,
> against the ancient foe, but set it free
> from him who goads it to perversity.
>
> This last request we now address to You,
> dear Lord, not for ourselves—who have no need—
> but for the ones whom we have left behind. (*Purgatorio* XI:16–24)

Dante uses the occasion of the penitents' prayer for the living to address the reader directly on the importance of prayer in the lives of the living.

> If there [in Purgatory] they pray on our behalf, what can
> be said and done here on this earth for them
> by those whose wills are rooted in true worth?
>
> Indeed we should help them to wash away
> The stains they carried from this world, so that
> Made pure and light, they reach the starry wheels. (*Purgatorio* XI:31–36)

Prayer not only is that which facilitates the intercommunion of the living and the souls in Purgatory, but it also drives *Purgatorio*'s pervasive concern for the restoration of human community grounded in an anthropology rooted in the irreducible relationality of the human person.

Dantean Forgiveness and Modern Accounts of Forgiveness: Kristeva, Arendt, Jankélévitch, and Guardini

The Dantean innovation of the Lord's Prayer around the petition of forgiveness recalls the driving principle of the Purgatorian drama: the grace and gift of forgiveness. In Canto I of *Purgatorio*, Dante, the poet, in the encounter with Cato sets up a paradoxical relation between grace and mercy and law and justice. Cato personifies the tradition of Roman law. Cato views with alarm his sighting of Virgil and Dante: "Who are you—who, against the hidden river/ were able to escape the eternal prison?/... The laws of the abyss—have they been broken?" (*Purgatorio* I:40–41, 46). As Mazzotta (2014) keenly observes, Cato, in a way, is "a stranger to the world of Purgatory" (p. 121). It does not occur to him that Dante and Virgil may be the recipients of a Divine action—Grace, which is inexplicable by natural or human law. Virgil explains to Cato that "it is a power descending from above/ that helps me guide him here" (*Purgatorio* I:68–69).

In Dante's economy of forgiveness, grace and the gift of forgiveness do not exculpate or excuse wrongdoing and transgression but transcend them for the sake of repairing the harm done—to the person, the human community, and creation. In this respect, *Purgatorio* and the Christian tradition, to which it gives poetic expression, resonate in unison with twentieth- and twenty-first-century thinkers' excited interest in forgiveness as indispensable to cultural, social, and political wellbeing and development. Scott (2010) is among those who privilege poetry, art, and ritual over juridical means to achieve these ends. Their use of metaphor, symbols, and the multivalent quality of language opens up "fresh insights into processes of resolution and reconciliation" (p. 3).

Among Scott's chief influences in thinking about the poetics of forgiveness are Julia Kristeva and Hannah Arendt. Kristeva's writings range widely— encompassing philosophy, literary criticism, semiotics, psychoanalysis, and feminism—and include a book-length examination of Arendt (Kristeva, 2001) A practicing psychoanalyst, her interest in forgiveness proceeds from the 'maladies of the soul' and the general malaise she sees in her patients (Kristeva, 2010). She derives her understanding of forgiveness mainly from psycholinguistics and semiotics. It turns on her unique use of the French word, '*pardon*,' stressing its second syllable, '*don*,' which means gift and suggests that forgiveness is a gift.

Forgiveness, for Kristeva (2002), is a 'never-ending practice' gifted to a person distinct from the person's wrongdoing. Forgiveness does not nullify judgment and punishment. There is no immersion in Lethe—the river of forgetfulness—to distance oneself from memories of wrongdoing, as Dante, the pilgrim, experiences at the summit of Mount Purgatory (*Purgatorio* XXXI). Transgressors will not be granted forgetfulness of their actions, but the ability to start over. Kristeva (2002) believes that forgiveness can be mediated effectively through painting—especially Georgia O'Keefe—but also through music and creative, poetic communication.

Kristeva's accounts of forgiveness rely heavily on Arendt's (1958) discussion of forgiveness, which in turn rests on an Augustinian conception of forgiveness. But, whereas Kristeva develops the idea of forgiveness in its relation to human interiority, Arendt develops it toward the communal and political. Arendt's concern is how forgiveness works in the sphere of the worldly in which men and women disclose themselves to others through their speech and actions. Arendt's (1958) rich account of human action takes its prompt from her reading of Dante's *Monarchia* and is the necessary prelude to her concept of forgiveness.

> For in every action what is primarily intended by the doer, whether he acts from natural necessity or out of free will, is the disclosure of his own image. Hence it comes about that every doer, in so far as he does, takes delight in doing; since everything that is desires its own being, and since in action the being of the doer is somehow intensified, delight necessarily follows ... Thus, nothing acts unless [by acting] it makes patent its latent self. (Arendt, 1958, p. 175)

By speech and action, men and women create webs of human relationships and, along with them, unpredictable consequences. Speaking and acting of necessity result in good and harm. Arendt states:

> Because the actor always moves among and in relation to other acting beings, he is never merely a "doer" but always and at the same time a sufferer. To do and to suffer are like opposite sides of the same coin, and the story that an act starts is composed of its consequent deeds and sufferings. (p. 190)

The inevitability and irreversibility of the adverse effects of human action find their remedy in "the faculty of forgiving" (p. 237). Forgiveness is a release from the consequences—emphatically not the erasure of a bad or transgressive act. Forgiveness allows one to begin anew, to continue to act freely in the world. It appears to change reality by undoing through speech and action that which seemed irreversible. Such transformative power, without which men and women would be imprisoned by wrongful acts, is inherent in "the potentialities of action itself" (pp. 236–237). What activates this potentiality is 'respect,' which for Arendt is something like Aristotle's conception of *philia*—a kind of friendship but "without intimacy and without closeness" (p. 243). Such friendship regards a person from whatever distance exists between him or her and the other. It is not dependent on a person's résumé of accomplishments or qualities. "Respect," writes Arendt, "because it concerns only the person, is quite sufficient to prompt forgiving of what a person did, for the sake of the person" (p. 243). Insofar as one's speech and actions have a bearing for good or ill on others, forgiveness is always a communal act. We can never forgive ourselves because

> we are dependent upon others, to whom we appear in a distinctness which we ourselves are unable to perceive. Closed within ourselves, we would never be able to forgive ourselves of any failing or transgression because we would lack the experience of the person for the sake of whom one can forgive. (p. 243)

Before settling on respect as the motivating force for forgiveness, Arendt considered love as a motive for forgiving. She acknowledges the value of the Christian principle "that only love can forgive because only love is fully receptive to who somebody is, to the point of being always willing to forgive him whatever he may have done" (p. 243). But ultimately, such love, "by its very nature, is unworldly" (p. 243) and ill-suited to the political sphere of human action. It applies, if at all, to a narrowly circumscribed sphere of human relations.

Arendt (1958) departs from her Augustinian influences by holding that forgiveness does not require an action coming from outside the natural order of human existence, such as grace. Curiously, Arendt premises her account of human action, and ultimately forgiveness, on her interpretation of Dante's conception of self-definition in *Monarchia*. But then she moves in a radically different direction from him by drastically circumscribing the power of love in human affairs. Whereas for Dante in the *Purgatorio* and in the entire *Commedia*, all of creation moves and is governed by the economy of love (e.g., *Purgatorio* XVII).

To be sure, friendship or *philia* is a kind of love, according to Lewis's (1960) typology of love. But Arendt's conception of friendship, which she prefers to call 'respect,' has little in common with Lewis's account of friendship or the warmth of the friendships in *Purgatorio* primarily between Virgil and Dante, but also between Casella and Statius. Such friendship, as Barolini (2014) notes in his commentary on Canto II of *Purgatorio*, is one of the cantica's great themes: "there is no theme that has deeper roots in Dante's poetry than that of male friendship." By contrast with friendship as we find it in *Purgatorio*, Arendt's (1958) concept of friendship or respect is an arms-length relationship, "without intimacy, and without closeness" (p. 243).

A contemporary of Arendt's, Vladimir Jankélévitch comes closer to Dante's conception of forgiveness inasmuch as it insists that true forgiveness must involve an authentic relation with another person and be prompted by something outside of human nature and potentialities. Like Arendt, Jankélévitch was Jewish and his extensive range of philosophical writings drew heavily on Greek, Roman, and Christian sources without committing to any particular religious confession. Jankélévitch (2005), as explained by his translator Andrew Kelley, holds that "true forgiveness must involve a real relation with another person" (p. xxi). For

Jankélévitch, the act of forgiveness is of "the order of grace" and "supernatural" in character, inasmuch as forgiveness is not merely to overcome hatred for an offense, "nor to rally around the thesis of innocence" (p. xxiii). Rather,

> forgiveness consists in this, that my opinion on the subject of the guilty person precisely has not changed; but ... it is my relations with the guilty person that [are] modified, it is the whole orientation of our relations that finds itself inverted, overturned, and overwhelmed. In the process, "hatred" turns into "love." (p. xxiii)

Jankélévitch (2005) shares in common with Arendt and Dante the natality that results from forgiveness. "Forgiveness," writes Jankélévitch, "is literally epoch-making in both senses of the word: It suspends an old order, it inaugurates the new order" (p. 149). With Kristeva, he sees forgiveness as a gift. The gift of forgiveness institutes new relations among men and women, and inaugurates "a second youth, *a vita nuova*" (p. 150). Forgiveness also has ontological consequences because the person forgiven knows a joy "reserved for those of who have rebounded from non-being into being" (p. 150).

The power of forgiveness to create the world anew takes on extraordinary significance in the theology of Guardini. Like Arendt, Guardini favors the Augustinian tradition of theological reflection. It is likely that Guardini's theology directly influenced Arendt in some measure since, as noted by Krieg (1995), she attended his lectures at the Friedrich Wilhelm University in Berlin during the 1920s. Guardini's account of forgiveness begins with the nature of sin. He acknowledges one's personal responsibility for sin, but because we exist in an intricate web of relations with others and the world, it is "impossible to speak of the sin of the one" (Guardini, 1954, p. 147). Sin opposes the moral order and natural order by imitating Lucifer's attempts to dethrone and degrade his Creator. It opposes the sacredness of human persons, human community, and the creation that sustains and nurtures them. In the end, "sin does not remain in the solitary cell of the human conscience, but swiftly spreads to become a community of error" (p. 149). Sin's communal nature resonates in unison with Arendt's theory of human action insofar as the irrepressible need for a person to act in the world inevitably has consequences for the human community.

In his commentary on the cure of the paralytic in Mark's gospel (*Mark* 2:3–5), Guardini focuses on the extraordinary words of Christ: "My child, thy sins are forgiven." To the scribes observing this scene, these words are blasphemous. "Who can forgive sins but God?" (*Mark* 2:7–8). Guardini (1954) suggests that more than the ability to walk, Jesus read a deeper yearning of the paralytic: his desire for forgiveness. He wanted to be rid of his sin, "really rid of it" (p. 150). In the deepest part of his conscience, he wanted to be entirely freed from guilt. This deepest desire of the human heart to be sinless and guiltless cannot be realized through merely human power, an ethical system, or religious principles. It is possible only from the outside, from revelation, from God. Guardini explains:

> God lives beyond the reaches of good, and therefore of evil. He himself *is* the good, but in inconceivable freedom; freedom from all ties, even from ties as ultimate as the conception of good. Such freedom renders him more powerful than sin. It is the freedom of love. Love is not only kinder, more alive than mere justice ... Such then the love that enables God to rise and, without in the least impairing truth and justice, to proclaim: Thy sin no longer exists. (p. 150)

For Guardini, genuine forgiveness is not only a force that allows for creating anew, as we see in Kristeva, Arendt, and Jankélévitch. It is "as far superior to creation, as love is to justice" (p. 150). The *Genesis* account of creation out of nothing stands as an unfathomable mystery, but even more so is the power of forgiveness.

> All human concepts are completely lost when faced with the mystery of God's power to render a sinner sinless. Such creative power emanates from the pure liberty of love. Between the states of sinfulness and sinlessness lies a death, a destruction in which the sinner is submerged, in order to be lifted from it into a new existence. (p. 150)

Like Jankélévitch, the joy of being set aright is primarily an ontological event—rebounding from non-being to being, raised from ruin to a new existence. For Guardini, such joy finds its expression in poetry, festivity, and liturgy. Dante gives expression to this sort of joy in the most dramatic liturgical event in *Purgatorio*: the emblematic pageantry at the summit of Mount Purgatory.

Leading the pageant (*Purgatorio* XXIX) is a seven-candle candelabrum. The richly symbolic number seven, suggests the seven churches of the book of *Revelation*, the seven gifts of the Holy Spirit, and the seven terraces of Purgatory proper (as noted in Mandelbaum's translation of Alighieri, 1320/1982; and the Sayers translation of Alighieri, 1320/1955). Seven also signifies the plenitude of God's forgiveness. "Then Peter went up to him and said, 'Lord, how often must I forgive my brother if he wrongs me? As often as seven times?' Jesus answered, 'Not seven, I tell you, but seventy-seven times'" (*Matthew* 18:21–22).

Continuing in Canto XXIX of *Purgatorio*, processing behind the candelabrum are twenty-four elders signifying the twenty-four books of the Old Testament; four animals, the four Gospels; a chariot, the Church; the griffin—with a lion's body and an eagle's head and wings—the dual nature of Jesus. Seven women clothed in white, green, and red come next. As Hollander and Hollander (2003) explain in their commentary, three of them walk alongside the right side of the chariot, representing faith, hope, and charity; four walk alongside the left side, representing prudence, justice, fortitude, and temperance, the four cardinal virtues. Prudence has three eyes to see the past, present, and future. Recapitulating the symbolic number seven of the procession's start are seven elders representing seven authors of the New Testament: St. Luke's *Acts of the Apostles*; the letters of St. Paul; the letters of Sts. Peter, John, James, and Jude; and *Revelation*.

This elaborate and spectacular liturgical procession seems at first to be heralding another public liturgical event, a ceremony of marriage. At the moment anticipated since Canto II of *Inferno*, Beatrice appears to Dante, the pilgrim, in "a white veil" (*Purgatorio* XXX:32). But what follows is not a wedding, but a public liturgy of confession, a rite that entails one's self-accusation of sinfulness, contrition, forgiveness, and reparation. The reunion of Dante and Beatrice is anything but warm and happy. Its tone is harsh, with Beatrice sharply reproaching Dante's failure to keep to the straight path and setting his desires on worthless things. He acknowledges the truth of Beatrice's charges and with tears of contrition confesses: "Mere appearance/ turned me aside with their false loveliness,/ as soon as I had lost your [Beatrice's] countenance" (*Purgatorio* XXXI:34–36).

Dante's confession occurs after the purgation of the seven terraces, and the purifying fire at the entrance to the earthly paradise. Nevertheless, Dante, the poet, requires a public confession before the angelic choirs, the Church, and Beatrice. Beatrice to Dante:

> Had you been silent or denied
> what you confess, your guilt would not be less
> in evidence …
>
> But when the charge of sinfulness has burst
> from one's own cheek, then in our court the whet-
> stone turns and blunts our blade's own cutting edge. (*Purgatorio* XXXI:37–42)

As in Canto I, Dante here presents the tension between Divine Filiation and humility. The self-shaming and humbling act of confession occur together with Beatrice's admonition to stand erect with the dignity of a son of God, ready to act. For she reminds him that he is a man and not a child.

> As children, when ashamed, will stand, their eyes
> upon the ground—they listen, silently,
> acknowledging their fault repentantly—
>
> so did I stand; and she enjoined me …
> "… lift up
> your beard …"
>
> I knew quite well—when she said 'beard' but meant
> my face (*Purgatorio* XXXI:64–69, 74–75)

Finally, the act of confessing rectifies Dante's desires: "The nettle of remorse so stung me then,/ that those—among all other—things that once/ most lured my love, became most hateful to me" (*Purgatorio* XXXI:85–87).

What follows is Dante's immersion in Lethe guided by Matilde and accompanied by the chanting of the *Asperges me* from *Psalm* 51, *The Miserere*. As in the liturgy of Baptism, the descent into the water symbolizes the death of sin and the rising up, the state of purification. Esolen's (Alighieri, 1320/2004) gloss on the immersion in Lethe highlights the ontological significance of forgiveness. Drinking the waters of Lethe for pre-Christians meant total forgetfulness of the travails of life. By way of contrast, Dante's drinking of Lethe's waters is a restoration to Edenic innocence. Dante enters the waters of Lethe to purify the entirety of his life. After which the remembrance of sin is "something extrinsic" to the new person he has become through the grace of forgiveness. As Esolen explains, "It [sin] forms no part of his being. He does not so much forget as regain" (Alighieri, 1320/2004, p. 491).

The Serious Playfulness of *Purgatorio*

Purgatorio is a prolonged liturgy, a performance, aimed at the reordering of human loves through forgiveness, and ultimately setting things aright between the person, others, and God. It is a space of poetic playfulness. But as Guardini (1997) would be quick to remind us, it is also serious in ensuring that its playfulness—a version of what Mazzotta (1993) calls "*theologia ludens*"—ought not be de-coupled from the truth it expresses and to which it allows us access. Like poetry and the poetic imagination, Guardini (1997) views the liturgy as a space of repose—not escape—with an indirect effect on human affairs. It has, writes Guardini,

> something in itself reminiscent of the stars, of their eternally fixed and even course, of their inflexible order of their profound silence, and of the infinite space in which they are poised. It is only in appearance that the liturgy seems detached and untroubled by the actions and striving and moral position of men and women. For in reality it knows that those who live by it will be true and spiritually sound and at peace to the depths of their being and that when they leave its sacred confines to enter life they will be people of courage. (p. 95)

These stars, the "starry wheels," are the endpoints of the Purgatorian pilgrimage. When Dante and Virgil climbed out of Inferno to the shore of the isle of Mount Purgatory, they "saw four stars/ not seen before except by the first people./ Heaven appeared to revel in their flames" (*Purgatorio* I:23–25). This moment of *con-sidere*, of thinking and being with the stars, calls to mind for Dante the memory of "the first people," the first community of human persons, which before the fall, had rightly ordered their loves. Restoring this right order for Purgatorians requires the arduous climb up Mount Purgatory, sustained and encouraged by a covenant of friendship, to the place where they will find "the first people."

Notes

1 Unless otherwise noted, all translations of *Inferno* and *Purgatorio* are by Allen Mandelbaum (2004).
2 All Biblical quotations are drawn from Jones (Ed.) (1966) *The Jerusalem Bible*.

References

Alighieri, D. (1955). *The comedy of Dante Alighieri: Purgatory* (D. Sayers, Trans.). Penguin Books. (Original work published 1320)
Alighieri, D. (1990). *Il Convivio* (R. H. Lansing, Trans.). Garland Library of Medieval Literature. (Original work published 1304–1307)
Alighieri, D. (2003). *Purgatorio* (J. Hollander & R. Hollander, Trans.). Anchor Books. (Original work published 1320)
Alighieri, D. (2004). *Inferno* (A. Mandelbaum, Trans.). Bantam Dell.(Original work published 1320)
Alighieri, D. (2004). *Purgatorio* (A. Mandelbaum, Trans.). Bantam Dell.(Original work published 1320)
Alighieri, D. (2004). *Purgatorio* (A. Esolen, Trans.). Modern Library.(Original work published 1320)
Arendt, H. (1958). *The human condition* (2nd ed.). University of Chicago Press.
Barolini, T. (2014). Purgatorio 2: The earth clock: Embracing the human. *Commento Baroliniano*, Digital Dante. Columbia University Libraries. Retrieved from: https://digitaldante.columbia.edu/dante/divinecomedy/purgatorio/purgatorio-2/
Brueggemann, W. (2003). *An introduction to the Old Testament: The canon and Christian imagination*. Westminster John Know Press.
Guardini, R. (1954). *The Lord*. Regnery.
Guardini, R. (1957). *Prayer in practice*. Pantheon.
Guardini, R. (1979). *Sacred signs*. Michael Glazier.
Guardini, R. (1997). *The spirit of the liturgy*. Herder & Herder.
Hawkins, P. S. (2006) *Dante: A brief history*. Blackwell.
Holloway, J. H. (1993). *The Pilgrim and the book: A study of Dante, Langland and Chaucer*. Peter Lang.
Jankélévitch, V. (2005) *Forgiveness* (A. Kelley, Trans.). University of Chicago Press.
Krieg, R. A. (1995). *Romano Guardini: Proclaiming the sacred in a modern world*. Liturgy Training Publications.
Kristeva, J. (2001). *Hannah Arendt*. Columbia University Press.
Kristeva, J. (2002). Forgiveness: An interview with Alison Rice. *PMLA, 117*(2), 278–295.
Kristeva, J. (2010). *Hatred and forgiveness*. Columbia University Press.
Jones, A. (Ed.) (1966). *The Jerusalem Bible*. Doubleday & Company.
Lewis, C. S. (1960). *The four loves*. Harcourt Brace.
Lundberg, M. (2011). *Tonus peregrinus: The history of a psalm-tone and its use in polyphonic music*. Routledge.
Mastrobuono, A. C. (1979). *Essays on Dante's philosophy of history*. L. S. Olschki.
Mazzotta, G. (1993). *Dante's vision and the circle of knowledge*. Princeton University Press.
Mazzotta, G. (2014). *Reading Dante*. Yale University Press.

Ratzinger, J. (1986). *The feast of faith: Approaches to a theology of the liturgy*. Ignatius Press.

Scott, J. (2010). *A poetics of forgiveness: Cultural responses to loss and wrongdoing*. New Palgrave Macmillan.

Singleton, C. S. (2000). In exitu Israel de Aegypto. *Dante Studies, 118*, 167–187.

Thurston, H. (1908). Cincture. In *The Catholic encyclopedia*. Robert Appleton Company. Retrieved December 5, 2019 from New Advent: http://www.newadvent.org/cathen/03776a.htm

Tucker, O. S. B. D. J. (1960). In exitu Israel de Aegypto: The divine comedy in the light of the Easter liturgy. *American Benedictine Review, XI*(1), 43–61.

Von Hildebrand, D. (1943). *Liturgy and personality*. Longmans.

Webb, H. (2013). Postures of penitence in Dante's Purgatorio. *Dante Studies, 131*, 219–236.

Williams, C. (1994). *The figure of Beatrice: A study in Dante*. Boydell & Brewer.

Wolterstorff, N. (2018). *Acting liturgically: Philosophical reflections on religious practice*. Oxford University Press.

Wright, N. T. (1988). *The epistles of Paul to the Colossians and to Philemon: An introduction and commentary*. Eerdmans.

Wright, N. T. (1994). Jerusalem in the New Testament. In P. W. Walker (Ed.), *Jerusalem past and present in the purposes of God* (2nd ed., pp. 53–77). Baker.

Chapter 12

Storytelling: Dante, Freud, and their Models of Eros

Hattie Myers

Hannah Arendt (1968) wrote that "no philosophy, no analysis, no aphorism, be it ever so profound, can compare in intensity and richness of meaning with a properly narrated story" (p. 22). Dante and Freud wanted their visions and theories to not just address reality, but to profoundly transform it. Like Arendt, they both knew that the way this transformation could occur would be through a properly narrated story. In psychoanalytic treatment, the 'properly narrated story' takes form within the psychoanalytic relationship. As Freud created it, this relationship became the vehicle through which any person's story could emerge and transform. In the *Divine Comedy*, this is reversed. One single man's 'properly narrated story' became, in Dante's hands, a way to transform all men.

On the surface, there is little connection between Dante's vision of a Christian afterlife and Freud's model of the psyche. And why should there be? The story of a medieval prophet born on the cusp of the Renaissance and the story of a nineteenth-century neurologist born on the cusp of postmodernism bear little connection. In this essay, I do not apply a psychoanalytic lens to Dante's great poem, nor do I have any interest in giving psychoanalysis a theological spin. But bringing them together on their own terms is another story.

Dante and Freud envisioned the kind of order intrinsic to the human condition which, if revealed, in Dante's words, might "remove those living in this life from a state of misery" (Alighieri, 1892, p. 199) or, for Freud, aiming lower, "might turn misery into everyday unhappiness" (Freud, 1895/1909, p. 120). Dante didn't make up the idea of a Christian afterlife, and Freud didn't invent the idea of an unconscious, but their models of eros allowed for a new understanding of the differentiated causes and depths of human suffering. All stories begin with desire—so does this one.

Like Aristotle and Kant before them, Dante and Freud were interested in the relationship between the nature of reality and the nature of our souls. Unlike Aristotle or Kant, Freud and Dante are not best remembered for their speculative theories on moral or natural philosophy. Rather, they are part of a tradition perhaps more in line with Augustine, who in his *Confessions* turned inward to understand nature and the soul. Unlike Augustine, however, Freud and Dante recognized that the complexity and depth of their own desires could not be relinquished. It was this unusually personal and philosophical engagement with the problem of desire that gave them the solid foundation they required to create a new way to ameliorate human suffering.

Freud and Dante recognized that conflicting desires lie at the heart of all human misery. For Dante, the problem was cloaked in medieval Christian concerns related to free will and predestination: How was it that men could be free while at the same time subject to a greater transcendent force? Six hundred years later, Freud struggled with an analogous knot: How can we become the master of our own house given our unconscious instinctual nature?

The unified theories that Freud and Dante developed to address these conundrums were based on similar models of eros. How they came to understand desire enabled them to confront these metaphysical problems without resorting to dualisms or nonparadoxical ways of thinking.

By way of ushering in his new discovery, Freud used *The Interpretation of Dreams* (1900/1913)—and in particular chapter seven—to explore the depth and contours of the psychic reality. He describes psychic reality as emanating from a dark and unknowable source, where the meshwork of associations is particularly close and branches out in every direction into the intricate network of our world of thought. The libidinal wish, said Freud, which is at the center of every dream, every psychic experience, emerges like a "mushroom out of this mycelium" (p. 416). Freud called this obscure spot the 'navel' of the dream and emphasized that unknowable point is not locatable in space so much as in time. Freud cautioned his readers that he was using spatial metaphors to describe what were actually temporal phenomena. The metaphors, he cautioned, should not be taken for reality itself.

These psychoanalytic concepts laid out in *The Interpretation of Dreams* were to be Freud's earliest blueprint for a unified model of psychic reality which, in its most complex rendition, was a closed multileveled, tripartite structure that had no edge and within which any thought or image could be associated to another. The year was 1900.

The unified clarity of Dante's vision was unveiled to him only in the final hours of his journey, reportedly in the year 1300. There are about twenty lines in *Paradiso* XXVIII where Dante describes seeing the point from which, he said, hung the heavens and all of nature. Dante leaned on Aristotle to add philosophical heft in his effort to rhetorically describe the truth of what he beheld. In a discussion related to the 'unmoved mover' as a final cause and supreme good, Aristotle says, "It is on such a principle then, that the heavens and the natural world depend" (*Metaphysics* XII:7). Dante took this philosophical abstraction to heart, and with it, he visualized a universe consistent with thirteenth-century Christian theology. Dante described seeing the heavens and all of nature concretely suspended from a God upon whom the heavens and all of nature depend and circle around. By using the Italian word '*depende*,' which connotes both a psychological abstraction and a concrete physical relationship—like the English phrase 'to lean on'—Dante linguistically joined physical complexity and psychological depth of vision. Dante himself depends, throughout his poem, on the flexibility of words and images to convey the complexity of connected parallel universes where different spheres of space are mirrored and held together by time and speed. He leans on language.

How did Freud and Dante develop these different visions of reality that were powerful enough—as Lawrence Friedman suggests about psychoanalysis, and Teo Barolini suggests about the *Divine Comedy*—to challenge our human inclination to see reality in dualistic and nonparadoxical terms? To answer this question, it is necessary, as Wallace Stevens wrote, to examine "the resemblance between things" (1942, p. 71). Using two different stories and means of storytelling, it seems likely that Freud's and Dante's models of eros contributed—if not enabled—them to envision a complex structure of reality, which in turn they would use to explain and transform our human condition.

Freud wrote in a footnote added in 1910 to his 1905 *Three Essays on the Theory of Sexuality* (1920) that,

> The most striking distinction between the erotic life of antiquity and our own no doubt lies in the fact that the ancients laid the stress upon the instinct itself, whereas we emphasize its object. The ancients glorified the instinct and were prepared, on its account, to honor even an inferior object, while we despise the instinctual activity in itself and find excuses for it only in the merits of the object. (p. 30, n. 13)

Different from the ancients and unlike their contemporaries, Dante and Freud neither glorified nor despised desire. Rather, they placed their understanding of drive at the center of their understanding of how change occurs. Freud defined instinctual activity or 'drive' as a concept that he situated on the interface between soma and psyche. Because drive itself was an abstraction, the reality of a drive could only be inferred from its manifestation—or in Freud's words, its 'derivative'—in action or thought.

For Freud, drives were key to understanding the structure of our psyche. In the *Three Essays on the Theory of Sexuality* (1905/1920), he laid out his phylogenetic description of the development of drives, which became a story of psychosexual phases. Later, in his metapsychological papers, he described the vicissitudes of the drives and their role in psychic functioning and suffering. Freud's seminal works showed how the sources, aims, objects, and force of our drives—as reflected in thoughts, dreams, symptoms, and actions—become not only a way to map psychic reality, but also a way to understand how we engage with the world. Freud created a therapy out of these theories in which the intensities, conflicted aims, and displaced objects of human desire could be experienced, put into words, and transformed in the context of a unique therapeutic relationship.

What was the story of Freud's drive theory at the turn of the twentieth century? Freud was an empiricist. He developed his understanding of drives in the context of the scientific premise that, in the natural world, all objects come to a state of rest unless otherwise acted upon. Within this perspective, Freud posited that the aim of drives must always be trained toward relieving tension and achieving a state of homeostasis. In accordance with these natural laws of physics, Freud believed that unopposed by consciousness or the demands of reality, there was an energic force that would naturally move to drive ego and id more closely together in an effort to achieve a frictionless, conflict-free state. The implications of Freud's drive theory, following these principles of constancy, led to his nirvana principle, or the death instinct. The end of all internal tension would result in a state of inertia. This bit of existential darkness notwithstanding, the fullness of Freud's drive theory allowed a way for him to understand psychic transformation, psychic health, and psychic pathology. "Drives," Freud said, were "demand[s] made upon the mind for work in consequence of its connection with the body" (1915, p. 122). Over the course of his lifetime, Freud's ideas would become increasingly more precise as he endeavored to explain exactly how it was that work happened.

Dante also understood desire in highly abstract terms. In his earliest poetry, Dante recognized that love moved his heart in inexplicable ways, and he concluded as Freud had that love was neither material nor intellectual. The *Vita Nuova* was a collection of Dante's early poetry mixed with later prose, in which Dante interpreted, in hindsight, the complexity of his desires in relation to his experience and dreams. While in the *Vita Nuova*, Dante said that he had spoken of love in concrete bodily terms, but love, in fact, was not a substance. Channeling Aristotle, Dante concluded that love was an "accident of a substance" (*Vita Nuova* XXV). Trying next to get better purchase not just on the essence of love but also on its trajectory, Dante tried his own hand at philosophy to better understand the problem of shifting desire. Dante's philosophical musings were recorded in a treatise he called the *Convivio*. Much in the way that Freud's neurological tract *Project for a Scientific Psychology* shadows *The Interpretation of Dreams*, the *Convivio* was Dante's scholastic forerunner to the *Divine Comedy*.

In the *Convivio*, Dante explained his idea that goods or objects—*bene*—are taken in through the eyes and their images unfolded in the heart. Initially, the soul desires simple things—an apple, a woman, a horse, money—and then the aim of desire becomes truer and objects become better. For example, a goodness that could be shared by everyone might be a better goodness to possess because there is no limit to it and, therefore, no harm done to anyone in having it. Later illustrating this point in the *Divine Comedy*, Dante wrote, "love is the seed in you of every virtue/ and of all acts deserving punishment"[1] (*Purgatorio* XVII:104–105). Desire, in abstract, non-psychological terms, brokered neither a positive nor negative valence; it was a motion. And for better or worse, it was desire that moved the soul.

For Dante, desire's spiritual motion embodied the Christian soul, and for Freud, the drive's energic molding of man's psyche was neither glorified nor vilified but lay at the center of both their arts. It was from this center that Dante and Freud set forth on paths yet uncharted. Freud's psychoanalysis rested on his understanding of drives inherent to our psychic development. In Dante's *Commedia*, desire was embodied as spiritual motion. Both men believed that this energic force would, if not impinged upon, be pulled—or be inclined—toward an ideal, conflict-free, tensionless state that, as long as we are alive, is actually unachievable.

Of course, Dante's theory of desire led to quite a different story.

As a medieval Christian, Dante knew that humans had two ways to access God and assess truth so that desires could be harnessed and directed toward our better good. First, Dante knew that God could only be accessed through Christ's mediation. The dual qualities of Christ literally being both man and God provided the necessary transitional bridge between humanity and heaven. Secondly, Dante knew that only during life can a man's capacity to reason allow him to differentiate good from bad in order to better direct the trajectory of his desires. Because inclinations can only transform in time, souls require time to transform.

While we are living, the aims and objects of our desires as they continue to develop come to map the character of our souls. Dante explained that human desire can be too strong or too weak; it can be aimed toward the wrong object or the right object for the wrong reasons. Our ability to direct our fate and transform our souls is made possible through the use of our reason in tandem with our desires. In other words, as explained in *Purgatorio* XVII, we have the free will to act, or not, on our inclinations. After life, there is no more time to act; in the afterlife, desire is justly met.

On the surface, it might seem that Dante's description of the afterlife of a soul whose desires are met has some resonance with Freud's description of an autoerotic state of primary narcissism—a kind of return to the beginning of life prior to the experience of any object outside the self. This, I think, would be a profoundly reductionistic misreading. A more accurate parallel of Dante's model of desire in the afterlife may be found in Freud's description of perversions. In perversion, Freud revealed, our instinctual life unites under the sway of desire unmediated by time or space. In the afterlife, when there is no longer time nor space, Dante also imagines that desires are mediated by only our own tendencies. In the abstraction of the afterlife, the inclination of each soul is perfectly and justly met in Dante's world, whether in heaven or hell, again, for better or worse.

Freud and Dante shared a common mission. These two cartographers of our souls were determined to understand the paradoxical aspects of human nature in order to address our suffering. The task to which they set themselves required new arts powerful enough to contain the concrete, affective, philosophical, psychological multiple meanings of any one story. While the power of psychoanalysis and the *Commedia* would come to depend upon the capaciousness of language and the centrality of relationships, it was their makers' understanding of eros that gave these arts a common foundation.

Note

1 Unless otherwise noted, all *Commedia* quotes are the Mandelbaum translation and may be found in Columbia University's Digital Dante: https://digitaldante.columbia.edu./

References

Alighieri, D. (1892). *A translation of Dante's eleven letters* (C. S. Lathan, Trans.). (G. R. Carpenter, Ed.). Houghton Mifflin and Company.

Arendt, H. (1968). *Men in Dark Times*. Harcourt Brace Javanovich.

Freud, S. (1909). *Selected papers on hysteria* (A. A. Brill, Trans.). The Journal of Nervous and Mental Disease Publishing Company. (Original work published 1895).

Freud, S. (1913). *The interpretation of dreams* (A. A. Brill, Trans.). Macmillan. (Original work published 1900).

Freud, S. (1915). *Drives and their vicissitudes. The standard edition* (Vol. 14). W.W. Norton & Company.

Freud, S. (1920). *Three essays on the theory of sexuality* (A. A. Brill, Trans.). Nervous and Mental Disease Publishing Company. (Original work published 1905). [e-publication: https://www.sigmundfreud.net/three-essays-on-the-theory-of-sexuality-pdf-ebook.jsp].

Stevens, W. (1942). *The necessary angel: Essays on reality and imagination*. Vintage Books.

Chapter 13

Purgatory as a Metaphor for Therapy and Associated Ethical Implications

K. L. McFarland and Tommy Givens

While journeying up Mount Purgatory with Virgil, Dante ascends to the second terrace where those guilty of envy reside. He writes:

> And as the sun brings no help to the blind,
> So for the shades in the place that I speak of
> The light of heaven withholds its radiance.
>
> An iron thread pierces and sews up
> All of their eyelids, as is done to falcons
> Still so wild they recoil at keeping quiet …
>
> … And on the other side of me there sat
> The devout shades who wet their cheeks with tears
> Which seeped out through the terrible stitched seams. (Alighieri, 1320/1987, *Purgatorio* XIII:67–72, 82–84, Cotter translation)

Descriptions such as these and other sundry purgations fill the second book of Dante's masterpiece, bringing one to wonder how such suffering can possibly be related to therapy. Yet, can it not be said that there are often healing moments of shared suffering within therapy? This paper will endeavor to use Purgatory as a primary metaphor to explore the role of suffering within the therapeutic process. The first section of this paper elaborates on this metaphor and the concept of purgation that may be occurring within therapy. Following this, this chapter presents a concept of engaging in therapy with the dead, proposing that the actions of the dead are still playing out in the lives of the living and that some of these too need to be purged. Finally, this essay closes with an exploration of the ethical question of evil, considering whether suffering can be instrumentalized towards healing or if this is a problematic cheapening of suffering and potentially a form of retraumatization.

Therapy as Purgatory

Many psychological theorists have used metaphors to describe the process that occurs within a therapeutic setting. As noted by Todd (1985), Jung described therapy as confessional; but this current presentation examines the thesis that therapy could also be viewed as purgation. To contemporary readers, Dante's *Purgatorio* may seem little different from his *Inferno*. The troubling and sometimes horrific images Dante imagined are overwhelming, so it can be difficult to see how any good could come from such suffering or whether such suffering can be understood in terms of the good that comes from it. However, parallels can be found between Purgatory and the therapeutic process. Therapy, like Purgatory, occurs in a liminal location that is set apart from everyday experience. And, like in Purgatory, in therapy, clients process the consequences of past actions in their personal history. Additionally, the role of the therapist is similar to that of Virgil in Dante's *Purgatorio*, in that the therapist is a unique supportive companion through the journey rather than an omnipotent expert. The following sections explore these concepts in more detail.

Therapy as Liminal

The Divine Landscape of Dante's *Commedia* includes the expected categories of the heavenly Paradise and hellish Inferno, but also the middle space of Purgatory. This is situated on the Earth and imagined as an immense mountain of nine levels. While Dante imagines the location of Purgatory as on the far side of the planet Earth, it is still in a location that is profoundly other, like the Inferno or Paradise. It constitutes a middle ground that is a place of transition and movement rather than fixedness. The souls that Dante finds on the various levels of Purgatory are on a journey of cleansing, and Purgatory itself is not a final destination.

Looking to therapy, it too is a type of middle ground. The psychological space of the therapy room is an in-between place that is set apart from the normal interactions of life. The therapeutic relationship is distinct from other social interactions, and the frame of therapy gives it a structure that is not present in other relational settings. This separateness allows clients emotional and relational space to contemplate their life and be purposeful about how they want to improve themselves. Ideally, therapy has a similar movement towards the goal of personal health, and therapy itself is not a final destination. Just as a soul in Purgatory desires to move on into Paradise, the clients in therapy desire to find healing and move on in their life. This analogy breaks down here slightly in that a client may complete a course of therapy and then later require a return to therapy for additional support, whereas the soul in Paradise does not need to ever return to Purgatory.

Lacan proposed that normal rhythms of life are disrupted by the Sabbath in a way that helps define and challenge expected understandings of the normal (Reinhard & Lupton, 2003). One could say that both therapy and Purgatory are similar in that they are disruptions of the expected rhythms of life and afterlife. Purgatory and therapy are both places of pause before continuing forward. The existence of that pause helps travelers/clients understand more fully where they are coming from and where they are going. Without that pause, some understanding may still be present, but the pause—be it Sabbath, Purgatory, or Therapy—allows room for deeper processing to occur.

Processing as Purgation

The neologism 'Purgatory' did not come into existence as a noun and location until the middle of the twelfth century, as theologians grappled with how to understand the afterlife (Le Goff & Goldhammer, 1986). As the *Online Etymology Dictionary* ("purge," n.d.) informs its readers, prior to this, the verb 'purge' grew from the Old Latin '*purigare*,' taken from the roots '*purus*' "pure" and '*agere*' meaning "to set in motion." This purification process was distinct from the process of salvation. The existence of Purgatory addressed the theological challenge of what happens to people who were baptized as Christians but died without fully confessing their sins. According to Catholic theology of the twelfth century, they would still be impure and therefore, unable to ascend to Paradise where no sin is allowed. Yet they were also baptized believers and, therefore, unable to descend into the Inferno. Purgatory provided a theologically necessary space for the cleansing and purification of impure believers, readying them to move on in their heavenly journey.

Clinicians do not often speak using terms of purity, cleansing, sin, and purgation, yet conceptual parallels may be found. Events and circumstances sometimes occur within clients' lives that prevent them from achieving their desired goals, be it personal health, relational satisfaction, or any one of a number of presenting problems. These preventative struggles are likely the result of multiple interacting factors (Galatzer-Levy, 2017), so the therapist cannot point to a struggle with alcoholism or borderline behavioral patterns and simply label it a 'sin' to be purged. Yet a goal of therapy may still be to process such challenges and, hopefully, to learn to manage them so forward progress can be made towards the client's ultimate goals and health.

An apt example of this within psychological theory can be found in trauma-informed interventions. As extensively presented by the research of van der Kolk (e.g., 1994), some individuals are unable to neurologically process the memory of trauma in ways that non-traumatic memories are processed. Therefore, they have difficulty moving on in their lives in the wake of a traumatic event. Intrusive memories 'haunt' the individual, to use the language in line with Dante, and PTSD symptomatology may follow the specters and demons of unconsolidated traumatic memory. According to the well-known work by Herman (2015), when responding therapeutically to a client who has experienced trauma, therapy must progress through three main stages: establishing safety, remembrance and mourning, and reconnection. The therapist must provide a safe space for clients to be able to emotionally process the events that occurred, which then will ideally allow them to move forward in life. This is very similar to the concept of Purgatory. The location of Purgatory is not in the dangerous hellscape of the Inferno, nor is it among the living where further sin can occur. It is a set-apart location beyond Earth but before Paradise. In this safe location, souls can truly remember and mourn their past.

Traumatized clients are most often victims. The purging of therapy allows them to be purified to some extent of the 'sins' committed against them, as well as their own potentially maladaptive choices. Therapy does not set out to intentionally cause pain to the client, as this would be horribly unethical and directly opposed to the primary mandates of therapy. But it does provide a place for pain that already is within the client to emerge and be honored in an emotionally cathartic way. This is with the goal of allowing the client to recall, experience, then reconsolidate traumatic memories in ways that, as Herman (2015) recommends, are not affectively disruptive. And, like Purgatory, there is—ideally—no rush or time limit imposed upon the client for how long it takes to be 'cleansed' of the torment of past trauma. It can be said that this language is not quite appropriate since the reconnection after trauma is not a perfect reconnection, and there cannot be a complete purgation of a history of trauma. But trauma can be processed, healing can be had, and forward motion in life is possible.

Guide or Companion

As Dante journeyed through the various levels of the Divine Geography, he did not travel alone. His guide through the Inferno was the righteous pagan Virgil and then Beatrice led him as far as she was permitted through Paradise. Dante stayed with Virgil through his time on Mount Purgatory, yet the wise Greek was unable to answer some of Dante's questions as he had in the Inferno (e.g., *Purgatorio* VI:30–48). Virgil, according to Dante, does not belong in Purgatory because he wasn't baptized in life; therefore, he did not know the paths of the mountain as well as he knew the paths of the underworld. He instead became a companion to Dante, rather than a guide. Virgil was able to answer some of Dante's questions but still continued to spur him on. Then, at the appropriate time and place, Virgil left Dante in Beatrice's capable hands. Dante later mourned the loss of Virgil but continued upward and onward into Paradise.

In many ways, the role of the therapist is similar to the role of Virgil in *Purgatorio*. The therapist has wisdom to offer, but it is limited as the therapist is treading the unknown paths of the individual who sits across from her or him. This is more of a companion role than that of a guide, and while it is a supportive role, it is limited and not omniscient. This is important within this larger metaphor because Virgil has no authority within Purgatory. He only observes, responds, and occasionally recommends. Virgil is not responsible for the pain that exists on this mountain, nor is he called to the same path of Dante. His role is to support Dante's mission. And ultimately, God, not Virgil, orchestrates the painful healing that occurs on Mount Purgatory. In this chapter's final section on ethics, we offer more about the nature of this suffering.

Similarly, therapists are a removed participant in the lives of their clients. They are supportive, but that support is purposely limited by the ethical frame of therapy, allowing clients to make their own decisions and lead their own life. The expertise of the therapist is available to the client, like Virgil's wisdom was to Dante in Purgatory, but it is not an omniscient expertise. And, like in the

Commedia, therapists cannot orchestrate the processing that occurs, but can only facilitate it through their own theoretical and practical formation as a therapist. And ultimately, within therapy, it is clients who choose how they will engage in the therapeutic process and determine how the healing progresses.

Therapy with the Dead

In this section, we explore the concept of what it is to interact with the dead in a therapeutic setting. Obviously, this is not a suggestion of holding an in vivo seance or engaging in paranormal activity with the client in the session. As interesting as that might be, this paper instead explores the idea that the actions of the dead have repercussions that last into the present day. This section explores this concept starting with Dante's engagement with the dead, then an examination of psychological theory, and closes with a presentation of how Protestant Christian theology can engage the topic.

The Dead in the Commedia *and Roman Catholicism*

Catholicism has a long history of interacting with the dead, beginning with Jesus Christ Himself. The theology of a postmortem life allows for the possibility of the living communicating with the dead. The most obvious example of this is the Catholic practice of praying to the Saints, asking them to intervene for the good of the living. Within Dante's *Purgatorio*, however, the situation was reversed. The souls he encounters asked Dante to remember them when he returns to the land of the living, so that Dante may encourage faithful Christians to pray that their time in Purgatory will be shortened.

The tripartite structure of Dante's Divine Geography portrays souls in distinct levels, with each requiring a different response from the living. Souls in Hell are to be remembered as infamous examples and warnings and are also to be remembered as the people behind corrupt policies and systems still at play in Dante's day. The living were to learn and change their ways so they could avoid the punishments described in *Inferno*. The souls in Purgatory were indeed examples of what not to do, but they were less extreme examples, likely easier to identify with for the average reader. The living were to learn and change their ways, but they were to also remember the dead in their prayers. This is unique to *Purgatorio*, in that the living can help the dead and shorten their suffering. Finally, the souls in Paradise are also examples, but they are examples to follow. The Catholic Saints, among others, reside in this vast domain, and it is a place where the dead can intercede with God to ease the suffering of the living.

Within Psychology

It has been said that even when one is working with an individual client, the room is full of people that the client brings in with them (A. Dueck, personal communication, 2017). This is referring to all of the relationships, past and present, that create the complex dynamical systems of clients' lives, shaping their psychology (Juarrero, 2002). Therapists are trained to consider what systemic pressures, such as socio-economic status and culture, contribute to their clients' lives and psychological needs, but the scope of this consideration is typically synchronic and seldom extends beyond the client's lifespan. In theory and in practice, the conversations surrounding social embeddedness generally refer to the living participants in the client's life. One exception to this rule would be grief work or the long-term processing of the loss of a particularly important individual in a client's life. However, it could be argued that every client is impacted by the dead, whether she or he is aware of it or not. Contemporary Western society does not like to think about or discuss the dead as many other cultures have and do, so it could potentially be called a blind spot within the psychological framework of many Westerners.

This tendency is beginning to change somewhat as research regarding the presence of intergenerational trauma progresses (Bezo & Maggi, 2018). Researchers are discovering the present, negative, psychological repercussions of events that may have occurred several generations in the past (Brothers, 2014). For example, 2019 marked the four-hundredth anniversary of the arrival of the first African slaves to 'American' soil (Noe-Payne, 2019). This event and the eventual establishment of slavery in the United States continues to profoundly affect the lives of African Americans, but also still impacts racial dynamics for all people groups in this country. The actions of the dead are still resonating four hundred years later, and many struggle to purge the impact of this systemic trauma from their lives. If moral/religious language is added, the transgression/sins—and virtues—of past generations shape the realities of the present. Viewed from the paradigm of complexity theory, the sins and virtues of past generations have shaped the landscape of possibilities for the living (Juarrero, 2002). This is not a deterministic shaping, where the living have no free will and their choices are predetermined by past generations. However, the inherited landscape of possibilities does constitute various limitations a person may or may not have. It may be incredibly difficult for a person to climb out of inherited poverty or fight the tide of systemic racism, but it isn't impossible (Juarrero, 2002).

Regardless of what the presenting problem may be, a clinician may be aided by exploring a client's ancestry as much as possible. It can be potentially overwhelming knowing how far back to go or what is relevant. But it can also be surprising what clinically relevant material comes up with a simple prompt like 'tell me about your grandparents.'

Within Protestant Theology

In the last section, we presented a brief overview of the traditional Roman Catholic understanding of Purgatory. Yet, this sketch did not look at Protestant perspectives, even as these are difficult to integrate. This is due to the fact that Protestant theologies concerning the afterlife are usually binary visions of Heaven and Hell, rather than the nuanced triadic Divine Geography that Dante envisions. The dead, to the average Protestant, are immediately taken to Judgment then whisked to Heaven or Hell, leaving no room for interaction with the living. Prayers should be offered only to God, not to intermediary Saints, and afterlife destinations are final, so there is no point in praying for the dead. Thus, it seems that there are few solid theological reasons in the minds of living Protestants to conceive of the dead as present, with the exception of personal loss.

But this traditional Protestant theology does not negate the previous paragraphs regarding engaging the dead in therapy. Regardless of the postmortem destinations of previous generations, their actions still have shaped the present reality that living people of the world must navigate. The Hebrew Bible reflects this phenomenon in its report that children endure the consequences of their ancestors' sins (*Exodus* 20:5–6; *Deuteronomy* 5:9), while it also prohibits intergenerational legal accountability (*Deuteronomy* 24:16; *Ezra* 18:20). This is an important distinction, which allows for the reality of inherited behaviors, traumas, and privileges—for good or ill—while providing a legal and theological basis for protecting a child from punishment for the actions of past generations. This is a subtle nuance, but an important one.

When considering a general Protestant perspective on the dead, it could be argued that the current theological paradigm is impoverished. Of course, caveats must be made regarding the presence of great diversity within various Protestant traditions. But the mental severing of the dead and the living may be more of a cultural development than a product of sound theological reflection. As has already been stated, the Roman Catholic theology surrounding the dead allows for far more interaction, as do the vast majority of indigenous non-Western religions. It is possible that inherited philosophies from the West—namely Cartesian dualism, the rise of scientism, and the Enlightenment's obsession with reason—kept Protestant thinkers from engaging the mystical in ways to which Roman Catholics were not averse.

Looking to the Old and New Testaments, there is not a clear outline of the heavenly geography that explicitly presents details for how to engage with the dead. Mention of Abraham's bosom (*Luke* 16:19–31), Gehenna (*Matthew* 5:29–30; *Mark* 9:43–47), the New Jerusalem, Heavens, and Earth (*Revelation* 21), and other such locations are referred to or described, but not explained. Protestants argue for and against the existence of a literal hell (Bell, 2011; Givens, 2016), the location of the New Heavens and Earth, and if damnation is eternal. The only thing Protestants seem to agree about on this topic is a general rejection of the idea of Purgatory, with notable exceptions such as C. S. Lewis (1952/2009).

However, it is possible that an understanding of Purgatory can be accepted from a Protestant perspective, though not in the traditional Roman Catholic sense of the term. The above-mentioned verses surrounding children experiencing the consequences of their ancestors' sins (*Exodus* 20:5–6; *Deuteronomy* 5:9) could be viewed as a form of Purgatory. It could be said that as each generation encounters the impact of the prior generation's sins, these can be cleansed by God as God works through communities and individuals. If people are indeed surrounded by a cloud of deceased witnesses (*Hebrews* 12:1), then it is possible that the dead are affected by the purging of their sins through the working out of the consequences of these sins in subsequent generations. This would likely be simultaneously good and painful to observe. As God's redemptive hand moves through the centuries, God redeems both the children and the ancestors.

One can easily imagine a different Protestant theologian arguing strongly against these ponderings. Certainty about this topic is impossible. Thus, spiritually-mindful clinicians do not have preset methodologies for how to engage the dead in ways that are ethically responsible and theologically thick. Pluralistic theologies will argue for and against any theory regarding the dead. Additionally, this paper examines only Christian theology and does not begin to touch various perspectives on the dead from other religious frameworks.

For the clinician, the overall encouragement would be to engage the dead while honoring the theological tradition of the client. Additionally, both clinicians and psychological theorists must take into account the presence of the dead in the academic heritage of Western theology and psychology. Polarized examples like Freud's rejection of religion and Jung's spiritual explorations exist within the annals of psychology's history. Similar comparisons could be made within theological circles. However, this essay is not recommending a thoughtless mystical leap of faith into the supernatural. It is true that pseudoscience is alive and well, and both theologians and researchers are wise to proceed carefully. But as postsecular philosophies are spreading in contemporary thought (Callaway & Taylor, 2019), it is important to purposefully consider how the concept of interacting with the dead might make sense, and to take account of other spiritual issues held within the client's existential and ontological worries.

Ethical Challenges

The final section of this paper addresses the ethical challenges that can be presented in response to using Purgatory as a metaphor for therapy. This concern mainly grows from the imagined sense of Purgatory as a place of imposed tortures by a vindictive deity. This section addresses this problem through a brief exploration of an example from Dante, then a more detailed presentation of the problem of evil and suffering through the lens of St. Thomas Aquinas.

Suffering in Dante's Purgatorio

This paper opened with a quote from the *Commedia* when Dante and Virgil ascended to the tier of the envious and saw, with horror, that the penitents' eyes were sewn shut. Dante does not minimize the jarring nature of this penance, but he includes the phrase "as is done to falcons,/ still so wild they recoil at keeping quiet" (*Purgatorio* XIII:71–72, Cotter translation). In medieval falconry, this practice was called 'seeling.' It developed in response to the reality that when a falcon is newly caught, it is terrified of everything and may seriously injure itself if it is startled by its new environment. Falconers today consider seeling cruel and instead utilize a falconry hood that covers the bird's eyes. But there is always the possibility that the hood may fall off, endangering the bird. So medieval falconers advocated for the use of seeling the falcon's eyes, for the bird's safety, while it became habituated to the sounds and smells of its new world. This time was also used to help it become used to and recognize its owner's voice. The medieval falconers did not believe that seeling hurt the falcons because they saw no evidence of pain when they engaged in this practice, so they did not believe they were being cruel (Frederick II, 1248/1961).

The parallels are immediately apparent with Dante's apt illustration. The envious were distracted by the lust of the eyes, so their sight was taken from them while they learned to be calm in the presence of a new Master. When they developed this self-control—and would no longer harm themselves by the temptations of the eyes—they would then regain both their sight and their freedom to continue on towards Paradise. When one considers the cultural context of the illustration, it seems far more understandable that Dante describes this consequence in *Purgatorio* and not *Inferno*. It is not pleasurable, because it is indeed a painful purging, but if the medieval falconers did not think seeling hurt the falcons, then Dante's metaphor feels a bit less cruel. (A brief note on the ethics of falconry as a sport: As Holderman (2010) notes, 70% of wild raptors die within their first year naturally. Contemporary falconers who catch young wild birds often train them for several years then release them as experienced hunters. Ethical practitioners of the sport consider this a way to support wild populations by helping young birds survive their vulnerable first few years. Released birds quickly revert to wild behaviors.)

Suffering in Healing

So, must we recoil at the notion of healing done by means of suffering? Is all such healing evil? Examples abound where healing is found on the far side of suffering, such as the 'no pain, no gain' mantra of some athletes, to the 'this will just pinch a little' warning before the dentist injects Novocain, to the pain of chemotherapy when battling cancer. Pain and healing often go together. Indeed, perhaps the existence of things like pain-stopping medications has shifted our understanding of suffering. Pain has come to be unilaterally equated with evil, but is this accurate? Pain can be said to be an important signal to the body that there is a problem that needs attention. Thus, this pain is not evil but good!

However, purposefully inflicted pain is a separate issue. One can see the essential difference between the pain inflicted by a medical doctor with the larger goal of recovery and the pain inflicted by an abuser. Self-mutilation is another form of inflicted pain, which is yet another ethical question of its own. But like the medical doctor, the therapist is mandated to act with the client's best interest in mind. Hence, to purposely set out to 'purge' a client's past traumas without the client's invitation or blessing could be seen as unethically inflicted suffering. Yet, *with* the client's consent, the therapist is tasked with knowingly guiding the client into a certain kind of pain. The suffering of the traumatized client has already been inflicted, and the fundamental role of the therapist is to be one of support and care in the face of processing past pain. But this may involve bringing the pain to the present so it can be honored and processed, even as the therapist must proceed carefully to prevent retraumatization.

But what of God and God's role in the generational traumas that are passed through the ages? If the therapist is facilitating healing but God is enacting it, God is apparently involved not only in the original trauma but also the purgative pain whereby it is healed.

This theodicy has troubled theologians for millennia. Looking back to learn from the dead, St. Thomas Aquinas—a contemporary of Dante in the thirteenth century—himself followed the wisdom of the dead by drawing from St. Augustine of Hippo—a fourth-century North African theologian. As explored by McCabe (2010), Aquinas built upon Augustine in his proposition that evil is a distortion of created beings rather than something essential to created beings. In other words, when God created the heavens and the earth, the essential nature of creation was good at its foundation. However, this good creation was distorted, and this distortion is what is now called evil.

Thus, according to Aquinas, God is not the creator of evil but of good, and God opposes the evil that distorts this good creation. Aquinas argued that God is shaping the consequences of evil, not accepting them as final, molding them towards God's divine and good goals. God repurposes the consequences of evil to move created beings to oppose evil and be healed, and this may be understood intergenerationally as a kind of purgation.

These consequences are described in Christian scripture by the complex term, 'death' (e.g., *Romans* 6:23). 'Death' names the manifold processes of decay that are fueled by human corruption, from the breakdown of the social fabric over generations to fertility-destroying disease among animals and human beings to drought, famine, and depleted soil. Yet, precisely these difficulties can provide the conditions in which human communities recognize their injustice and work together at reform. Thus, 'death' can be the food of rejuvenation and life, such that moral accountability is not a matter of retribution but the hope of redemption across generations. Thus, human accountability and the potential pain it engenders might be understood as hope for redemption.

The Christian faith thus informed holds that as God moves through history, opposing evil and working in and through death, God turns these distorting forces against themselves to bring about the redemption and restoration of God's good creation, effecting revitalization where death had come to reign. Through this pattern of repurposing the consequences of evil, God is simultaneously just, merciful, and filled with hope.

Limited Knowledge and Instrumentalization of Suffering

The difference between God and human medical doctors, therapists, or Dante's imagined purgations is that God's knowledge is complete. The finite knowledge of human healers allows for the possibility of potentially damaging 'healing' practices. Medieval falconers did not consider seeling painful, but human knowledge has progressed, so now the practice is not supported. Similarly, medical doctors no longer prescribe heroin. Psychiatrists do not perform frontal lobotomies. As human knowledge increases, ideally, methods of healing are refined and become less 'cruel.' But each generation must strive to engage in healing practices that minimize suffering while also bringing about healing, knowing that healing is not typically pain-free.

One might argue that any instrumentalization of suffering is problematic in that it cheapens the suffering or explains it away. But like purgation, therapy does not endeavor to belittle the gravity of harms committed or endured or to neatly justify the pain a client endures in the course of therapy. Rather, the therapist enters into the suffering with the client, which allows for healing through a recognition of the severity of the harm done and the often-complex kinds of pain it has caused. Suffering can be neither overlooked nor cheapened by explanations that truncate a client's healing process. Like Virgil, therapists must journey with the client through the pain of past mistakes and the wrongs of others, honoring rather than minimizing the suffering that has resulted.

Conclusion

To the medieval Christian, Purgatory was not viewed as cruel but delivered both justice and mercy, making room for a hopeful redemption. This essay has sought to present how therapy is similar to Purgatory in that it seeks to honor the pain of past torments and allow a space for that suffering to be presented and purged. Western psychology also must consider what it means to do therapy with the dead and be mindful of how the actions of past generations continue to have repercussions among the living. Finally, this chapter presents ethical challenges regarding the role of pain and suffering in the healing process and explores them from a theological perspective. Suffering must be carefully honored as a part of the path to healing, but not treated flippantly or cheapened. The ethical intent must always be a redemptive engagement of suffering with the ultimate goal of healing and wholeness.

References

Alighieri, D. (1987). *The Divine Comedy* (J. F. Cotter, Trans.). Amity House. (Original work published 1320).

Bell, R. (2011). *Love wins: At the heart of life's big questions.* HarperCollins UK.

Bezo, B., & Maggi, S. (2018). Intergenerational perceptions of mass Trauma's impact on physical health and well-being. *Psychological Trauma: Theory, Research, Practice, and Policy, 10,* 87–94. https://doi.org/10.1037/tra0000284

Brothers, D. (2014). Traumatic attachments: Intergenerational Trauma, dissociation, and the analytic relationship. *International Journal of Psychoanalytic Self Psychology, 9*, 3–15. https://doi.org/10.1080/15551024.2014.857746

Callaway, K., & Taylor, B. (2019). *The aesthetics of atheism: Theology and imagination in contemporary culture*. Fortress Press.

Dueck, A. (2017). Letter to Kelley McFarland.

Frederick II. (1961). *De arte venandi cum avibus (on the art of hunting with birds)* (C. A. Wood & F. M. Fyfe, Trans.). Stanford University Press. (Original work published 1248).

Galatzer-Levy, R. M. (2017). *Nonlinear psychoanalysis*. Taylor and Francis. https://doi.org/10.4324/9781315266473

Givens, G. T. (2016). *The ethical Burden of Hell: A critical retrieval of Gehenna, Hades, and Eternal Fire*. [unpublished manuscript].

Herman, J. L. (2015). *Trauma and recovery: The aftermath of violence–from domestic abuse to political terror*. Basic Books.

Holderman, F. W. (2010). *The California Hawking Club, Inc. apprenticeship manual: A starter guide for the prospective Falconer*. California Hawking Club.

Juarrero, A. (2002). *Dynamics in action: Intentional behavior as a complex system*. Bradford Book.

Le Goff, J., & Goldhammer, A. (1986). *The birth of purgatory*. University of Chicago Press.

Lewis, C. S. (2009). *The great divorce*. Harper Collins. (Original work published 1952).

McCabe, H. (2010). *God and Evil: In the theology of St Thomas Aquinas*. Bloomsbury Publishing.

Noe-Payne, M. (2019, August 23). It was 400 years ago that the 1st Enslaved Africans arrived in North America. In *Morning Edition*. Retrieved from https://www.npr.org/2019/08/23/753642877/it-was-400-years-ago-that-the-first-enslaved-africans-arrive-in-north-america

purge (n.d.). *Online etymology dictionary*. Retrieved from https://www.etymonline.com/word/purge?ref=etymonline_crossreference#etymonline_v_2891

Reinhard, K., & Lupton, J. R. (2003). The subject of religion: Lacan and the ten commandments. *Diacritics, 33*, 71–97. https://doi.org/10.1353/dia.2005.0023

Todd, E. (1985). The value of confession and forgiveness according to Jung. *Journal of Religion and Health, 24*(1), 39–48.

van der Kolk, B. A. (1994). The body keeps the score: Memory and the evolving psychobiology of posttraumatic stress. *Harvard Review of Psychiatry, 1*(5), 253–265.

Chapter 14

Dante's Economy of Words after Marx[1]

Matthew Elmore

1.

Scarcity is the foundation of history. It is the condition of our development, the force behind our industry. That was the claim of Sartre in his *Critique of Dialectical Reason* (1960, p. 202). Not quite a decade had passed since the death of Stalin, and in France, the intellectual scene was sharply framed by a problem with Marxism. On the one hand, the image of a classless future was dissolving; on the other, the image of revolution was deeply pressed into the French psyche. Intellectuals were often asked—as they themselves were asking—if a social system could ever be devised to satisfy all needs. As far as Sartre was concerned, the question was shrouded by myth. Hegel had been right to say that humans struggle against each other for power, but the conflict would never come to rest (Sartre, 1968, p. 34). Not that Marxism was thereby refuted; to the contrary, it was required, but on another foundation. Insecurity, not eschatology, demanded action on the part of the poor (Sartre, 1956, p. 658). Material disproportion was the core condition of Marxism—the condition without which Marxism would cease to be. Equity had to be seized again and again, never to reach an essential freedom from struggle. When equity materialized, it was unstable, prone to the interest of power. Therefore scarcity, as a phenomenon of political history, could not be divorced from human existence.

Some years later, Sartre gave an interview in which he made his claim more intimate. "I consider that scarcity is the phenomenon in which we live," he said. "Even here, among ourselves, there is scarcity in our conversation: scarcity of ideas, scarcity of understanding. I may not understand your questions or may answer them badly—that, too, is scarcity" (Sartre, 1981, p. 30). After decades in the public eye, Sartre had grown familiar with the inevitable occurrence of misunderstanding. His view of scarcity had thus intensified and broadened: The term was now applicable to the realms of thought and communication. Simultaneously, it resonated with common turns of phrase, as when one 'scarcely understands.' In the most mundane of examples, Sartre had located the most profound site of the problem. A fundamental lack recurs in every exchange, destabilizing every chance at clarity and comprehension.

2.

In what follows, I read Sartre's difficulty along Dante's lines. Perhaps more poignantly, I treat Dante's *Commedia* like a lens, inspecting two growing branches on the Marxist family tree. The first is traceable to Sartre, and it has since developed in the work of Žižek and Badiou. I see it taking off from a simple question: 'What is scarcity?' On the second branch, the recent work of Hardt and Negri draws from Deleuze and stems from a related question: 'How is scarcity revolutionized?'

The two questions appear compatible, as if to diagnose and treat the same thing. But the appearance is deceptive; each inquiry faces a horizon opposite the other. On the horizon of the first is nothingness: being lacks itself, so to speak, like an appetite. It is full only as it finds itself wanting. Every encounter with being is thus an encounter with its unavoidable absence; daylight is always falling into dusk. But against the other horizon, the converse: Being is not a vacuum but a fountain, emerging in a continuous dawn of multiplicity and difference. Every encounter with being is thus an encounter with its amplitude and possibility.

In sum, the two questions indicate opposed readings of material existence. Matter signifies either the void or the virtual—the absence or the presence of its potential fullness. Each, as a theoretical option, has born unique fruit. And each has objectified scarcity in its own way. The first question, asking 'What is scarcity?' has already assumed a deficit of being; the second, asking 'How is scarcity revolutionized?' has granted a surplus. Scarcity, we might say, is not one object but two.

3.

But both options, as branches of the same tree, have developed the same intuition: to extend the Marxist account of what eludes counting. That dimension, for each, is language. Verbal material exceeds the methods of economic measure; it is not strictly countable in terms of its loss or increase. Still, each horizon evokes one type of economic trend: Where Sartre observes language slipping into the void, Hardt and Negri observe its generativity and power. In either case, again, language is unfathomable as a material resource. Even if we can discuss it under the headings of loss or production, it exists in a kind of countless flow.

And in either case, Marx was right: Language is how we change the form of the material world (Marx, 1967, p. 178). Architecture is far less effective in his estimation: Marx compares the work of human architects to that of spiders and bees, stating that the worst human architect is set apart from the animal kingdom by the faculty of his imagination. The process of human labor involves the effect of images—first mental, then material. That notion, even on its own, is enough to provoke a serious look at the world of Dante's allegory—a world which was not another world *per se*. The *Commedia* was written "for the world which lives badly" (*Purgatorio* XXXIII:103). His poem was, if nothing else, a redress of this world's material greed. No wonder it has always had a context in Marxism; Engels himself once said Dante was a prototype of the party spirit (Marx & Engels, 2010, p. 271). But as I read him, Dante was far more than the spirit's prototype. He was its prophet. Not only did he anticipate the two questions above, he reconciled them, taking each further than either would dare journey on its own.

In the *Commedia*, human language is indeed a sign of the unfathomable. It cannot wrap itself around what it signifies, because its formation depends on what it is not: eternal love. Dante's lyrical being emerges in the created cadence of time, unfolding from and toward what exceeds him. He cannot exhaustively say what he sees. Nor, in the attempt, can he exhaust the matter of language. His soul is moved allegorically to the horizon of verbal creativity, where language is at once deficient and overflowing. He reads his own passions—desire, fear, grief, joy—as allegorically coordinated by the good, the enjoyable, finally replete in God. And he believes that without such a witness, the value of goods is signified only by their possible loss.

The science of economics operates on such a model, as Lionel Robbins said explicitly (2007). The scarcer the good, the greater its worth. Value, in this frame, is a quotient of worry: we may lose the good we have; we may not get the good we want. The production of a commodity is legible only in such a plotline.

Is there another light by which to signify nature? According to Dante, yes. The Good, reflected in the creation of language, is never spent. Neither can it be stolen from anyone confessing its reality. It exists only as shared. When another takes it, it is never gone. It is multiplied.

Part I: The Void

4.

Sartre has shown that scarcity is prior to every numeric derivative, and I take him to be right. In its most basic position, scarcity is a term of want. It names an absence found in the groans for a good not had. To say it another way, scarcity does not originate in the measure of resources *out there*, in the world beyond our bodies. It is a phenomenon *in here*, in the perceived relation of ourselves to whatever is out there. Not that scarcity is somehow conjured up by or confined to the self; we have a word for it, which is enough to demonstrate its communicability. It exists, broadly speaking, in a shared translation of human consciousness. I say 'human' because other animals, who no doubt suffer deprivation, do not name it as such. The phenomenon as we know it emerges from a nexus of capacities we call rational, ethical, and—I emphasize—linguistic. 'Scarcity' is a term made possible only by a specific mode of human grammar. If not for the sense that a belly *should* be full or that a meal *could* be lost, the term would have no utility. It is not concretely a thing. You cannot point to scarcity as you can a building or a fish or a ball. It is a narrated object, a noted absence—in a story, say, about a people who *should* be fed. As such, the term always evokes a potential future. It is an object we identify in the fear of loss and the desire for gain.

What habits of mind—what habitual reading of the world—enables *Psalm* 23's "I shall not want"? I am interested in Dante's answer. As in Augustine's *Confessions*, Dante's narrative is built on the promise of fullness, the promise of rest, of life at last freed of lack. Of course, the *Commedia* differs from Augustine's telling. It is a poet's journey through the netherworld. But to examine it only as the product of another genre, as distinct from the 'nonfictional' memoir of Augustine, is to miss the genre they share.

Augustine's conversion, we might recall, began when Ambrose demonstrated the power of allegorical reading (*Confessions* 5.14.24). By way of example, the Hebrew laws of sacrifice were read as executed. Jesus, fulfilling all righteousness, now defined the sacrificial figure. Allegorically, time worked in two directions: Israel's legal culture was the sign of its coming Messiah, even as Christ came to signify the meaning of the law. On one side, it was an allegory of what was to come; on the other, an allegory of what was fulfilled. Each Testament allegorized the other, which gave history its coherence. The world was not simply developing in a bare timeline. Ancient Israel was collocated in the Church, folded on the point of the incarnation. In Greek philosophy too, Christians had discovered aspects of the Word impressed into nature, written by pagans before its advent as flesh. Christ was seen folding all of history on his coming, creating not only two epochs but a retrospective parallel in the first, between Israel and the Gentiles. Neither body of literature was complete until the Word came to signify what the human could be. The body of Christ was where both were fulfilled, effecting a new kind of literary material.

This outlook, however alien to us now, held sway for centuries. It explains how Dante could read Virgil as a heavenly messenger, or how Aquinas could set Aristotle in a theological syllabus. It operated by the observance of "a fold in being," to borrow a term from Foucault (1970, p. 20). One entity always reflected another—asymmetrically in many cases. The Old Testament reflected the New; time mirrored eternity; humanity imaged God. Dante's *Paradiso* fits easily into this paradigm, extending all the way to the final vision of being: Souls reflect God until at last, God's very essence appears as "lume reflesso" [reflected light] (*Paradiso* XXXIII:127). At the heart of all being, divinity reflects itself—even as humanity, Dante paradoxically finds. The fold rises all the way into the triune fellowship. It is absolutely transcendent. There is no being beyond the fold.

Here is the key point: The real was always figurative. God the Word was both the fact and the figure of the real. Representation and analogy were not mere stand-ins for literal fact; the literal was unfolded in the world of figures. To repeat a quote first attributed to Hugh of St. Victor, "the whole visible world is like a book written by God" (Josipivici, 1971, p. 29). That is why Augustine could read himself, and indeed all of history, into a reflective communion with the divine. The material world and its characters were nothing if not signs of a deeper, self-reflective Creativity. On the same ground, Dante could novelize the world and his being in it. In the waning light of Scholasticism, at the dawn of the renaissance, the *Commedia* was a development of—not a departure from—Augustine's genre.

5.

Now, a brief word is warranted. If Dante's poem is irradiated by Augustine's writing, why does the poet mention the saint only twice in passing? It is a riddle that kept scholars busy in the early twentieth century, only to fall away when Carlo Calcaterra noted the absence of special episodes with a great many saints: John Chrysostom, Ambrose, Gregory the Great, Anselm of Canterbury, even the Apostle Paul himself (Calcaterra, 1942, p. 251). To that list, we can add Benedict, whom Dante seats in heaven next to Augustine and mentions only there.

It is quite possible that Dante's direct knowledge of Augustine was minimal, even though his debt to *Confessions* can be verified. In the minor work *Convivio*, Dante cites Augustine to answer an ethical question: Is it ever good to speak about oneself? Yes, Dante says, when it might benefit others.

> And this reason moved Augustine to speak of himself in his *Confessions*. Through the process of his life, which went from bad to good, and good to better, and better to best, he gave us an example and instruction which could not be provided by any other testimony so true as this. (*Convivio* 1.2.14)

Clearly, Dante cast himself on the same sort of pilgrimage. While it remains unclear if he knew Augustine's larger works, their traces are everywhere. How to explain this? Dante was heir to an old estate. Over the centuries, scholastics had built onto Augustine's property. Even if they sometimes remodeled its dwellings to fit the needs of their time, the lasting vintage of Augustine was never uprooted. Dante, perhaps without always knowing it, was a drinker of the ancient bishop's wine.

6.

I have begun with Sartre because he sets off down Augustine's path. In Sartre's view, scarcity names at least two hungers: one for understanding and the other for material goods. Unlike Augustine, Sartre believes these hungers signify nothing. They provoke an existential gape at a profound, unavoidable absence. I take Sartre's view to be a reflection of the medieval psyche—a reflection Dante would have recognized. But Dante gets beyond Sartre's dilemma because he can assume a great deal more about how the two hungers relate.

To begin with, Dante believes material hunger may be rightly or wrongly placed. And when it is misplaced, it has a skewing effect—a scarcifying effect—on understanding. Both hungers, material and mental, are jeopardized when vice warps reason. Hence, at the outset of the *Commedia*, Dante's character is lost in a dark wood. (Lostness, we should note, is a kind of mental scarcity: scarcity of context, scarcity of signification for a place.) Struggling to regain "la verace via" [the true way] (*Inferno* I:12), Dante has not merely drifted from the light; he has been chased into darkness by three beasts—a leopard, a lion, and a wolf—classically thought to symbolize lust, pride, and greed.[2] These three, says Aquinas, are the coordinating causes of all sin. They summarize one appetite for goods without God (*Summa Theologica* 1–2.77.5). In the language of *1 John*, the beasts are "all that is in the world." Hungry for material life, they de-sign the Good; rather, they re-sign it, claiming the world for themselves apart from the order of God's love.

Dante has altered the Johannine arrangement, placing pride—the lion—before greed—the wolf. Some commentators, noting this, have suggested the progression of a human lifespan: sins of youth, sins of manhood, sins of age.[3] If this is the case, then Dante's character, lost midway through life's journey, is driven furthest from the path by his desire for a plush retirement. The wolf is the empty pursuit of paradise on earth. She is the gaunt metamorphosis of the other two, which, in their final phase of habituation, are no longer beautiful or powerful. They are ravenous and malnourished—"carca ne la sua magrezza" [laden in her thinness] (*Inferno* I:50).

The move to read the bestiary like this, as an evolvement, is compelling and probably right. But it is also incomplete, because the wolf takes on sharper definition when Virgil interprets her existence and foretells her demise. "Many are the animals she mates with," he says, "and there will be yet more" (*Inferno* I:100–101). Not only is she the maturation of the other beasts, she is also potentially their mate and mother. Her starving frame produces all kinds of sin and reduces all sin back to itself. Thus, the wolf, over the other two, is Dante's analogue for 'all that is in the world.' And Virgil says as much: She is the figure let loose from hell by primal envy, and therefore, she is the sole prey of heaven's hound (*Inferno* I:109–111).

In a manner of speaking, every occupant of hell has been chased into it by the wolf—by the desire for what is not properly theirs. Because the wolf is multiform, souls are variously displaced, molded by whatever they wanted most in life. A classic illustration is found in the second circle, where souls are blown back and forth through the air like a flock of birds, doomed to fly forever without landing. These souls, Dante learns, are those who "subjected reason to appetite" (Alighieri, 1320/1966, *Inferno* V:39). Among them are Cleopatra, Dido, and Achilles—figures who display the restless outcome of the soul when fixed to another as its highest good.

Paulo and Francesca, whom Dante greets, are not well-known figures of literature, but tellingly, their adultery was inspired by the tale of Lancelot and Guinevere. Their sin was emulative, an allegorical performance of a literature they loved. By Francesca's account, she and Paulo are victims of the story, even as they are victims of love. But what, in this case, is love? Paulo can do nothing but weep, because the pair, together forever, is void of true consummation. In the final act of their being, the lovers allegorize the Good by showing what it is not. And that, for Dante, is the significance of hell. It is a perpetual scarcity of the Good, even though the Good is never scarce in itself. The episode is meant to give the reader pause: How does human nature mis-allegorize its own good? Envy, it seems, is the fundamental self-promotion of that possibility. It warps the reflective power of human agency, captivating desire in counterfeit signs of what is most desirable.

Dante thus replies to Sartre:

1) Vice, not appetite, signifies nothing.
2) The nothingness of vice is parasitic on the Good, clinging to its surface rather than seeking its depth.
3) Vice remains an allegory of the Good by negation, a warning sign of emptiness, visible against the horizon of true beatitude.

7.

Classically, a vice has scarcifying effects because it is also a kind of excess; it is infinite desire manifest in the wrong direction, toward what cannot sustain it. There is no more vivid picture than in the depths of *Inferno*, where Ugolino eats the head of his one-time captor, the Archbishop Ruggieri. A political prisoner, Ugolino was locked in a tower with his children, each of whom died of starvation before he did. He describes how he felt over their bodies in the dark for two days, calling their names to no avail. "Then hunger," he says simply, "won out over grief" (*Inferno* XXXIII:75). The tragedy is twofold: Not only was he forced to eat his children; the last days of his life, which he spent eating them, formed his final reason for being. Now in hell, his cannibalism has taken its true form. Wanting only vengeance—which is not to say divine justice—he may only be a consumer of his enemy. This, for him, is the final good, the final excess, the final nothingness. He consumes his captor, even as he himself is consumed by endless hunger. The episode calls to mind the words of St. Paul: "But if ye bite and devour one another, take heed that ye be not consumed of one another" (*Galatians* 5:15). This is the finale of hell, the final warp of the wolf's pursuits.

Ugolino's place—in the lowest rim with political traitors—corresponds with the picture at the close of Augustine's *City of God* (Freccero, 1986, p. 153). Human relations feed, so to speak, in one of two directions: communion or cannibalism. Ugolino's meal is thus poignantly opposed to the flesh of Christ, who invites his enemies to feed on him, but in so doing, changes them into friends.

8.

Two canines, one wild, one obedient, both seeking food: this is the poem's first great contest of opposites. Scholars are divided on the identity of the heavenly hound—The Holy Spirit? A figure from history? The *Commedia* itself? But the question requires no answer, provided we note the *type* of rivalry it is—or rather, what it is not: It is not a competition of equal forces. If the wolf is the evolution of three kinds of excess, the hound is strengthened by a greater three: "sapïenza, amore e virtute" [wisdom, love, and virtue] (*Inferno* I:104). While the wolf feeds on depletable goods, the hound feeds on endless plenty. His foods are immaterial, which is precisely what makes them hardier; he feasts on the very attributes originating all material things.

Wisdom, love, and virtue: these will resolve the perplexity of want. But how? If Dante is to understand—if he is to feed upon the hound's hardier goods—he will require two critical means: a pilgrimage and a fellowship. The divine foods cannot be given all at once, nor can they be self-prepared. They are necessarily spread out over a journey because they change the eater over time. And they are convivial, shared with others who have acquired a greater taste for it. (The divine food, after all, *is* another.)

John Freccero has traced a fitting parallel to the seventh book of the *Confessions* (Augustine, 397–398/2006), where Augustine recalls being "in the region of unlikeness" (Freccero, 1986, p. 153). After taking a second mistress, Augustine was at odds with himself. He had deduced by now that God was incorruptible, but he failed to see how this might affect his slavery to lust. Then, through the writings of some Platonists, he heard God as if from afar: "I am the food of grown men: grow and you shall eat me. And you shall not change me into yourself as bodily food, but into me you shall be changed" (*Confessions* 7.10). Dante's character must embrace the same Eucharistic possibility. He must learn to feed upon the Good, which, when consumed, will not grow scarce; it will instead transform his deficient nature into the sufficient nature of divine love.

Which is to say that Dante must feed upon an excess, a truth greater than his present power of reason. It is an intake of knowledge available only to faith. And what a strange faith it is, resting as it does on Virgil. The only way to regain the light is to follow a pagan through hell. Dante must see how everything refers to the Good, even the self-induced scarcity of the damned. But he wavers, frightened of what he does not understand. "Since if I come I will abandon myself,/ I am afraid my coming may be crazy./ You are wise; you are an expert at what I cannot reason" (*Inferno* II:35–37).

Dante's character evokes the problem of Sartre. 'How am I to signify my need?' The problem of scarcity is more acutely one of identity. 'What do I scarcely understand about myself?'

Part II: The Virtual

9.

One of my critical aims so far has been to show that scarcity is not, in the first place, a shortage of resources but a signifier of human desire. In making my point, however, I have bypassed an important question: In what sense is scarcity also a fact of materiality? In what sense is it rightly understood as a problem in the world of physical resources?

Hardt and Negri posed this question a decade ago, noticing a shift in the way we define the problem. Before the digital age, it seemed obvious that material goods were exclusive. They existed in one place at a time and belonged to one party at a time. But we now understand the opposite to be true, at least in many cases. I can download a book or a song, and I am not removing it from the natural number available to all. Its copies are effectively without boundary or quantity, reproducible in many places at once. For Hardt and Negri, this new mode of acquisition signifies a newly possible communism. It outmodes the logic which says, "if you have it, I cannot have it" (Hardt & Negri, 2004, p. 180). Downloadable goods disrupt the doctrine of nature most firmly established in John Locke's thesis on property (Locke, 1689/1960, *Second Treatise* §31, 36–38). How strange, then, that the Lockean doctrine continues to justify today's market structures. Digital goods, which could be released and reproduced almost infinitely, are monetized by artificial restrictions. Scarcity is unnaturally enforced. It is as if, without depleting and privatizing what is common, human nature will cease to be.

Hardt and Negri thus urge a new political identity upon the possessors of virtual reality. Their call is not owing to some recent mutation of our nature; it is grounded more deeply in the real. Locke's main mistake, they believe, was to take one class of goods as the only kind. The class itself is not up for dispute: "Material property, such as land or water or a car, cannot be in two places at once: my having and using it negates your having and using it" (2004, p. 311). But a second class of goods remains, and it is likely the more important, because it shapes the way we signify the first.

> Immaterial property, however, such as an idea or an image or a form of communication, is infinitely reproducible. It can be everywhere at once, and my using and having it does not hinder yours. On the contrary, as Thomas Jefferson says, ideas are enhanced by their communication: when I light my candle from yours they both seem to burn brighter. (2004, p. 311)

We will soon see that Jefferson reveals a great deal more than Hardt and Negri are ready to accept. But for the moment, we can commend their provocative use of his thought. Though famously influenced by Locke, Jefferson saw beyond the Lockean boundary. He understood the plain fact of an immaterial commons, an economy of ideas that only existed as spontaneously sharable and reproducible. Though less globally patent in his day, it has now materialized in digital networks, widening the hidden fissure in Locke's state of nature. And we, the virtual realizers, must rethink how to symbolize our relation to matter. It may turn out that 'the economy,' as we often compass the term, is merely the skin of an irreducible abundance. The goods we possess are not merely exclusive.[4] Some must be excessive. Some must exist only as they are shared and reproduced freely.

10.

But how do we pierce the rind for the fruit? How can we overcome the habits of scarcity if a deep virtual reality signifies a more progressive social arrangement? Hardt and Negri, in a rather surprising turn, indicate the necessity of love. Love is the only power strong enough to exceed the immediate 'mine and ours' of the nuclear, bourgeois family. They specify: "We need to recuperate the public and political conception of love common to premodern traditions" (2004, p. 351). That is, we ought to emulate early to medieval Christians and Jews. Readers may wonder if the authors have been converted from the materialism of Marx; after all, the practices they affirm took place in the auspices of divinity. But Hardt and Negri anticipate the charge and object to it. Love, they say, need not be a metaphysical reality. It was always "incarnated in the common material political project" (2004, p. 352). As soon as they seem to transgress Marx, they reclaim religious love for his tradition. But in so doing, they offer two solutions that are not neatly interactive. If immaterial goods evoke an alternative world structure, how is love properly reduced to materiality? Whence comes the power, the immaterial, or the material?

A serious reading of Dante is not only helpful but appropriate here. As a prime theorist of the love Hardt and Negri invoke, he shows that they are fainthearted about its implications. The politics of love must reflect an immaterial excess beyond human reckoning. If love transcends the private and familial—and for Dante, it must—it must therefore exceed the mortally political. It must be the very power moving the sun and other stars. It must entail not only the predictable order of nature but the miraculous, the resurrected, the incalculable. Only in a world with such motivity can political love enact itself beyond the seeming boundaries of nature. Only then can a political language emerge to signify a reality beyond the burden of scarcity.

II.

For Dante, words cannot fully signify love's reality: "trasumanar significar per verba/ non si poria" [to go beyond the human cannot be described in words] (*Paradiso* I:70). At the same time, love is the everlasting object of language. It always exists on the poetic horizon; there is always more to say about it, more ways to signify and allegorize its being. Human language thus exists in a strange relation to itself, because, like love, its capacity for sign-making exceeds our reckoning.

These two powers of language—to fathom and remain unfathomable—comprise one reason for Dante's continued circulation on the left. Among such thinkers is Cesare Casarino (a coauthor with Negri), who cites Dante's short *De Vulgari Eloquentia* (Alighieri, 1302–1305/1960) as a resource for theorizing revolution (Casarino, 2008, pp. 8–15). Though Dante's work is written in high Latin, it sets forth a case for the eloquence of vernacular speech. Notably, Dante's intent is not to prove the advantage of one regional vernacular—say, Tuscan; he rather believes in the nobility of "that which we learn without any formal instruction, by imitating our nurses" (*De Vulgari Eloquentia* 1.1.2). The vernacular is thus opposed to *gramatica*, the discipline of the learned, typically excluding women and the poor.

By opposing the vernacular to formal education, Dante makes two subtle points:

1) Rules of grammar do not precede the vernacular—they rather suggest its primacy.
2) There are not many vernaculars but one—the vernacular is whatever language is first taught to a child.

These points are followed by a third: God gave language to Adam not in any one specific tongue but in the capacity for one. The faculty of language is, in Scholastic terms, a potency—an ability waiting to be actualized. It is thus displayed by, but not the same as, any given language (*De Vulgari Eloquentia* 1.4.1–1.4.6). While the vernacular is realized in local forms of life, it is virtually suspended outside all geopolitical dialect and definition. Taking note of this, Casarino employs Dante to say that language always signifies the virtual possibility of being in common.

Along these lines, it is compelling that Dante chose Italian for his *Commedia*. Dante wrote the lyrics for a new mode of commonality, activating a new form of ascent for the uneducated class. Not only did he sentence certain clerics to hell, but his language broke from the Latin strictures of theology. There was now a vulgar Paradise of God that seemed to revive and yet diminish its formal counterpart. Any speaker of Italian, learning the poem by heart, could somehow become more native to a universal communion exceeding their own tongue.

A further point can be drawn here. If we are to follow Casarino in accepting Dante's theory, we must do more than merely invoke the virtual potency of being in common. We must retrace the link between the virtual and the virtuous. For Dante, our capacity for language implies the common possibility of becoming like God. At no point did Dante suppose the Italian tongue could be developed apart from the Godward potencies of nature. The *Commedia* was written to strengthen the politics of love, and correspondingly, to strengthen a people's language for it. How are we to fathom this? How can a given language signify the transcendence of itself? This is also to ask: How is universal love made particular in words?

12.

Beginning his treatise *On Christian Doctrine* (397–426/1958), Augustine reflects on how his teaching ought to be economized as a reproducible gift. "Everything which does not decrease on being given away is not properly owned when it is owned and not given" (1.1). Hardt and Negri have variously repeated the claim: There are two classes of goods, the first of which decreases by distribution. The second, when shared, remains undiminished. It was Augustine who first recognized this, citing the miraculous feeding of the multitudes:

> There were at one time five loaves and at another time seven before they began to be given to the needy; and when this began to be done, baskets

and hampers were filled, although thousands of men were fed. (397–426/1958, 1.1)

Does bread not belong to the first class of goods, which decreases the common store when distributed? In this case, no. The miracle, it seems, is an apocalypse of the second class. Tearing open the first class of goods, Jesus reveals the true precedence of the second. Here we find Augustine's metaphysical difference from Hardt and Negri, who think that love can be incarnated in material self-reference. The Gospel hangs everything on the opposite claim: materiality is only possible in the Word. The multiplied loaves are an allegory of creation, a work not finally captive to the politics of material power. (The evangelists make this clear, placing the miracle after the birthday feast of Herod, where wolfish appetite reigned supreme.) Augustine thus reads his own work allegorically, believing his words may be assimilated to the miracle.

> Just as the loaves increased when they were broken, the Lord has granted those things necessary to the beginning of this work, and when they begin to be given out they will be multiplied by His inspiration, so that in this task of mine I shall not only suffer no poverty of ideas but shall rejoice in wonderful abundance. (397–426/1958, 1.1)

If Augustine's ideas are multiplied freely, it is because their existence does not belong to Augustine. They signify the original Creativity of all things. A similar notion is found in Dante's introduction to *De Vulgari Eloquentia*: "I shall try, inspired by the Word that comes from above, to say something useful about the vulgar tongue." The words belong to the Word.

Dante, following Augustine, will agree with Hardt and Negri that scarcity is more of an outlook than a material fact. He will likewise agree that scarcity is transcended by means of ideas, shared in the vernacular mode of political love. But he will insist that when language alters the perception of scarcity (thus altering the problem itself), it is because love and language derive their true power from immaterial Being. They derive, that is, from the Word made flesh, who sets human nature free from corruption and loss.

Hardt and Negri have almost lighted upon this, but without metaphysics to 'torque' their desire upward (as Virgil teaches in *Purgatorio*), their project falters. For them, 'immaterial property' cannot truly signify the immaterial. It remains an empty signifier, falling back to corrupted matter. The immaterial, for them, is prone to obsolescence and decay—the very opposite of the Word made flesh. A downloaded book—even a book shared by all—remains bound in a computer process, embedded in the proprietary labors of upkeep and production. The same is then true for minds and language, mysteries that seem likely to shrink to the custodial narratives of neurology and healthcare. Virtuality is physicality. It is depreciable, like the economic scarcity it ought to resist.

Under these circumstances, Sartre is proven right: Scarcity and life cannot be divorced, and Jefferson's candle cannot signify what Hardt and Negri claim. Lighting my candle with yours may double our light, but it will increase the rate at which we are plunged into darkness.

Dante, however, believes that primal light is uncreated. If we will, we can possess it by reflecting it to others. Reflection is the condition of its being possessed, just as multiplication is the condition of its being received. This, for Dante, is how love is 'incarnated in the common material political project.'

A short anecdote will help make the point. Not long ago, I saw an intriguing piece of art called a lightpainting (see http://lightpaintings.com). The artist, a man named Stephen Knapp, had mounted dozens of glass fragments to a massive wall. Rather than mounting them flat, he hung them perpendicular to the surface so that they jutted out, facing each other at random angles. From a single light in the corner, Knapp produced some fifty rays of light, reflected between fragments in every direction across the wall's expanse. The work suggested something limitless, as if a single light's energy could be increased forever. It challenged a certain assumption about art supplies. Paint, when used, is used up; light, however, may be multiplied when used. This is how the *Commedia* portrays the divine economy, taught at first by Virgil on the purgatorial ascent. We will turn to that passage in a moment, but the matter of language deserves more immediate attention.

13.

A lightpainting, of course, is not free of depletion. The bulb will burn out; the store of glass will diminish. But with Dante, we are engaged in a fully allegorical universe. Light signifies the Being who first let it be. Nothing is ever reduced to absolute literality: there is no such absolute. The literal sense of things cannot come apart from the figurative. Even God, as the Word, is a sign of God.

Hardt and Negri have led us to the brink of the same vision, but they obscure it, flattening love to the horizontal plane. They signify love as 'incarnated' without the immaterial Word, and in so doing, they fail to see the resulting cacophony. They have proposed an immaterial economy of ideas, a boundless reproduction of common property. But it must be asked: What ideas will be digitized and multiplied? All? If so, how will this not lead to another kind of scarcity? Mere multiplication of ideas will not satisfy the human hunger for understanding. The yawning void of Sartre remains.

And there is a second problem. As neo-Marxists, Hardt and Negri advocate the overthrow of some ideas. How can they be sure the good ones will multiply? Is the network to be adjudicated? If so, how is it boundless? How does it not threaten to control the reproduction of some ideas? The network, drawn together by its own void of stability, is implanted from the start with the seeds of hegemony; it exists only as imperiled, risking its own overthrow by those it suppresses. Without saying as much, Hardt and Negri (2003, pp. 63–66) admit this, granting that revolutionary acts have no final end. Sartre's point is again proven true: Insecurity is the foundation of industry.

Let us consider the alternative. In Dante's world, the reproducibility of thought openly exists on more than one axis—not only on the horizontal but the vertical. The pilgrim finds himself on the incline, aiming to ascend, reproducing signs of the Good in his own words. The reproduction of a text, whether from *Proverbs* or Plato or *Playboy*, reveals human nature on both axes; we receive and reproduce whatever ideas seem to hold the most promise. It is just as the Greeks and Hebrews believed: emulation, that critical aspect of language learning, is a feature of wisdom's natural weave. We learn to speak as we learn to live. Hoping to ascend in joy, we follow the perception of exemplary teachers. Our perception is rooted in theirs. "In fact," says Dante, "we believe that for the human, it is more natural to be perceived than to perceive" (*De Vulgari Eloquentia* 1.5.1).

Augustine extends the same thought in *De Trinitate* (400–416/1887), carrying it to its metaphysical end: Our being is fully perceived by the Word of God (15.11.20). This is an article of faith—how else can one partially perceive being finally perceived? But the reproduction of language always evokes something like it. Language seeks consummate knowledge, springing forth from lack of it. To speak is to try to understand. Language thus evokes the Word, or else it evokes the void, as Sartre believed. But even Sartre's doctrine is an article of faith, and those who reproduce it live by his perception.

14.

Human words, for Augustine, are thus 'enigmatic' of the divine Word (*De Trinitate*, 400–416/1887, 15.10.19). Our verbality is like God's and yet not. Whereas we humans gain our verbal knowledge in the world of things, all things exist because the Word knows them (15.13.22). The divine Word is not created but creating. Still, at the very site of our difference from the divine nature, we bear its image. Human language, bound as it is in the process of learning and becoming, is inexhaustible. Its development reveals a deep and boundless creativity, like the very plenitude of God's own being verbal. Our language, as a creation, is always creating new things.

That is why in *Paradiso* XXVI, Dante borrows an image from Horace, picturing words as leaves on a branch (see Horace, *Ars Poetica* 60–63; also Homer, *Iliad* 21.463). Just as leaves fall and are replaced, the use of words is always in transition. In Horace, the image signifies mortality, the inevitable slippage of life into the void. But Dante inverts the emphasis, drawing focus to the leaf's origin and source of renewal. The image now calls to mind Christ's teaching in the Gospel: "I am the vine, ye are the branches: He that abideth in me and I in him, the same bringeth forth much fruit" (*John* 15:5). The image, in fact, is voiced by none other than Adam, whom Dante calls *pomo* [fruit] (*Paradise* XXVI:91). Adam is the figure of Dante's own poetic method, representing the human task of naming things and thereby constituting their verbal existence in the world.

The episode is verdant, rich with wild garden imagery, revealing the diversity of nature's flourishing. If nature inclines toward one final beauty, it is not thereby foreclosed. It is multiplied in its splendor. All kinds of new things might happen, as presented by the *Commedia*'s language. Drawing ever closer to God, Dante pushes vernacular Italian well beyond its former scope, establishing all kinds of new words to suit his needs. God's economy surpasses all easy classification; novel words are necessary to reflect the divine excess (Luzzi, 2010, p. 330; Schildgen, 1989, pp. 111–113). Thus, when Dante is lost for words, he is forced to make more. Scarcity, in this case, gives way to abundance.

If language is a multiplying phenomenon, Dante's lyricism demonstrates why. The possibility of a new expression, like the possibility of an echoed idea, is born in a cosmos already verbalized by love. We create language to share delight in what we cannot finally capture. And a well-crafted poem—a new creation ready to be read and repeated—puts the feel of it on our tongues.

15.

But how can we subsist on verbal material? Are the poor to be fed by words alone? No, but neither can we live by bread alone. Recall that Marx, from the beginning, was bent on articulating the worker's hope. His problem was the wage worker's alienation from his own fulfillment. Through the material dialectic, workers would one day be psychologically whole, no longer subject to an upper class. Marx indeed imagined a world beyond his senses, but he did not carry its implications far enough, as I am suggesting Dante did. Let us turn, then, to the teaching of Virgil, where Dante's character begins to see the operations of divine love in its pure economic form.

The pair has just departed the terrace of the envious, where Guido del Duca laments the futility of loving what cannot be shared: "O race of humans, why put your heart where trade is a negation of partnership?" (*Purgatorio* XIV:86–87). The phrase is puzzling, and Dante turns to Virgil for an explanation. The answer comes in the form of a contrast: there are two kinds of work, says Virgil. In the first, laborers split the good for which they toil. The second, however, is a process of multiplication: the more souls there are who say "nostro" [ours], the more good each soul has. This is the highest form of love, which Dante would understand if his desires were "torcesse in suso" [torqued upward] (*Purgatorio* XV:53). As is often the case, Dante's character remains stuck in the world of lack. How, if a good is distributed, can there be more of it? Virgil's answer is a concise primer on the Augustinian matter of charity.

Such an economy depends on "that infinite and ineffable good" (*Purgatorio* XV:67). The Good is first classified by what it is not: limited and describable. No volume—numeric or literary—can fathom it. To identify it properly, we must negate all things from it. This is no mere matter of subtraction: even 'zero,' the mathematical difference of all things from all things, belongs to the realm of quantity. The Good must surpass even the void of all things. It is *là sù*—above the limits of negation, so to speak. How then can we know it? Here is Virgil's answer: despite its transcendence and negativity, it "flows to love/ as a ray of light comes to a lit body" (*Purgatorio* XV:68–69). A loving person is an image of the Good, the way a person standing in the sun is an image of light.

Still, our knowledge of the Good never departs from the negation of limit. We can never find its boundary, because when it appears in the realm of quantity, it multiplies. The more souls there are who set their hearts above—*là sù s'intende*— the more there is to love. Each beloved soul becomes a mirror of the good to others, who then reflect the light to others, and on it goes forever. The trade of love is, therefore, quite unlike the trade of a commodity; it increases by distribution. Put another way: Love does not value what it does not have, because love is its own good. The more loves one has, the more loves one receives. This is the grammar: Love loves love. Love is the object and the action of every subject.

If this seems a fanciful politics, Dante's character agrees. Even as he begins his heavenly ascent with Beatrice, he questions its reality, working to calculate what he cannot. He wonders: How can souls in the lower spheres of Paradise feel no envy of those in the higher? The first soul to speak to him is Piccarda, who happily explains. In Paradise, love is the only desire of every soul (*Paradiso* III:7–87). Since every soul is uniquely created, all enjoy being filled in unique ways. Those in the lower spheres suffer no loss. Gradations of love do not set a limit to their flourishing; love is like a rainbow's colors. It is a liberation of uniqueness, a deliverance of diversity in one. John Took puts it well: "every soul called into communion ... enters into that truth in a manner wholly its own" (Took, 2006, p. 407). In other words, if Dante can be satisfied by the unique care he receives from Virgil and Beatrice, the souls in heaven are equally happy in their own mediated relations to the Good. Piccarda, like Dante and Virgil and Beatrice, reflects love as no one else can. God's love for others has not cost her any joy. If she were to conceive it that way, she would mistake the Good for a scarce resource. Further, she would deny her own love for others—the love reflecting God's love for her.

The display continues when souls in a higher sphere cry out to Dante, "Here is one who will increase our loves!" (*Paradiso* V:105). Love, Dante is learning, is utterly unafraid of sharing. It only exists as procreative; it seeks to multiply itself, or else it is not truly received. That is how eternity is manifest in time. Eternal Being does not merely expand forever beyond the horizon of our understanding. It produces more and more unique refractions of itself in the creativity of each witness. To hoard the gift is to mis-allegorize the plenitude of its goodness. Augustine says the same in *City of God* (413–426/1950):

> For the possession of goods is by no means diminished by being shared with a partner ... on the contrary, the possession of goodness is increased in proportion to the concord and charity of those who share it. In short, he who is unwilling to share this possession cannot have it; and he who is most willing to admit others to a share of it will have the greatest abundance himself. (15.5)

The theme is finally taken up by Beatrice herself in the uppermost sphere of *Paradiso*. As she prepares Dante for his vision of God, she expounds the metaphysics of love from its origin:

> It was not by having a good acquired for himself
> (that being impossible), but because his splendor
> could, re-splendoring, say, *I exist*,
>
> in his eternity without time,
> beyond every other comprehension, as it pleased him.
> Eternal Love was opened in new loves. (XXIX:13–18)

It is a variation on a theme from *Confessions*, where Augustine recognizes that God has no need; whatever is good is God's (7.10.17). Aquinas says the same: Goodness and being are one, because God is the origin and fruition of both (*Summa Theologiae* 1265–1274/1947, 1.5.1). But Dante puts the idea down in a profound rhyme. God cannot increase the store of his own Good. In God, there is no absence to necessitate acquisition—*acquisto*. Thus, the new loves of Love are created rather than acquired, repeating 'I am' in a way that suits their creaturely form—*Subsisto*.

Beatrice soon urges Dante to turn and see countless thousands of human mirrors, each unique in how they radiate the first light. When at last Dante gazes into the prime essence of Being, he sees that even there, the light is produced by reflection. The self-reflection of God is, at its heart, love for another. Dante, his eyes constantly adjusting to the splendor, sees what appears to be a human figure. The image is no doubt Christic, but Dante recognizes it by a personal pronoun: "nostra effige" [our image] (*Paradiso* XXXIII:131). And this is the final vision. Loving God, we love what is most truly ours: the self-image of divine nature; the beginning and end of human reflection; the love ascending from scarcity and death; the material life of communion.

Conclusion

16.

By the time of the *Commedia*, Dante's Florence was in a routine state of conflict. The unionizing movements of the non-elite *popolo* had achieved a new, protomodern version of the city-state, effectively redistributing the power of the old aristocracy. Political life was now staged as a competition of business interests. Statesmen, no longer allowed a position solely by patrimony, were required to affiliate with one of several tradesmen's guilds (Najemy, 2007, p. 246; Najemy, 2008, pp. 35–44). Dante himself enrolled in the guild of apothecaries, holding a variety of public offices before his exile. But once outside the city, appalled by its endless infighting, he turned his attention to writing.

For him, political representation had to entail a great deal more than group interest. He knew this from the philosophy of St. Thomas: every desire was evidence of one final Good. The dialectics of democratic life thus obtained their value from a common end. If the *demos* signified competing aims, those aims also signified the existence of a real, unified happiness. Good politics were, in a word, purgatorial. Society had to be mediated by an account of human characters seeking the Good of their nature.

Of course, such a conception now appears all but antiquated. Within three centuries, John Locke would trace the politics of fulfillment along a totally different plotline. Happiness, he said, is not one thing but many; not every man prefers cheese and lobsters (1690/1975, 21.55). His sentiment was humorous but powerful, because it signified the untethering of natural desire from its unified consummation. To him, the plurality of human taste indicated many private forms of happiness. The sign of human liberty was to read 'no trespassing'; private citizens were fully entitled to signify their own good, and if need be, they could do so by revolting against the claims of a tyrant. Liberalism thus produced a new symbolic relation to nature. Its government now belonged first to the individual, then to the majority.

Hence, if the *Commedia* can be read against materialism, its critique is not strictly of Marx. It is equally directed at Locke, and Dante reveals their common underpinning. Granted, the two made widely divergent claims: Marx believed in a single material end for humanity; Locke believed there were many. Marx was against private property; Locke was for it. But Marxism was nonetheless an outgrowth of Lockean problematics because, in both schemas, the peasant's revolt is justified by the common right to material existence. The same logic emboldens laborers to unite, to take arms when necessary, and abolish hegemonic power. Herein lies the correspondence of the left and the right to this day: liberty is deliverance from scarcity to self-possession. Whether self-possession will occur in many private estates or one held in common—that is our public debate.

But as Badiou and Tarby (2013) have noted, the political divide is now no more than a soft contradiction (pp. 3–4). Capitalism now configures the left and the right irreversibly. Sartre's view has proven accurate. In sum: I always feel inferior to the image of my fulfilled self. I am always in want. Furthermore, the image of my fulfilled self signifies a world ideally disposed to me, and I cannot help but want others to serve that ideal (Sartre, 1956, pp. 471–534, 658). The projection of a Proletarian Party could not solve the problem; its eschatology is merely a symptom of the same inferiority complex. We are basically a lack, an unstable existence which, taken on its own, is nothing. The self, like the Party, *is* a scarcity. We are not the sort of beings who can ever repose in ourselves, as Augustine said of God.

And the market very naturally capitalizes on our predicament. Consider the term 'upgrade.' It suggests a movement of ascent, yet there is no terminus. The marketed self is a climber toward beatitude, but the climb has no lasting achievement. A completed purchase, which held out the promise of a complete self, is soon overtaken by obsolescence and want. Necessarily so: The market produces the very lack it appears to resolve. The upgraded self is endless because our completion is figurative. This is what Marx failed to see, and it is why the figurations of capital have won the modern heart.

As Badiou and Tarby (2013) also say, true resistance now seems impossible without the conviction that "something needs to be done that escapes the law of the world" (pp. 3–4). And I believe this is Dante's gift to the present. He does not neatly solve our problem; he offers a richer one, reading the Lockean-Marxist sequence backwards: Scarcity is the *outcome*, not the *incitement*, of radical self-possession. As Sartre perceived, a self is not finally possessed by itself. Radical self-referral can result only in a form of domination, like Ugolino's cannibalism. Self-referral cannot signify a state of equality; it is parasitic on the hierarchy it denies.

The question then stands before us: What sort of enfranchisement do we seek? On the one hand, the narratives of Dante and Augustine signify a world in which the human heart finds rest in God. On the other hand, the world of Locke and Marx is one of self-possession, which Sartre discovered was a perpetual scarcity of being.

17.

We have seen that an 'immaterial commons' is indeed real. Strengthening the claim of Hardt and Negri, we can now signify it as a communion—even a communion of saints—by which the virtual is identified with the virtuous. Hardt and Negri are right: Virtual reality must refer to goods shared in a project of political love. But virtuality, therefore, invokes a guided ascent to the Good. Human nature, by ascending to the singular Good of its origin, is not foreclosed; it holds the possibility of surprises multiplied from eternity. Mirrors of the Good may always emerge in unique speech communities, novelizing their vernacular beyond its former scope. And if their language can be novelized, so too can their economy. Language produces material culture; on this, Dante and Marx agree. But only Dante can compel his readers to share the good by multiplying it, rooting themselves in the allegorical life of the divine image.

Augustine's term for allegorical was *uno atque altero*—'one and yet another' (*Confessions* 5.14, 5.24). Everything, for him, evoked a fold in being. The universe in which that fold appeared was one of gratuity and diversity, a cosmos in which the real was always conceptive, never reduced to a single 'self.' We could sketch Augustine's phrase along Gadamer's (1989, p. 296) lines, noting how a text, when read, coproduces meaning in excess of its authorship. But Augustine's idea is not precisely the same. Rather than promoting the unbounded subjectivity of a text, he pursues its unbounded fulfillment. In both cases, perfect knowledge of the author exceeds the reader. But Christian allegorical tradition rests, by faith, in the purposive authorial Good beyond the reader's mind.

In a way, Dante and Augustine agree with Sartre: we scarcely understand. But they signify scarcity by its allegorical end: communion. As Augustine once said to his parish, "the very desire with which you want to understand is itself a prayer to God" (1992, p. 48). Sartre's milieu can be transformed on these terms. By faith, the penitent see the nothingness of their hunger for goods without God. They also find themselves lacking words to express the Good into which they are called. Witness the poet in love, for whom language fails to exhaust newfound beauty. This type of scarcity, this sense of lack, cannot fail to produce abundant material.

For the allegorist, signs of the Good are virtually everywhere. They are, as it were, waiting to appear. Although God transcends the allegorist, God is given to her in a diversity of presences. The allegorist is called upward, joining the world as a unique sign of its origin, novelizing her communion beyond its present language. She learns to read herself in promise of I Am, who spoke to Moses from the burning bush, calling together a people out of their slavery. The work of allegory is not merely avant-garde, though it is very often novel. It rests on the hallowed ground of the sign. The burning bush, in all its novelty and resistance to former categories, is not merely new; it signifies the Good, as it was in the beginning, is now and will be forever.

By apprenticing herself to that undying fire, the allegorist illuminates the non-being of scarcity, emerging in fellowship from the malnourished places of envy and fear. Learning from others, she ascends into the paradisal overflow, transfixed by Eucharistic patterns along the way. Material goods will soon appear to be exponents of the infinite, given to multiply. As signs, they are valuable not for their scarcity but for their givenness. The allegorist will thus learn to possess the Good by sharing what she sees of it in others. Not only will she serve those in need, she will novelize need itself.

It is true that her experience must entail a kind of loss, but her lost life, had she kept it, could belong only to the wolf. Her loss is precisely the loss of what others find scarce. And as she releases the world of scarcity, she discovers the true Good of the world. The material politics of love entail sacrifice—which is not to say oblivion. It is to say communion. "Except a corn of wheat fall into the ground and die, it abideth alone: but if it die, it bringeth forth much fruit" (*John* 12:24).

Notes

1 This paper is an evolution of prior material for which the author holds the copyright. See Elmore, M. (2017). At a Loss: Dante's Antiphon to recent Marxist voices. *Glossolalia*, *8* (1), 2–33. Retrieved at https://glossolalia.yale.edu/sites/default/files/glossolalia_8.1_0.pdf.
2 Some have argued that it is unnecessary to affix a discrete sin to each beast (for instance Demaray, 1969). But the wolf is unmistakably a figure of greed in Virgil's exposition (*Inferno* I: 97ff).
3 See the note in the Sayers translation of Alighieri, 1320/1949, p. 75. Her reading is apt, given how Dante reads Virgil's *Aeneid* as an allegory for the three stages of man's maturation (*Convivio* 4.26, Alighieri, 1304–1307/1995). Also see Okamura, 2001.
4 Not all Lockean thinkers hold this view. Often, air and sunlight are considered non-commodities held in common. However, Locke believes that the common is without

value until it is privatized; the common goods of nature exist only as *potentially* valuable. Theoretically, air itself would more valuable if commoditized—as indeed shown in the marketing of water; this, for Hardt and Negri, is the impetus in question.

References

Alighieri, D. (1949). *Hell* (D. Sayers, Trans.). Penguin. (Original work published 1320).
Alighieri, D. (1960). *De Vulgari Eloquentia* (S. Botterill, Trans.). Società Dantesca Italiana. (Original work 1302–1305).
Alighieri, D. (1966). *Commedia*. Mondadori. (Original work published 1320).
Alighieri, D. (1995). *Convivio* (R. Lansing, Trans.). La Lettere. (Original work 1304–1307).
Aquinas (1947). *Summa Theologiae* (Fathers of the English Dominican Province, Trans.). Benziger Brothers. (Original work 1265–1274).
Augustine (1887). *De Trinitate* (A.W. Haddan, Trans.). Christian Literature Publishing. (Original work 400–416).
Augustine (1950). *City of God* (Marcus Dods, Trans.). Random House. (Original work 413–426).
Augustine (1958). *On Christian Doctrine* (D.W. Robertson, Trans.). Prentice Hall. (Original work 397–426).
Augustine (1992). *Sermons 148–183 on the New Testament* (E. Hill, Trans.). New City Press.
Augustine (2006). *Confessions* (H. Chadwick, Trans.). Oxford University Press. (Original work 397–398).
Badiou, A., & Tarby, F. (2013). *Philosophy and the event* (Louise Burchell, Trans.). Polity Press.
Calcaterra, C. (1942). *Nella Selva del Petrarca*. Lincio Capelli.
Casarino, C., & Negri, A. (2008). *In praise of the common*. University of Minnesota Press.
Demaray, J. (1969). The Pilgrim texts and Dante's Three Beasts. *Italica, 46*(3), 244–241.
Elmore, M. (2017). At a loss: Dante's Antiphon to recent Marxist voices. *Glossolalia, 8*(1), 2–33. Retrieved at https://glossolalia.yale.edu/sites/default/files/glossolalia_8.1_0.pdf.
Foucault, M. (1970). *Order of things*. Random House.
Freccero, J. (1986). *Dante: The poetics of conversion*. Harvard University Press.
Gadamer, H.-G. (1989). *Truth and method*. Continuum.
Hardt, M., & Negri, A. (2003). *Empire*. Harvard University Press.
Hardt, M., & Negri, A. (2004). *Multitude*. Penguin.
Homer. *Iliad* (S. Butler, Trans.). In *MIT classics archive*. Retrieved from http://classics.mit.edu/Homer/iliad.html
Horace. *Ars Poetica* (A. S. Kline, Trans.). In *Poetry in translation*. Retrieved from http://www.poetryintranslation.com/PITBR/Latin/HoraceArsPoetica.htm
Josipivici, G. (1971). *The world and the book*. Stanford University Press.
Locke, J. (1689/1960). *Two treatises of government*. Cambridge University Press. (Original work published 1960).
Locke, J. (1975). *An essay concerning human understanding*. Clarendon Press. (Original work published 1690).
Luzzi, J. (2010). "As a Leaf on a Branch…": Dante's neologisms. *PMLA, 125*(2), 322–336.
Marx, K. (1967). *Capital* (Vol. I). (S. Moore & E. Aveling, Trans.). International Publishers.
Marx, K., & Engels, F. (2010). *Collected works* (Vol. 6). Lawrence & Wishart.

Najemy, J. (2007). Dante and Florence. In R. Jacoff (Ed.), *Cambridge companion to Dante*. Cambridge University Press.

Najemy, J. (2008). *A history of Florence*. Blackwell.

Robbins, L. (2007). *An essay on the nature and significance of economic science*. Mises Institute.

Sartre, J. (1956). *Being and nothingness* (H. E. Barnes, Trans.). Washington Square Press.

Sartre, J. (1960). *Critique de la raison dialectique*. Gallimard.

Sartre, J. (1968). *Search for a method* (H. E. Barnes, Trans.). Vintage Books.

Sartre, J. (1981). *The philosophy of Jean-Paul Sartre*. Open Court.

Schildgen, B. D. (1989). Dante's neologisms in the Paradiso and the Latin rhetorical tradition. *Dante Studies*, *107*, 101–119.

Took, J. (2006). "S'io m'intuassi, come tu t'imii" ('Par'., IX.81): Patterns of collective being in Dante. *The Modern Language Review*, *101*(2), 402–413.

Wilson-Okamura, D. S. (2001). Lavinia and Beatrice: The second half of the *Aeneid* in the middle ages. *Dante Studies*, *119*, 67–93.

Index

Because names such as Dante, Virgil, and Beatrice as well as references to the *Vita Nuova* and *Commedia* appear throughout this volume, these terms are not indexed. 'Phenomenology' appears throughout the first part of this volume as well and, thus, does not receive indexing.

2001: A space odyssey 73–78

Adorno, T. 61–62
Albertus Magnus 61, 151
alchemy 19, 114, 117–120
alterity 19, 21–22, 31, 34–36, 126–127, 134, 159; debt to the other 114–115, 138; the other xiv, xvii, 22, 31, 45, 93, 116, 124, 126–127, 129, 131, 138, 152, 155–156, 162, 164–165, 175–177, 180, 208, 216, 220; the Other xiv, xvii, 19, 33, 35–37, 48, 61, 63, 67, 72, 95–96, 116, 126, 129, 131, 134, 138, 148–149; otherness 16, 19, 21–22, 31, 34–35, 37, 56–57, 64, 90, 160, 162; other-than-self 83, 93, 95
apophaticism xiv, 29, 34, 44, 59, 60, 61, 67, 78; apophatic spirituality 20, 23, 28
Aquinas *see* Thomas Aquinas
Arendt, H. 174–178, 183
Aristotle 8, 13, 46, 54, 57, 61, 64, 65, 115, 145, 147, 156, 158–160, 175, 183–184, 186, 204
Asay, T. 9, 18, 21–23, 26, 33, 40, 43, 45
Augustine of Hippo 9, 11, 15, 21, 22–23, 36, 39, 41, 81, 116, 136, 139–140, 161, 175–177, 183, 198, 204–205, 207–208, 211–212, 214–219; and Presence 9, 19, 22, 25, 29, 33, 45
Avicenna 64, 65, 150

Bacon, R. 57, 65
Barolini, T. 147–151, 176, 185

being-in-the-world 33, 82, 94; *see also dasein*
Bernard of Clairvaux 86

Clarke, A. C. *see 2001: A space odyssey*

dasein 25, 33, 80, 85, 87, 91–92, 96, 106, 115, 137
Deleuze, G. 11, 43–44, 60, 202
De Monticelli, R. 16–17, 24, 40, 124
Descartes, R. 13–14, 33, 55, 64–65, 99; Cartesian 25, 31, 194
Dionysius 22, 58, 59, 67
Duns Scotus xvii, 13, 14, 38, 51–70; and univocity of being 38, 51, 53, 54, 56–58, 60, 66–67, 73

Eckhart von Hochheim (Meister Eckhart) 58, 68
epistemology xv–xvi, 6–10, 13–14, 19, 29, 33, 38, 48, 53–55, 60, 64–65, 74, 90, 113–114, 116, 118, 121–122, 134, 138–139, 156
epoché (bracketing, phenomenological reduction) 10, 19, 25, 32–33, 40, 46, 97–98, 124, 133
existentialist 80, 92, 94, 96
existential-phenomenology xvii, 9, 12, 20, 26, 29, 117

falconry 189, 196–197, 199; and seeling 197, 199
Foucault, M. 60, 65, 204

Francis of Assisi 8, 23, 116, 139–140;
  Franciscan spirituality and theology 8,
  15, 56, 57, 117, 126
Franke, W. xvii, 7, 12–13, 20, 23–39,
  72–73, 75, 78, 98, 105, 114, 121, 124,
  139, 156
Freud, S. 11, 19, 133–134, 183–187, 196

Gadamer, H.-G. 21, 24, 53, 156–159, 219
grace 8, 17, 34, 73, 89–91, 95, 123,
  137–138, 149, 151, 156, 160–162, 174,
  176–177, 180
Guardini, R. 165–167, 177–178, 180

Hardt, M. & Negri, A. 202, 208–213,
  219, 220n4
Harrison, R. P. 7, 12, 15–16, 18–21, 23,
  27–31, 40, 116
Hawkins, P. S. xvii, 14, 155–156, 164,
  167–168
Hegel, G. W. F. 9, 45, 63, 65, 201
Heidegger, M. 4, 9–11, 18, 21–22, 24–26,
  29, 33, 39, 46–47, 68, 75, 85, 92, 96,
  105–106, 114, 115–117, 127, 137,
  139–140, 156–157
Henry, M. 12, 54
Henry of Ghent 65, 66
hermeneutics xvi–xvii, 12, 18, 23–26,
  29, 45, 52, 80, 99, 102, 108, 113,
  116, 121, 127, 138–139, 156, 158;
  hermeneutic regression 16
Hildebrand, D. von 164–165, 167
Hillman, J. 38, 72
Husserl, E. 9–12, 22, 25, 29, 32, 45–46,
  53–55, 97–100, 102, 109–110, 115,
  124, 140

imaginal 19, 22–24, 38–39, 42, 76,
  117–118
ineffable xvi, xviii, 5, 13, 20, 23, 29,
  34–37, 39, 44, 46, 56, 69, 73, 75–76, 78,
  125, 132, 215

Jankélévitch, V. 176–178
Jung, C. G. 3, 29, 38, 45, 47, 72–73, 77,
  113–114, 117–118, 120, 122, 135,
  189–190, 196

Kant, E. 52–53, 55, 60, 62, 68–70,
  100, 156, 183
Kierkegaard, S. 63, 94–95
Kristeva, J. 174–175, 177–178
Kubrick, S. *see 2001*: A space odyssey

Levinas, E. xiv, 10–11, 19, 22, 33–38, 54,
  61–62, 114, 131, 134, 139
Locke, J. 209, 218–219, 220n4
Luke, H. 3–4, 111n4

Marion, J.-L. 12, 54, 156
Marx, K. 201–203, 210, 213, 215,
  218–219
Milbank, J. 60–62, 114
modernity xv, 9, 12–17, 38, 41–42,
  51–56, 58–66, 68, 70, 92, 114, 118,
  119, 147, 219; peri-modernity 118;
  postmodernity xv–xvi, 4, 11, 15–17,
  33–34, 37, 39–41, 44, 54, 61–62,
  113–114, 117–118, 127, 136, 183;
  premodernity xv, 4, 12, 14, 31, 34,
  42, 92–93, 114, 118, 210; proto-
  modernity 217
Monticelli, D. 45–48, 105–106, 109, 121

Neoplatonism 53, 59
Nicholas of Cusa 52, 68

ontology xv, 6, 18, 21, 25, 29–30, 33,
  37–38, 45, 54–56, 59–60, 64, 66, 80,
  82–86, 88, 90, 97, 113, 115, 164,
  177–178, 180, 196
Other *see* alterity

peri-modernity *see* modernity
Petrarch 15–16, 127
Plato 52, 54, 115–116, 145, 208, 214
postmodernity *see* modernity
premodernity *see* modernity
proto-phenomenology xvii, 4, 9, 14, 38,
  116, 136
Pseudo-Dionysius *see* Dionysius
psychotherapy 113, 122, 127, 129–130,
  133–135, 138–139

Radical Orthodoxy 60, 114
Richard of St. Victor 38–39
Ricœur, P. 10, 12, 156, 158
Romanyshyn, R. 73, 114, 117–119

Sartre, J.-P. 102, 106, 201–203, 205,
  207–208, 213–214, 218–220
Sokolowski, R. 158–160
Spinoza, B. 51, 60
Suárez, F. 60, 65–66

Thomas Aquinas 8–9, 23, 58, 61, 66, 116,
  139–140, 151, 159, 196, 198, 204, 206,

217–218; Thomistic 15, 39, 62, 89, 121, 128, 133, 160
Tillich, P. 80, 92
Took, J. xiv–xv, 15, 20–21, 23, 92–96, 105, 216

ultraphenomenology 32, 35, 37, 139

Vico, G. 52, 66

William of Ockham 55, 56

For Product Safety Concerns and Information please contact our EU
representative GPSR@taylorandfrancis.com
Taylor & Francis Verlag GmbH, Kaufingerstraße 24, 80331 München, Germany

www.ingramcontent.com/pod-product-compliance
Lightning Source LLC
Chambersburg PA
CBHW071827300426
44116CB00009B/1462